THE PRIMARY
THAT MADE
A PRESIDENT

★

THE PRIMARY THAT MADE A PRESIDENT

John F. Kennedy and West Virginia

★

Robert Rupp

The University of Tennessee Press / Knoxville

Library of Congress Cataloging-in-Publication Data

Names: Rupp, Robert O., author.

Title: The primary that made a president : John F. Kennedy and West Virginia /
Robert Rupp.

Description: First edition. | Knoxville : The University of Tennessee Press,
[2020] | Includes bibliographical references and index. |

Summary: "This book examines an enigma: How did a small Appalachian state,
overwhelmingly poor and Protestant, become a key player in the political future
of John F. Kennedy? While the primary proved to be an unpredictable campaign boost
for JFK, the 1960 West Virginia contest also brought to light a host of social issues that
would play a part in the overall story of Kennedy and the 1960s. The West Virginia
primary meant the end of a taboo that kept the Catholic faith out of American politics;
the rise of the primary as a political tool for garnering delegate support; the beginning
of a nationwide confrontation with Appalachian stereotypes; and the seeds for what
would become Kennedy's War on Poverty" —Provided by publisher.

Identifiers: LCCN 2020015420 (print) | LCCN 2020015421 (ebook) | ISBN
9781621905738 (hardcover) | ISBN 9781621905745 (pdf)

Subjects: LCSH: Kennedy, John F. (John Fitzgerald), 1917–1963. | Presidents—United
States—Election—1960. | Primaries—West Virginia—History—20th century. | West
Virginia—Politics and government—20th century.

Classification: LCC E837.7 .R87 2020 (print) | LCC E837.7 (ebook) | DDC
973.922—dc23
LC record available at https://lccn.loc.gov/2020015420
LC ebook record available at https://lccn.loc.gov/2020015421

To L.G.R.

CONTENTS

ILLUSTRATIONS

ACKNOWLEDGMENTS

I have spent two decades studying the 1960 West Virginia primary and over that time have been grateful to many, including the staffs at the John F. Kennedy Presidential Library and Museum, the Minnesota Historical Society, the West Virginia Archives and History, the staff at the West Virginia Wesleyan College Library for their help and their interlibrary loan efforts, and to West Virginia Wesleyan College for their support.

I also would like to thank the state organizations that sponsored the conferences honoring the anniversaries of the 1960 West Virginia primary.

I also appreciate those who have read and made comments on the manuscript in various forms over the years, and to those associated with the University of Tennessee Press for their insightful comments and recommendations. I also want to acknowledge editing support from Roxy Todd and Rachel Rosolina.

I also must acknowledge and thank Anna Macias and David Jennings at Ohio Wesleyan University and J. Roger Sharp and Ralph Ketcham who were my mentors at Syracuse University. They all provided excellent examples of scholarship, teaching, and encouraging students.

And finally, I have to thank all of my students who have made teaching so enjoyable and rewarding, and especially the students who enrolled in my "Kennedy, Catholicism, and Charisma" course at Wesleyan and conducted interviews with and collected documents from people across the state of West Virginia.

INTRODUCTION

The 1960 West Virginia presidential primary is arguably the most storied contest in modern American politics. And yet, John F. Kennedy traveled so quickly from being a dynamic presidential candidate to a martyred president that many forget his debt to West Virginia in his quest for the Democratic presidential nomination. Kennedy himself acknowledged this debt when he returned, as president, to the state to celebrate its centennial on June 20, 1963. At that event, he declared, "I would not be where I am, I would not have some of the responsibilities which I now bear, if it had not been for the people of West Virginia."[1] Besides propelling Kennedy to the Democratic nomination, the West Virginia primary changed the face of politics by advancing religious tolerance, foreshadowing future political campaigns, influencing public policy, and perpetuating regional stereotypes. This book will examine these four themes as well as other aspects of this important political contest in the Mountain State 60 years ago.

Advancing Religious Tolerance

When the president spoke at the centennial celebration in Charleston that day, he didn't mention the difficulties his campaign faced during the nearly five weeks spent campaigning across West Virginia, the most prominent of which was his Catholicism. In those weeks, the press and the candidate turned the primary into a referendum on religious tolerance.

The religious issue became an important factor in the West Virginia contest after the Wisconsin presidential primary on April 10, 1960. Prior to that, Kennedy and his advisors viewed the West Virginia primary as an easy contest that would serve as an insurance policy if opponent Hubert Humphrey remained in the fight after Wisconsin. In fact, a December statewide poll of Democratic voters by Lou Harris showed Kennedy beating Humphrey in West Virginia 70 to 30 percent.

But everything changed after that Wisconsin primary. While Kennedy handily beat Humphrey with 476,024 votes to 366,753, the press credited his victory to a strong turnout of Catholic voters, who composed 30 percent of Wisconsin's population. And a new post-Wisconsin Lou Harris poll of selected precincts showed Kennedy trailing Humphrey 60 to 40 percent, with the explanation that before the Wisconsin primary, West Virginia voters didn't know Kennedy was a Catholic. Now they did.

As a result, the primary caught the attention of the nation and beyond as a test case for religious bigotry. As Parkersburg newspaper editor James Young summed it up, "West Virginians will either bury their prejudice, or they will bury John Kennedy."[2] A Kennedy victory in a state where Catholics made up only 4 percent of the population would demonstrate that a Catholic could get Protestant votes. But a defeat would be attributed to one factor: prejudice.
On election night, Ken Kurtz of WSAZ television in Charleston explained that the election hinged on "how [Kennedy's] Roman Catholic religion will sit at the polls with West Virginia's heavily Protestant voters," with Kennedy steadfastly denying that his religion "should have or has had much influence on the election."[3]

West Virginia voters agreed with the candidate: Kennedy won in a landslide, carrying 50 of the 55 counties and collecting almost 61 percent of the popular vote.[4] The *Charleston Gazette* described the results as a "devastating victory" that should prompt reconsideration by those party professionals who held Kennedy "at arm's length because of doubts that a Roman Catholic could be elected to the White House."[5]

As president, Kennedy reminisced about the West Virginia primary with his friend Ken O'Donnell one evening at the White House: "Just think, if I had buried Hubert in Wisconsin, we would not be sitting here now."[6] His statement led O'Donnell to claim that this one primary election allowed Kennedy to "lick the religious issue in a showdown test that certainly must be a monument in American political history."[7]

Foreshadowing Future Political Campaigns

The second impact of the West Virginia contest was how the primary provided a preview of future political campaigns. Not only were presidential candidates chosen in popular elections instead of party back rooms, but they also needed more money to run a campaign, and they needed to spend that money in a particular way to appeal to voters. The Kennedy campaign in the Mountain State prefigured modern presidential campaigns in expenditures as well as its allocation to television and the mounting of an impressive, statewide organization. Ralph McGill of the *Atlanta Constitution* called Kennedy's victory a "dramatic example of what thorough, if expensive, organization can produce if handled by professionals."[8]

Joe Kennedy famously said they were going to sell his son "like soap flakes."[9] To accomplish that promotion in West Virginia, the Kennedy campaign previewed what McGill called the "latest scientific mechanisms" in its use of television, polling, and computers.[10] The campaign focused on creating an image of a candidate that Joe championed as the first popular-culture political celebrity, boasting that John's picture on a magazine cover boosted sales.[11]

Influencing Public Policy

The distance between Boston, Massachusetts, and Charleston, West Virginia, may have been 800 miles, but the distance between John F. Kennedy and West Virginia seemed far more when he started his campaign in the Mountain State. This was most apparent when his life experience stood in stark contrast to that of his primary opponent, Hubert Humphrey. While the Minnesota senator had witnessed up-close poverty, the Massachusetts senator had little exposure to it until he started campaigning in West Virginia.

Kennedy's experience in West Virginia became a teachable moment for the future president, one that influenced the policies of his administration and the direction for the nation, especially regarding federal attention on Appalachia. The candidate's exposure to poverty provided motivation for a food stamp proposal and the Appalachian Regional Commission (ARC), and it helped plant the seeds for a future War on Poverty. Several of those programs, like the food stamp program, survive today.[12]

Kennedy was personally affected by the poverty, poor nutrition, joblessness, and hopelessness he saw firsthand in West Virginia. He spent time passing abandoned miners' homes, with boards over windows called Eisenhower curtains, and considered it his "education." Ramie Barker, who would become a senior advisor to West Virginia governor Earl Ray Tomblin, says, "Traveling around here changed him. He learned to become a president." Barker notes that he "saw wives line up for surplus government food, and he heard about kids who saved their school milk for younger siblings at home."[13]

During the last week of the campaign Kennedy emphasized "he was glad that he entered the West Virginia primary because it gave him an opportunity to see the plight of men who have lost work because of automation." Referring to the primary, he said that "This is the best school, the hardest school, and in many ways the most somber school of learning about this problem."[14]

As Richard Goodwin wrote "Kennedy was in West Virginia to win an election. But in that struggle he was learning more about America; about that underside of American life that he had never experienced so personally, intimately." Goodwin related that midway in the West Virginia primary campaign, Kennedy came to the Washington office and, commenting to no one in particular, said: "You can't imagine how those people live down there. I was better off in the war than they are in those coal mines. It's not right. I'm going to do something about it. If we make it." Then he added ironically: "Even if they are a bunch of bigots."[15]

In his televised debate, Kennedy emphasized how his almost five weeks in the Mountain State would impact his presidency by saying, "A President can hear about those problems (in West Virginia)—he can read reports—but unless he has spent a month here, seeing it for himself and talking with people, he cannot fully grasp this state's urgent need for action."[16] But this recognition of the state and promise of action for the state had an important geographic component as the candidate went on to state that "For America is not just Chicago and Los Angeles—it is Logan and Beckley and Welch as well."[17] The candidate often reminded his audiences that he had been in the state so long, that he learned the geography of the Mountain State. He knew the difference between Charleston and Charles Town; had been the only presidential candidate to have come to Welch three times, or visited Collins High School twice and knew "where Slab Fork is and has been there."[18] Never before had a presidential contender spent so much time in a state, and it could be argued that never before or since had a future president learned so much.

The experience motivated Kennedy to back up the promises he made to West Virginians during the campaign with concrete public policy programs based on governmental help. Key to these programs was the philosophy that these once proud and able people weren't poor and malnourished because they deserved it, but because of circumstances beyond their control.[19]

In regard to policy, the contest brought national attention to the economic problems in Appalachia and kindled Kennedy's interest in fighting rural poverty, which ultimately led to the creation of a number of initiatives and programs by Lyndon Johnson. But such attention and subsequent action came at a price. The so-called "rediscovery" of white poverty in the upland South brought with it increased attention to stereotypes. Appalachia in general and West Virginia in particular were portrayed negatively in popular culture and mainstream media.[20]

Perpetuating Regional Stereotypes

The fourth impact of the primary campaign rests both in its challenge to and perpetuation of stereotypes of the state and region. On the upside, the outcome of the primary undermined outsiders' low expectations of state residents, who confounded conventional wisdom due to the strong Appalachian value of judging people on an individual basis. After the election, a West Virginia newspaper argued, "Sen. Kennedy's victory proves what some of us have been trying to say all along. That West Virginia is not the hotbed of religious prejudice some of our distinguished visitors have supposed it to be. We have our religious feelings, to be sure, and here and there they run deep and bitter, but in a purely political campaign, they are not decisive."[21]

The downside, however, was reflected in reports of West Virginia as an impoverished state, with photographs often showing hard times on gaunt faces. Appalachia had always been victim of such caricatures, but it was made worse in the spring of 1960 by the invasion of the national press with negative coverage that exaggerated the role of religious bigotry while resorting to stereotypes of the region.[22] Charleston reporter L. T. Anderson pointed out "West Virginia was badly portrayed to the nation. It was pictured as a kingdom of defiant, vulgar, gross and stupid bigotry."[23]

When the Massachusetts senator began his nomination effort, Ben Bradlee of *Newsweek* asked him at the end of 1959 if he thought he could win. Kennedy answered, "Yes, if I don't make a single mistake myself and if I don't get maneuvered into a position where there is no way out." In other words, he could never finish second in any primary, or get into a situation like Harold Stassen did in 1948, where everything was riding on one event (the Oregon primary) and he blew it.[24] After the Wisconsin primary, the West Virginia contest unexpectedly became that one event that could derail Kennedy's quest. It became an election that the candidate had to win.

Contenders Contrast

The primary candidates' personal histories could not have been more different. Kennedy was born into a wealthy family in a Boston suburb and given a million-dollar trust fund at the age of ten. Humphrey was born in Wallace, South Dakota (population: 600), in a room over his father's drugstore. While Kennedy was educated first at a prep school and then at Harvard, Humphrey had to leave the University of Minnesota after one year to help manage his father's store during the Great Depression and didn't return until six years later.[25]

Humphrey never became wealthy, and the poverty Kennedy observed in West Virginia was the poverty Humphrey had witnessed and experienced growing up in South Dakota. One time when Senator Robert Byrd was introducing the Minnesota senator in West Virginia, he said, "And Senator Humphrey knows what it is like to go to school in the snow in tennis shoes."[26]

There were also striking personality differences that appeared to favor Humphrey. The Massachusetts senator could be charming and charismatic, but Humphrey was a poor boy from the Midwest with a folksy campaign style and a long record of support for federal programs.[27] Although both of their platforms promoted a myriad of federal programs, Humphrey was seen in tone and in content as the more populist candidate—a factor that should have benefit-ted him in the Mountain State. As Louis Bean, Humphrey's pollster, observed earlier, Kennedy would be a less attractive candidate in the hollows of West Virginia[28] than the "homespun Humphrey, whose father championed William Jennings Bryan—the populist three-time Democrat presidential nominee."[29]

Campaign Style

Each candidate was effective on the stump, but each had a different campaign style. A reporter noticed that John Kennedy "does not know the art of being folksy and is too intelligent to attempt it. So, he plays it straight." On the other hand, "Senator Hubert Humphrey is the naturally folksy type. It does not ap-pear out of character for him to be bouncy. He always is. He has the gift of out-going friendliness. It's a corny recipe, but it is as natural with Hubert Humphrey as his quick smile, his undenied good will and compassion for his fellow man."[30]

The West Virginia presidential primary in 1960 provided a vivid contrast between the candidate from Massachusetts and the constituency of the Moun-tain State. A look at the iconic *Life* magazine photograph of the candidate and coal miners in May 1960 reflects the early awkwardness of that intersection between Kennedy and Appalachia, as well as Kennedy's determination to over-come it. In the photo, the candidate, in his expensive London-tailored suit, sits in the middle of a ring of standing miners covered in coal dust after they fin-ished their shift. While he appears engaged as he talks with one miner, all of the other miners are standing with their arms folded or their hands in their pockets.[31]

This photo captures what could be seen as an alien encounter between the candidate and his temporary Appalachian constituency, when into this rural, Protestant, and poor state came an urban Irish-Catholic millionaire who was more attuned to the nuances of big-city politics than to the cadences of Appa-lachian political culture.

Time columnist Hugh Sidey certainly had his doubts about the fit of John Kennedy and West Virginia. He recalled wondering how this "young, busy-haired" Harvard-educated, millionaire with an Ivy League look, a strange re-ligion, and a Boston accent would do in this poor, southern, Bible-Belt state.[32] He observed the contrast when the two contenders campaigned on consecu-tive days in Beckley, West Virginia. On the first day, he attended a Humphrey rally that featured guitar player Jimmy Wolford, who warmed up the audience by singing to the melody of the popular *Davy Crockett* song: "Hubert, Hubert Humphrey, man for you and me." The next day, Kennedy came to town with a sound truck blaring his campaign song: Frank Sinatra singing "High Hopes,

He's Got High Hopes." Sinatra's revised lyrics were: "Everyone is voting for Jack, Cause he has what all the rest lack / Jack is on the right track / Cause he's got high hopes." The contrasts in music, dress, and manner prompted Sidey to think that Kennedy didn't stand a chance. In terms of background, image, and voting record, his opponent had the advantage.[33]

Despite Sidey's initial doubts, however, he later noted that West Virginians loved the Kennedy glamour. Far from being alienated by the Kennedy style, many voters were attracted to it. In a region of poverty, a visit by the Kennedys became a campaign manager's dream, and as the electioneering progressed, many voters came to embrace this aristocrat who would keep his suit coat on even in the coal mine.[34]

Six Trends

The candidates' uneven resources, combined with the importance of the outcome, help explain six trends that marked the five weeks leading up to the West Virginia primary vote on May 10, 1960.

The first trend was the increasing use by the Kennedy camp of resources. While Humphrey had budget problems, the Kennedy campaign had unlimited access to funds for television advertising, organization, slating, and much more.

The first trend triggered the second trend: the escalating attacks by Humphrey on Kennedy's spending. It wasn't until the third week of the campaign that Humphrey raised this issue directly. At a campaign stop in Keyser, he said, "I can't afford to run through this state with a little black bag [of money] and a checkbook." Later that day at Kingwood Humphrey complained, "I'm ganged up on by wealth."[35] The Kennedy camp countered with the incredulous claim that they had spent 20 percent less than Humphrey in the campaign. Full accounting of campaign expenditures did not have to be reported, so any hard numbers were elusive. However, few took Kennedy's claim seriously, and later estimates had Kennedy spending close to a million dollars on his West Virginia primary campaign.[36]

The third trend was an increasing bitterness between the two candidates. At first neither would attack the other or even mention his opponent. But with so much at stake for each, and without accurate polling to judge where voters were leaning, the truce in Wisconsin evaporated in West Virginia.[37] The Kennedy camp, whose candidate had the most to lose, ultimately encouraged FDR Jr.'s last-minute attack on Humphrey's draft status.[38]

The increasing hostility in the final weeks prompted reporters to compare the electoral contest to another struggle familiar to the state and nation, the Hatfield-McCoy feud. Ironically, during the televised debate, when the contenders faced their largest audience of the campaign, neither candidate displayed the bitterness seen on the stump.[39]

The fourth trend was an extended argument over the "underdog" factor. Humphrey argued correctly that, in terms of resources, he was the underdog. But the Kennedy campaign continued to promote their candidate as a victim both of religious bigotry and a gang-up by Lyndon Johnson and other contenders for the Democratic presidential nomination. Kennedy supporters argued that these two factors gave an unfair advantage to Humphrey.

Adoption of the "underdog" mantle benefitted Kennedy in a number of ways. First, it created sympathy among voters in a culture that was sensitive to the unfairness of life. Second, it served to diminish expectations for Kennedy. If he lost, he could argue that he lost not to Humphrey, but to a gang of opponents, all of whom lacked the courage to enter the state's primary. He could also trace his defeat to religious prejudice in the state that reflected the innate bigotry of West Virginians. In fact, John Kennedy cited both factors as reasons he needed to spend vast sums in West Virginia that he hadn't spent in Wisconsin—and he may have believed it.

The fifth trend was the unexpected national attention the primary generated. Unlike New Hampshire or Wisconsin, the West Virginia presidential primary had never had an impact on nomination efforts in either party. It was just a "beauty contest," divorced from the selection of delegates to the national nominating convention. One could win the primary and get no delegates. But the significance of the West Virginia contest changed when the Wisconsin race failed to end Humphrey's nomination effort. Before the Wisconsin vote, Humphrey's active participation in West Virginia was uncertain. But the explanation for Humphrey's loss in Wisconsin (Catholic voters) and the unexpected closeness of the vote (he carried four of the ten congressional districts) encouraged the Minnesota senator to challenge Kennedy in West Virginia.

Humphrey's decision set the stage for a contest in May, but two factors contributed to the attention that fight generated. The first was demographics. Of the remaining primaries, West Virginia had the fewest Catholic voters, and it was the only remaining one where Kennedy had serious opposition. It represented the best hope for John Kennedy to exorcise the notion that Catholicism was an electoral handicap in presidential elections.

While the timeline explains why the media came to the Mountain State, the uncertainty surrounding the result explains the story's attraction. Horserace journalism wasn't possible because the answer to the question "Who is ahead?" was not available to the press, public, or politicians. No one had access to state-wide polling, which meant one had to rely on Lou Harris's "selected precinct polling," or newspaper polling, which was even more flawed.[40] Everyone had to wait until the votes were counted on Tuesday night, May 10, 1960. Before then, the media only had access to pundits and anecdotal polls of voters, none of which could predict who would win.

The sixth trend in the West Virginia campaign was the uncertainty of how the religious issue would play out in the electoral arena. In 1960 it was difficult to predict how the Democratic electorate in West Virginia would vote, even more difficult to understand how religion would impact their voting. The situation was made more uncertain by conflicting information. The last time a Catholic candidate ran in a West Virginia presidential primary, in 1928, Democrat Al Smith easily beat a weak opponent, but he was overwhelmed in the general election that November. Catholic animosity in the 1920s was more open and easier to gauge, and although hostility was prevalent in 1960, it was more restrained.

The situation wasn't helped by reporters from outside the state who were more eager than their West Virginia counterparts to uncover and highlight bigotry in the state. The out-of-state press appeared to focus more on the low percentage of Catholics in the state (four percent) than on the low percentage of church membership (41 percent). They were also more interested in the bigoted comments of a few than on the apparent libertarian leanings of the many.

Historiography

It has been six decades since the five-week intersection of candidate John F. Kennedy and West Virginia affected the electoral history of America. Although many historians acknowledge the significance of the primary, the event has inspired only two monographs and one book-length narrative.

The first monograph on the contest was written by newspaper reporter Harry W. Ernst shortly after the primary.[41] His 31-page work provides many of the stories, insights, and quotes that future books on Kennedy and his presidential election would use to describe their sections discussing the West Virginia primary.[42] Three decades later, Daniel B. Fleming wrote the first book on the primary campaign (*Kennedy vs. Humphrey, West Virginia, 1960*, 1992). His work provided a detailed investigation of the primary, but unfortunately, the work is out of print.

If the 1960 West Virginia primary lacks books or monographs, it does not lack discussion. Summaries of the contest are present in almost all of the many biographies of John Kennedy and in the studies of his 1960 presidential election effort. The sections, however, are short—usually less than 19 pages.

Any discussion of historiography of the West Virginia primary must begin with Theodore White's seminal book on the 1960 presidential race, *The Making of a President*,[43] which changed how political campaigns were covered. His work, published in 1961, transformed the modern narrative of election coverage from simple stories filed by reporters to grand, sweeping historical dramas.[44] In his 18 pages on the West Virginia contest, White focused on Kennedy's effort to overcome West Virginian voters' prejudice toward Catholicism.[45]

White, however, did not assume a neutral stance in his narrative. If Ernst was positive about the Kennedy campaign, White was reverential. He admitted later that he had "moved or was drawn across the line of reporting to friendship" with the candidate.[46] As a result, the book's narrative promotes what Stephen Ambrose called the "Teddy White thesis"—the idea that "Kennedy ran a brilliant campaign, while Nixon committed blunder after blunder" in the general election.[47] Such a perspective explains why White's pages on West Virginia don't investigate such disquieting factors as the expenditures of Kennedy or the smear against Humphrey.

Kennedy speechwriter and court historian Ted Sorensen reflects White's insider and pro-Kennedy view of the primary. In his nine pages on the contest, he highlights the religious issue in West Virginia without a full exploration of why it failed to materialize, and downplays the attack on Humphrey by noting that apologies were given.[48]

The plethora of historical literature on John F. Kennedy's life and the 1960 presidential election accelerated in the early twenty-first century with the publication of more than six books on the two topics. The recent scholarship on the 1960 West Virginian presidential primary shows a continued consensus on both the significance of the event and the superiority of candidate Kennedy. But the recent literature also offers a more balanced account of the man and his times, and a pushback to what one historian has called "Theodore White's hero worship."[49]

W. J. Rorabaugh (*The Real Making of the President,* 2009) provides the harshest critique of White's book. Calling Kennedy a master deceiver, he contends that previous accounts of the contest ignore Kennedy's manipulation of reporters and the questionable activities of his supporters.[50] Edmund Kallina (*Kennedy v. Nixon: The Presidential Election of 1960,* 2010.) challenges historians to revisit religious prejudice in the Mountain State and to explore the shortcomings of the Fourth Estate.[51] Such concerns are raised by Thomas Oliphant and Curtis Wilke (*The Road to Camelot,* 2017), who claim that White romanticized Kennedy's campaign and exaggerated his perilous position. Their claims undercut White's celebratory narrative of the event, but slight the worries that many contemporary observers consistently advanced.[52] The role of religion and Kennedy's strategy on the issue is explored in Chapter Two.

The role of anti-Kennedy forces in the West Virginia primary has been explored in David Corbin's 2015 monograph ("John F. Kennedy Plays the 'Religious Card"). Corbin, who was Senator Robert C. Byrd's speechwriter, overestimates the strength of the Byrd-led Kennedy opposition in the state, but he does provide evidence of press failings—a recurring theme in recent scholarship, which is addressed in chapter four of this book.[53]

The role of the Kennedy campaign in foreshadowing future politics, first highlighted in White's book, has continued to be explored in recent works on the election. In this regard, Gary Donaldson (*The First Modern Campaign*, 2007) argues that the 1960 general election prefigured presidential campaigns in terms of the construction of "the manufactured candidate . . . who could be made to appear to be something he was not." While he does not directly discuss image-making in his short discussion on the West Virginia contest, his thesis is explored in Chapter 3 of this book, which examines Kennedy's careful promotion of personas that would resonate in the Mountain State.[54]

Chapter Overview

Unlike the numerous Kennedy biographies and 1960 presidential election histories, this book concentrates solely on the 1960 West Virginia presidential primary. As a result, it can explore in-depth the events of that primary that other scholarship has not. This book is only the second book-length manuscript on the contest, and it is the first written by a political historian.

This investigation of the 1960 presidential primary includes, for the first time, an examination of the campaign ads Kennedy ran in the West Virginia primary, as well as the videotape of his televised debate in Charleston. Other resources that were unavailable to previous authors include articles from 30 state newspapers, available now on the West Virginia Division of Culture and History website ("Battleground West Virginia: Electing the President in 1960"). The book also used information from the conferences in 1990 and 2010 celebrating the anniversary of the primary. Panels at the two gatherings offered insights and stories from participants such as reporter Ken Kurtz, folk guitarist Jimmy Wolford, and Kennedy advisors Ted Sorensen and Richard Donahue. Finally, I made use of interviews and projects from "Kennedy, Charisma, and Catholicism: 1960 West Virginia Presidential Primary," a course that I've taught over the past two decades at West Virginia Wesleyan College.

Chapter one, "Kennedy's Quest and the West Virginia's Political Landscape," provides a survey of the political landscape that Kennedy confronted in West Virginia, as well as his efforts to set up an organization there and take the front-runner status in the state. Although the state's presidential primary was not a priority when he started his quest for the presidential nomination, it became one after his tainted victory in Wisconsin on April 5, 1960. And although he won that primary by more than 100,000 votes, many in the press credited his victory to support from Catholic voters, who constituted 30 percent of the state's population.[55]

Chapter two, "Kennedy Adopts a Religious Confrontation Strategy," explores how Kennedy tried to diffuse the religious issue in West Virginia by adopting a strategy of religious confrontation. His handling of the religion issue can be divided into two parts: before and after the Wisconsin primary. Before the April 5 Wisconsin vote, Kennedy deployed a "discuss and dismiss" approach, raising the issue only in a controlled media environment and never in his campaign speeches. But after the Wisconsin primary, he employed a confrontational strategy by openly talking about religion on the campaign trail in West Virginia and using television ads featuring him and featuring Franklin Delano Roosevelt, Jr. While the strategy posed a risk by bringing attention to his liability, it had a number of benefits and would become part of his general election campaign in Houston when he addressed the Greater Houston Ministerial Association.

Chapter three, "Food, Family, and Flag," examines Kennedy's need to employ more than just a confrontational strategy on religion to win the West Virginia presidential primary. Rather, he required a new political identity, which championing the "three-F" strategy could provide. This trifecta of issues—food, family, and flag—resonated throughout West Virginia where they addressed local concerns and values.[56] In fact, a focus on these three issues attracted voters in the Mountain State and offered an opportunity for them to see Kennedy as more than the Catholic candidate. The three-F strategy offered the opportunity to portray the candidate as the second FDR, a family man and a decorated veteran. Of the three issues, food and its corollary of economic development was the most important. Its adoption by Kennedy would bring national attention and federal help to the state and the region. The family issue was easy to use because it was so unique. It was the first time in American political history that a family clan had so impacted American presidential politics. Finally, the flag was the easiest to exploit. Kennedy was a legitimate war hero with medals who had a well-publicized story in a war that resonated in a state with one of the nation's highest rates of military service.

Chapter four, "The Press Reports," looks at the role of the Kennedy campaign in exploiting the financial, organizational, and media disparity between the Humphrey and Kennedy operations in West Virginia. The Kennedy campaign effectively used campaign tools such as a private plane and television ads that set a new standard for future presidential efforts. The senator who wrote an article for TV Guide on television as "new force in politics,"[57] used it in the Mountain State to reach voters in four ways: campaign ads, a documentary on PT-109, a television program, and a televised debate. His actions represented a full-court press to use the medium of television to craft personas for the candidacy. Besides examining Kennedy's use of modern tools of presidential campaigns, the chapter also explores the controversial role of the press, which failed to predict the Kennedy landslide in the West Virginia campaign. In its investigation of press bias, the chapter also explores three prominent journalists—William "Bill" Lawrence of the *New York Times*, Benjamin Bradlee of *Newsweek*, and national columnist Joseph Alsop—whose close relationships with the candidate raise questions both about their reporting on the primary in particular and of the relationship between a reporter and the reported in general.

Chapter five, "On the Campaign Trail," presents a timeline of the five weeks of the campaign efforts of Kennedy and Humphrey in the Mountain State. The chapter traces the exhaustive schedule of the candidates, which included at one time ten stops for Kennedy and 18 for the indefatigable Humphrey. Chapter five explores the intense campaigning across the state by both candidates, while Chapter six focuses on the legacy of the campaign. The bitterness of the campaign in the final days raised concern among national party leaders and prompted an agreement by the campaign managers that both candidates would refrain from personal attacks during the historic televised Charleston debate in the last week of the campaign.

Chapter six, "Conclusion," reviews the significant legacy of the primary to the state, the nation, and American politics. Besides advancing Kennedy's political career, the contest helped open the presidency to Catholic candidates, and impacted public policy. From food stamps to highway funds, Kennedy as president fulfilled his campaign pledge to help the state and the region. His support of the Area Redevelopment Act signaled an new era of attention on the Appalachian region. The short-term legacy of programs can be measured, but the long-term impact of the primary on presidential campaigning and regionalism is much more difficult to measure, though probably more important. The primary ushered in an infusion of money, television, and image-making that impacted the direction of presidential campaigns for the rest of the century. In addition, the negative coverage of the press promoted and exaggerated regional stereotypes that the region still faces.

Generations after his campaign for the presidency, John F. Kennedy continues to cast his shadow across our political landscape. No other president serving so short a term has left such an impact on the American public or generated so much scholarship.

Chapter 1

KENNEDY'S QUEST AND WEST VIRGINIA'S POLITICAL LANDSCAPE

You know, if we work like hell the next four years,
we will pick up all the marbles.

—John F. Kennedy to Dave Powers,
the day after Thanksgiving 1956[1]

Part 1: 1960 West Virginia's Political Landscape

An irony of American political history is that the political future of John Kennedy in the spring of 1960 rested with Democratic voters in West Virginia. Although the state's presidential primary was not a priority when he started his quest for the presidential nomination, it became one. The Massachusetts senator faced great political risk. A loss in the May 10 primary would undermine his "win all selected primaries" strategy and confirm that Catholicism was a liability in presidential politics. But a win would propel him to the nomination.

The political landscape that Kennedy encountered in West Virginia would be more difficult than Wisconsin, where he had just successfully battled Senator Hubert Humphrey. The Mountain State was starkly different in demographics, economics, and religion. Its voters were fewer, poorer, less educated, and, most importantly, less Catholic. While Wisconsin's population was 30 percent Catholic, West Virginia's was four percent, the second lowest in the nation. Only Utah had a smaller percentage of Roman Catholics.[2] And surrounding it all was the uncertainty of victory. As one Kennedy advisor noted, West Virginia was like an iceberg: "What's on top looks good, but it's very hard to figure out what's below."[3]

Carved out of an existing state during the Civil War, West Virginia was created in 1863 when Congress authorized, and President Abraham Lincoln approved, statehood for what had been an area of the commonwealth of Virginia. Lincoln's quick and controversial recognition of West Virginia statehood prompted Virginia's governor, Henry A. Wise, to declare it a "bastard child of a political rape." He and other Virginians resented the loss of one-third of their territory in the only boundary alteration in the Civil War. But a future Supreme Court ruling upheld the legality of the new state.[4]

The statue of Lincoln on the grounds of West Virginia's capitol honors his part in creating the state, but its formation can be traced to historic sectional tensions within the commonwealth of Virginia. For decades, the citizens living west of the Blue Ridge Mountains correctly believed that the government in Richmond had not addressed their concerns or paid attention to their region.[5]

Their grievances were aggravated by differences between the Tidewater and Appalachian areas of Virginia, most significantly the lack of a large slave population in the western part of the state. That region's support to enact gradual emancipation in 1832, and its lack of support for secession from the Union in 1861, reflected this sectional divide. This antagonism eventually played itself out on the battlefield as well, when the western counties contributed more Union than Confederate volunteers.[6] One hundred years later, when Kennedy courted voters in this state, its politics was more parochial, partisan, and personal than in many others.

Parochial

The first of these three Ps of West Virginia politics refers to its political insularity. Although industrialization had connected the state with the rest of the nation via commerce and transportation by the late twentieth century, West Virginia avoided the two most significant political movements of post–Civil War America. It was bypassed by populism, that "bottom-up" political rebellion that swept the South and West in the 1890s. Likewise, it had no counterpart to the "top-down" political reform of progressivism that swept the North and Midwest in the early part of the twentieth century.[7] The closest the state came to mirroring either of these reform movements was in the administrations of Democrat E. (Emanuel) Willis Wilson (1885–1889) and Republican Henry D. Hatfield (1913–1917). Wilson mounted a populist campaign in 1884 that challenged monopolies and railroads, while Hatfield initiated as governor such progressive reforms as primary elections and utility regulation.[8]

West Virginia also had few charismatic or powerful political leaders who could overcome what John Alexander Williams calls an "enduring and complex sectionalism" found in the relatively small and homogenous state.[9] Only two politicians were able to exert long-term control over state politics. The first was Republican senator Stephen B. Elkins, who from 1895 to his death in 1911 operated the state's first political machine. The second was M. M. Neely who, with the help of organized labor, fashioned a Democratic political machine in 1940 that impacted state politics for next two decades.

West Virginia is the only state that lies entirely within the borders of the region designated by the federal government as Appalachia. Appalachia came into national consciousness as a distinct region and people soon after the Civil War, when writers such as John C. Campbell, author of *The Southern Highlander and His Homeland*, portrayed the mountainous south as a homogenous area out of touch and out of step with the rest of the country.[10] In 1978, however, Henry Shapiro effectively challenged the mythical unity of this region and its population.[11] Recent scholarship has also undermined this idea of a coherent region inhabited by a homogeneous population. Ronald L. Lewis, Ronald D. Eller, and other historians have revealed Appalachia to be more complex and diverse than originally portrayed.[12] As Lewis observes, "Industrializing Appalachia was a matrix of cultural interaction among very diverse races and cultures."[13] Recent scholarship has also affirmed the role of activism in the region. These findings undermine the stereotype of reticent and powerless Appalachians.[14]

But the politics of the state did not often reflect the changes that industrialization and diversity brought to it. The amateur legislatures, lame duck governors, and lack of party machines continued. While West Virginia was connected economically with the nation, and its population was becoming more diverse, its politics lacked strong leadership or bold reform, in part because of its constitution, its continued sectionalism, and its domination by business interests, specifically the coal industry.[15] In regard to the latter, the state government's minimalist approach to policymaking from the end of the Civil War through the New Deal allowed the large economic interests to dominate its economy and politics.[16]

While West Virginia avoided the reform movements of populism and progressivism, it was impacted by Franklin Roosevelt's national actions and legislative agenda in the 1930s. The president earned a special place in the hearts of many West Virginians for his aid to the state during the Great Depression and for his encouragement of unions, which became, for the first time, a powerful player in the state's politics. In part because of Roosevelt's popularity, the 1930s would mark the beginning of an 80-year dominance of the Democratic Party in West Virginia.[17]

Partisan

When Kennedy ran in the 1960 presidential primary, West Virginia was in the middle of one of its many partisan periods. Although the state has had two major parties since its creation in 1863, it has rarely had a competitive two-party system. The success of both Elkins and Neely, who were of different political parties, reflected the roller-coaster ride of the legendary partisanship that characterized West Virginia politics during the first century of its history.

From 1863 through 1960 the state had four distinct phases of party dominance. The first period witnessed Republican control from 1863 through 1871. During the second period, 1872 through 1896, all five of the governors elected were Democrats. The Democratic party slipped into minority status with the election of 1896 when West Virginia followed the Republican tide that swept every part of the nation except the South.

The GOP takeover in the Mountain State in 1896 set it apart from the southern states to which West Virginia is often linked. During the next generation, West Virginia Democrats elected only one governor. The standing of the party was so poor that in 1924, Democratic presidential candidate John W. Davis, a West Virginia native, didn't carry his home state.

The fourth and longest period of party dominance started in 1933 when the Great Depression and Franklin Roosevelt's New Deal altered the political landscape of West Virginia and the nation.[18] Economic hardship favored the Democrats' call for an activist government, and President Franklin Roosevelt became a political saint in the state. For the rest of the twentieth century, West Virginia Democrats would maintain a two-to-one edge in registration, maintain majorities in both houses of the state legislature, and, with the exception of two Republican governors, shut out the GOP in almost all statewide executive offices and US Senate races.[19]

Since West Virginia in 1960 was essentially a one-party state, the most important election was not in November, when Democrats opposed Republicans in the general election, but in May when fellow Democrats faced off in contested primaries. As a Logan County politician observed, "Most of our work was over the day after the primary."[20]

A legacy of intense partisanship didn't mean a lack of political competition on the county level. The intra-party discord among Democrats during the primary meant that in most counties you had an ingroup that controlled most of the local offices and an outgroup in opposition. Each faction was usually motivated more by patronage than ideology. Such a situation presented a minefield for the Kennedy primary campaign as it tried to reach voters by wooing local factions.

When John Kennedy came in 1960 to campaign, the Mountain State was entering its second generation of Democratic supremacy. The party hadn't lost a single gubernatorial or presidential election between 1930 and 1952.[21]

Unfortunately for Kennedy, the one interruption to what would be a hundred years of Democratic domination occurred in 1956. In that election the GOP gubernatorial candidate, Cecil Underwood, was swept into office due, in part, to President Dwight Eisenhower's national landslide, and to a late-developing scandal that undermined Underwood's opponent. The unexpected Democratic losses in 1956 had implications for the Kennedy primary campaign four years later. First, it meant there would be no Democratic governor to play a role or court in the primary contest. Second, it meant that an already-decentralized party would be further weakened. By 1960 the state organization was at a low point both financially and politically. The decline was attributed in part to the Democrats' loss of patronage—an important factor in strengthening party organization.[22]

Personal

The most common adage of politics in the state is, "Everything is political in West Virginia but politics, which is personal." As Kennedy's state campaign manager, Bob McDonough, explained to Larry O'Brien, the keys to winning West Virginia were the county unit and personal contact. To win a statewide race, a candidate needed to have a local focus and employ retail politics.

Mounting a successful campaign in West Virginia would be a county exercise. But the Kennedy supporters soon discovered that for county political leaders, the 1960 presidential primary was not a priority. They were more interested in getting their candidates for local office on the general election ballot than in gathering votes for the presidential beauty contest. In the minds of many local leaders, an endorsement of Kennedy was at best a distraction and at worst a liability, as the controversy over his religion might lose rather than attract voters.[23]

Three factors heightened the local and personal focus in West Virginia politics. The first was the state's topography. West Virginia earned its nickname, the Mountain State, for being the most mountainous state east of the Mississippi River. Its terrain is so rugged that it has only one natural lake. If flattened, West Virginia would cover Texas. Such topography encouraged regionalism by discouraging easy intrastate transportation. Although train travel after the Civil War would help connect the state with the outside, ground transportation within the state remained difficult into the twentieth century.

West Virginia's boundaries also undermined a sense of political unity. Although small in size, the state is not compact. The heart-shaped state has four geographic districts and two distinct panhandles. The Northern Panhandle is a narrow stretch of land wedged between Ohio and Pennsylvania, and the Eastern Panhandle is separated from the rest of the state by mountain ranges.

The dispersal of cities highlights the state's lack of geographic unity. Four of its five largest cities lie at its borders—Parkersburg is right next to Ohio, Huntington next to Kentucky and Ohio, Wheeling next to Ohio and Pennsylvania, Bluefield next to southern Virginia, and Martinsburg next to northern Virginia, Maryland, and Washington, DC. Only the state capital, Charleston, rests in the center of the state.[24]

West Virginia cities are scattered, small, and few in number. In 1960, West

Virginia was in the top five most rural states in the nation, sharing the distinction with South Dakota, Vermont, Arkansas, and Mississippi. While 70 percent of Americans were classified as living in an urban area in 1960, 40 percent of West Virginians lived in cities of 2,500 or more. Only eight cities had populations of more than 20,000, and only two (Charleston and Huntington) had populations of more than 80,000.[25]

Finally, the state's 1871 constitution amplified a local political focus by encouraging rampant regionalism. Reflecting a distrust of powerful politicians, the document limited governors to one term and made legislators part-time political amateurs. Assigning a lame-duck status to elected governors inhibited their power in office and undermined any chance to become a dominant political force in the state. Making the legislative sessions short and the pay meager meant all legislators had outside jobs.[26]

The state's topography, boundaries, and constitution help explain why, for many citizens in 1960, the epicenter of political power resided not in Charleston, but in their county courthouse. County-elected officials, from county commissioners to assessors, had more contact with the voter than the politicians in Charleston. On the local level, the most powerful office was county sheriff, since that person both collected taxes and had the power to arrest you.[27] In such a political dynamic, one can understand the reluctance of local county politicians to get involved in the presidential primary, as that contest had no immediate benefit to the local slate of candidates being offered up in all the counties across the state.

This was the challenging political landscape that John Kennedy confronted in the spring of 1960. First, there was not that much interest in the presidential primary. Second, there was no single dominant politician or cadre of powerful leaders within the state Democratic Party for Kennedy to court. Third, Kennedy had to conduct a micro and not a macro campaign and spent weeks on face-to-face encounters. He had to wage an intense ground game, visiting individual counties and courting a plethora of local Democratic officials.

Corruption

Politics in the Mountain State was not only more parochial, partisan, and personal than in many other states—it was also more corrupt. Author and reporter Theodore White waxed eloquent on the corruption of West Virginia that stood in contrast to clean and decent politics of Wisconsin and Minnesota. Excluding the states of the south, White ranked West Virginia among those states whose politics "are the most squalid, corrupt and despicable." Using the metaphor of the family in *Tobacco Road*, White assigned the Mountain State to the "Jukes family of America politics," a group that included Indiana, Massachusetts, and

Texas. The latter two were home to Kennedy and his future running mate, Lyndon Baines Johnson."[28]

The association of the Mountain State and political corruption goes back a long way. A political cartoon from the early 1900s highlighted the state's reputation by showing the state's two US senators, Davis and Elkins, leaning on (pork) barrels of money, each holding a checkbook with their name on it and smiling at each other. At the top is "The West Virginia Problem." Obviously the 1904 cartoon saw the senators' free-flowing money as a problem.[29]

And it continued into the future. Wally Barron won his party's gubernatorial nomination in the same 1960 primary that selected John Kennedy. As governor, he would greet President Kennedy when he came to West Virginia to celebrate its centennial on June 22, 1963. But years later, Barron was convicted of jury tampering and sent to federal prison. Furthermore, political corruption in West Virginia was bipartisan. In 1990, former Republican governor Arch Moore was sentenced to five years in prison.[30]

A national audience saw the corruption when, a week before the primary, *Life* magazine published a four-page article titled "In Logan County, the Half-Pint Vote, Slating and Lever Brothers." The "half-pint vote" referred to those in the county who sold their vote for a half pint of whisky or a sum of cash ranging from two to four dollars.[31] The Lever brothers were two election commissioners who discussed how they would "help" voters by going into the voting booth and providing assistance. Their grins in the half-page picture suggested that their help ensured that the correct lever was pressed. Commenting on their work, one Logan politician said, "Man, on Election Day they play the levers in those voting machines like *Auld Lang Syne*."[32]

While White's generalization that the state had "sordid" politics could be applied to many counties in West Virginia, it overlooked the regional differences across the state in terms of machine-controlled counties. Most counties south of the Kanawha River were dominated by a political faction, but the counties in the north were less machine organized. Wood County in the west along the Ohio River, for example, had several factions contending rather than a dominant group.[33]

Slating

A unique and often misinterpreted practice in West Virginia elections was slating, which refers to the often-misunderstood procedure of assembling a list of candidates selected by a political faction in a county. Essentially, a slate was a list of candidates that the local political faction endorsed. Sometimes the list was printed and handed out in leaflet form, and other times it was printed in a newspaper or passed on to voters orally.

The key was to have a candidate's name on the correct slate—the list sponsored by a dominant county faction or associated with the county's most successful politician. Such linkage increased a candidate's chances. In counties that had different factions, there could be two or three slates of candidates. A candidate's preference would be to make it onto the slate of the "ins"—the dominant faction in the county. But if that wasn't possible, a candidate would seek endorsement by the "outs," who opposed the dominant county faction.

As Dan Fleming points out, the process was neither new to American elections, nor crucial to victory since West Virginia voters in most of the state made up their mind without the aid of slates.[34] But in 1960 it was an important part of electoral process, especially in the so-called southern coal counties, where it was considered a tool that ensured victory in a primary.

Three factors help explain slating. The first has to do with the primary's competitiveness. Given the poor state of the Republican party, the spring primary was the most important election of the year. After a candidate won the Democratic nomination in May, the election in the fall would, in many counties, be a foregone conclusion. Hence the stakes were high.

The second factor is the length of the West Virginia primary ballot, which in 1960 was one of the most cumbersome in America. A Charleston voter that year faced 53 individual choices of candidates. When the *Charleston Gazette* reproduced sample ballots for subdivisions in Kanawha County, the project required three standard newspaper pages.

Because of the ballot's length, the chief county registrar encouraged voters to familiarize themselves with it in advance.[35] He urged them to study the sample ballots printed in both Charleston papers, mark it at home, and take the newspaper or sample ballot with them to the polls. Such action would ensure that they could "vote correctly and as rapidly as possible."[36] As White points out, "Such a mystifying ballot requires simplification for the voter" and slating provides that simplification."[37] A slate of preferred candidates could be of practical use to the average voter, as it expedited what would be a long process.

The third factor is financial: slating offered an easy way to fundraise. County organizations or political factions would usually assess the candidates a fee to be placed on their slate. The expected fee varied by office. A candidate for governor, for instance, would pay more than a candidate for House delegate. Refusal to pay the fee meant you were left off the slate. The *Life* article quoted a future state senator, Dan Dahill, who said that in Logan County it cost $5,000 to be slated for most offices, but the standard fee for sheriff was $40,000.[38]

What could be called "paying the candidate's fair share" of campaign expenses in a county could also be labeled as a shakedown or legalized bribery. But slating was a method for county organizations to finance their election mobilization efforts. Most of the money would be used to underwrite campaign expenses, though certainly some stayed in the pockets of the political bosses or head of the county political faction.[39]

Slate donations were used to pay campaign workers, buy half-pint bottles, pay voters, and hire election-day drivers who would take voters to the polls. The drivers normally received $25 to $50, and they were expected to bring relatives and friends. The money raised would be used in voter mobilization efforts, although there are many stories where the candidate "fees" for being placed on a slate were used for private gain rather than public voter mobilization.[40]

The 1960 presidential primary offered a new experience for an old practice. Local bosses could seek contributions from either candidate—especially Kennedy, who had greater need and even greater resources to get slated in key counties. But it is important to understand that the presidential primary held no prospect of state patronage or power for the county leaders. Since their chief concern was to get their slate elected, their most immediate priority was to make sure the presidential candidate they endorsed would not be a drag on the local or regional slate.

Both presidential candidates used slating in an effort to win county support. According to Humphrey cochairman Bob Barrie, Hubert Humphrey and (even more so) Muriel Humphrey were horrified by slating. While the candidate did play the game eventually, he did so with less money and less success than his competitor.[41]

In Logan County, Humphrey paid money to get on the slate of party boss Ray Chafin. In public, the leader of the most powerful faction stood by the Minnesota senator, but when the Kennedy campaign made a larger offer, Chafin switched on Election Day—the name on his slate list in two of the three districts was Kennedy's.[42]

The story is told that on election night, when returns indicated a Kennedy win in Logan County, an enraged Barrie went to Kennedy headquarters in the Kanawha Hotel and confronted Pierre Salinger, press secretary for the Kennedy campaign: "'We bought Logan County and you bought it back.' 'Yes,' replied a smiling Salinger, 'and that is not all.'"[43]

Humphrey was at a disadvantage, both in terms of his late start and his lack of funds. He later wrote that he lost in the bidding war because his campaign expenditures were "peanuts" compared to those of the Kennedy organization. When aide Herb Waters told people that the Humphrey campaign was prepared to spend up to $25,000 to get on the slates (an amount that shocked Humphrey), Waters said, "I was laughed out of the office because it was not enough."[44]

O'Brien estimated that the Kennedy campaign paid $100,000 for slating.[45] In an interview, he said that the $5,000 spent to slate Kennedy in an important county represented the largest payment for slating. But slating was not a practice in most of the 55 counties, and if at least $100,000 was spent on it, either the number is suspect or much more money went to less important counties.

O'Brien relates a story about the time he called Phyllis Maddock, a secretary in charge of the money, on the hotel house phone and whispered, "Bring me five." Phyllis, who kept the money in a suitcase under her bed, gave him $500 instead of the $5,000.[46]

In his West Virginia primary contest, John Kennedy would use the new tools of wholesale politics, such as television, and the old practices of retail politics, such as slating and direct interaction with voters. He was battling on the tilted field of a state that did not fit the profile of most states. The risk of combat in this landscape was great, but the benefits of winning against Senator Hubert Humphrey were greater.

Part 2: JFK's Strategy and Early Start

Any examination of the 1960 West Virginia presidential primary must begin with the fact that presidential primaries at that time were not taken seriously. To use Harry Truman's phrase, they were "only eyewash" and not the avenue to nomination they would become after 1968.[47]

Ever since 1832, presidential candidates had been selected by a party convention. This quadrennial assembly of delegates was governed not by popular vote, but by party leaders who often engaged in behind-closed-door deal making to select a suitable candidate. Which meant that until 1960, party leaders were in control of the nominating process, not primary voters. So it is not surprising that most serious presidential contenders for the Democratic nomination in 1960 did not enter state primaries. Of the five major Democratic presidential contenders that year, only two did: Senator Hubert Humphrey from Minnesota and Senator John F. Kennedy from Massachusetts.[48] They would confront each other twice—first in Wisconsin on April 8 and then in West Virginia on May 10.

Of the 1,523 delegates who would be at the 1960 Democratic convention in Los Angeles, only 584 came from states with primaries. This meant that almost two-thirds of the delegates wouldn't be chosen by a primary election. Party bosses controlled the delegate selection in the 34 non-primary states. Additionally, many primary states would support a "favorite son"—the governor or senator or another prominent politician.

The purpose of pursuing a primary strategy in 1960 was psychological, not quantitative. A string of primaries would not yield many delegates, but it would help convince party leaders who controlled the majority of delegates at that summer convention in Los Angeles.[49]

Believing that the primary was his only path to the nomination, Kennedy mounted an extensive primary strategy that reflected both his front-runner status and his financial strength. In contrast, Hubert Humphrey planned a selective primary strategy that reflected his long odds and short funds. His long-risk campaign plan was to arrive at the convention with a nucleus of 150 to 200 delegates—enough to influence the party platform and position himself for a possible shot at the nomination. Humphrey later wrote that his nomination was "about a ten-to-one long shot. Still there was that chance."[50]

In the fall of 1959, West Virginia was on Humphrey's list of five possible states, and on Kennedy's list of ten states for consideration. But little attention was given to it by either campaign, and few could foresee the impact West Virginia would have six months later on the political landscape of the nation in 1960.[51]

There were certainly many reasons for John Kennedy not to enter the West Virginia presidential primary. Its delegation was small (only 25 delegates) and not bound to the primary result. In addition, he had no support from the state Democratic leadership. All of the House delegation and both US senators refused to support him. In fact, Senator Robert C. Byrd actively campaigned against Kennedy and would voice the "stop Kennedy" rationale that "If you are for Adlai Stevenson, Senator Stuart Symington, Senator Johnson, or John Doe, this may be your last chance to stop Kennedy."[52]

Another reason to avoid the West Virginia primary was that while it was long on history, it was short on impact. It did not have the tradition of New Hampshire, the nation's first primary, or the legendary history of Wisconsin, which had in the past undermined the presidential hopes of General Douglas McArthur in 1952 and the comeback hopes of Wendell Willkie in 1944.[53]

As *Charleston Gazette* reporter Harry Hoffman pointed out in January 1960, the Mountain State primary did not share such a proud history. In his article headlined "Primary Won't Elect a President," the veteran political reporter noted the fate of past primary winners. While Al Smith won it in 1928, "so did many lesser-runs such as perennial presidential candidate Harold Stassen." Concluded Hoffman "You don't get elected president by winning the West Virginia primary."[54]

In the end, Humphrey couldn't resist the temptation that the profile of West Virginia offered him. It was a state with strong labor backing, vast unemployment, and a small percentage of Catholics. Moreover, it was far enough away from home that a victory would make his appeal seen nationwide.

After Humphrey entered the contest, John Kennedy flew to Charleston on February 4, 1960, and officially registered for the primary. Kennedy entered six of the possible 16 primaries held that spring. On the flight back he showed reporters a Lou Harris poll from December of 1959, which showed him with a commanding lead (70 to 30 percent) over Humphrey. In his report Harris noted that "If the Wisconsin results are inconclusive, then West Virginia seems like a good testing ground for Kennedy to win a conclusive and decisive victory over Humphrey." Harris concluded that a concentrated effort in West Virginia "can result in a handsome victory and a powerful weapon against those who raise the Catholic can't win bit."[55]

While the Harris poll found anti-Catholic sentiment in the electorate, it was not enough "to have any deleterious effect on the outcome." He did offer, however, caution about the role of the national media when he suggested that "a careful eye" be kept on the role of religious prejudice in the state because it was such an "explosive issue and *is being fanned so faithfully by the fourth estate*" (italics mine).[56]

What Harris feared came to pass when the press in Wisconsin focused on the religious issue, appearing to generate national attention on Kennedy's faith. When voting returns from Wisconsin suggested that Kennedy had trouble getting Protestant votes, he went from being the front-runner for the Democratic nomination to the "Catholic candidate" who needed a primary win in an overwhelming Protestant state. And West Virginia went from being an asset—a firewall if Wisconsin didn't work out—to a dangerous liability. A trap, not for Humphrey, but for Kennedy, who discovered that his lead in the state vanished as concerns about his religion surfaced.

Starting after the Wisconsin primary on April 5 and lasting until Election Day in West Virginia on May 10, 1960, the nation watched the most competitive presidential primary of 1960 as Kennedy and Humphrey faced off in the Mountain State. A lack of accurate statewide polling data, and the uncertainty of the religious issue, would ensure that doubts dominated those five weeks of intense campaigning.

Organization

Fortunately for Kennedy, he had an early head start in organization in West Virginia. An organization had been assembled, a local staff was put in place, and access to funds appeared unlimited. The trap was set if Humphrey decided to continue his quest beyond the Wisconsin primary and contest Kennedy in the Mountain State.

Five weeks before the May 10 contest in West Virginia, Wisconsin held the first competitive primary between the two candidates, John Kennedy and Hubert Humphrey, who had selected the "primary route" to the Democratic presidential nomination.[57] The Wisconsin battleground in 1960 proved to be a costly campaign for Kennedy. It ended with an indecisive victory that set the stage for the West Virginia primary.

Going into that contest, the press identified Kennedy as the frontrunner, and many believed that a victory there would mark the end of Humphrey's campaign. The reasoning was that if the Minnesota senator could not win his neighboring state of Wisconsin in April, he would drop out of contention before the West Virginia primary in May.

But that expectation, like so many in American presidential politics, would not be accurate. Although John Kennedy won the Wisconsin primary by 100,000 votes, his win was not convincing enough to take Humphrey out of contention. The Kennedy camp made the mistake of raising the expectation that they might carry all 10 congressional districts. On election night, their candidate carried only six.

The significance of the primary was not so much in the results as it was in the reporting of the results. Specifically, the media attributed Kennedy's victory to a strong turnout of Catholic voters, both Democratic and Republican, who composed 30 percent of Wisconsin's population. The numbers supported this analysis. Of Wisconsin's ten voting districts, Kennedy won all five industrialized districts with Catholic majorities, lost all four rural districts with predominantly Protestant majorities, and narrowly won the one district that was evenly divided. His Wisconsin victory was disparaged because it came disproportionately from the four of the state's heavily Catholic Congressional Districts: Fourth, Fifth, Sixth, and Eighth.[58] Even Joseph Alsop, a columnist sympathetic to Kennedy, claimed that his religion helped him in the Catholic districts of east Wisconsin and implied that his religion hurt him in the western Protestant region where he was shut out.[59]

On election night the Kennedy family and close advisors listened to election returns in the suite at the Pfister Hotel in Milwaukee. Theodore White, who was in the room that night, described the candidate's demeanor. "Taut of face, unsmiling, sensing himself wounded, he prepared to leave for the TV studios to thank the people of Wisconsin for the victory he knew was not a victory."[60]

Seeing the expression on her brother's face as he studied the returns on election night in Wisconsin, Eunice Kennedy Shriver asked him, "What does it all mean?" He replied, "It means that we've got to go to West Virginia in the morning and do it all over again. And then we've got to go on to Maryland and Indiana and Oregon and win all of them."[61]

Kennedy's resignation that night reflected the fact that his first major contested primary did not turn out to be the expected one-and-out for Humphrey. Not only did Humphrey stay in the race, but the religious issue surfaced.

After Kennedy's tainted victory in the Wisconsin primary, his lead appeared to evaporate, as many West Virginia voters identified Kennedy as a Catholic, seemingly for the first time. Also for the first time in his quest for the presidential nomination, things went wrong. The anticipated Humphrey trap had become a possible Kennedy nightmare.

After the Wisconsin contest, Kennedy told a different version of the primary results than that offered on primary night. Although his organization had touted it as a big win, Kennedy later wrote *Washington Post* reporter Chalmers Roberts that "As for Wisconsin, I am reminded of the story of the old Frenchman who was asked what he had done during the French Revolution. He replied, 'I survived.' That's the way I felt about Wisconsin."[62]

How he felt about the upcoming primary in West Virginia was even more enlightening. In a letter dictated to another correspondent he voiced his concern: "Thank you for the cognac. I would like to say that I am planning to keep it to sip during the warm spring nights. Unfortunately, last night I begin to think about West Virginia and drank the whole bottle."[63]

Charleston Meeting

Coming off his "tainted" primary win in Wisconsin, Kennedy found himself in unexpected trouble in the Mountain State—a fact brought home dramatically to his team when they met with the campaign workers in the Kanawha Hotel in Charleston the day after the Wisconsin contest. Bobby Kennedy, Larry O'Brien, and Kenny O'Donnell had just flown from Milwaukee on Kennedy's private plane, the *Caroline*, and were taken directly to the meeting.[64] When Bobby asked the campaign workers if there were problems, a man stood up and shouted, "There's only one problem. He's a Catholic. That's our God-damned problem."[65] According to O'Donnell, the workers told the Kennedy team that they were getting abuse and ridicule from friends and neighbors for supporting a Catholic.

"Overnight our whole situation in West Virginia had changed," O'Donnell recalled. "All of the careful and hopeful planning for a successful campaign in this Southern border state, which would bring Kennedy into the Los Angeles convention as the leading contender, was on the brink of going down the drain." Bobby Kennedy "appeared pale and in a state of shock."[66] If Bobby was in shock, his brother was in disbelief. Hearing the bad news, John responded by reminding Bobby of the favorable Harris poll. To which Bobby replied, "The people who voted for you in that poll have just found out that you're a Catholic."[67]

With the stage set for a hard fight in the Mountain State, those who attended the strategy session in the Kanawha Hotel formulated a plan. The blueprint for victory that came out of that tense Charleston meeting was a two-pronged strategy for Kennedy to use in West Virginia. First, he would confront the religious issue, and second, he would promote a "three-F" issue strategy—food, family, and flag—that would resonate in the state.[68]

Early Start

Luckily for his campaign, John F. Kennedy entered the West Virginia primary with a head start in organization. He had taken an interest in the Mountain State as early as June 1958 when he had his pollster, Lou Harris, conduct the first survey of voters done in a state outside Massachusetts.[69] A year later, West Virginia was one of the states polled when the Kennedy campaign was identifying possible state primaries to enter. At that time, West Virginia appeared favorable as a state south of the Mason-Dixon line. In the end only two other states in the south had primaries: Florida, which supported favorite son Senator George Smathers, and Maryland, where Kennedy ran unopposed.

In addition to polling the state, he also visited West Virginia at least three times in 1959. One visit took him to Welch for a fundraiser in McDowell County. There he met the powerful political boss Sid Christie for the first of many times. Christie had to go downtown to buy the senator a dress shirt when Kennedy's luggage was lost. But an important friendship began, and on election night Kennedy would carry the county with 80 percent of the vote.[70]

But most importantly, Kennedy had in place a statewide organization almost a year before the May 1960 primary. The effort to organize West Virginia had started in January 1959, and by April the Kennedy camp had recruited Robert P. "Bob" McDonough, a Parkersburg business man who ran a printing company. A fellow Catholic who was devoted to the candidate, McDonough served without pay in his role as state organizer.[71]

Ken O'Donnell describes McDonough as "one of the most skillful and knowledgeable Democratic politicians in the state." This view was shared by the Kennedy staff, who gave him the nickname Our Man in Havana after the film starring Alec Guinness as a spy in Cuba.[72]

McDonough's job was to be not only the Kennedy camp's spy in West Virginia, but also their teacher about West Virginia. In this regard, his most important task was to convince them that the Mountain State was not Massachusetts. The Kennedy campaign in the former could not be just a rerun of his successes in the latter.[73]

Larry O'Brien, a close Kennedy advisor, had developed the classic Kennedy campaign in Kennedy's home state. The campaign involved voter receptions, tabloid handouts, and telephone calls. Based on his successful work, he had written a 64-page manual that outlined these tools and procedures. But when O'Brien proposed this approach to McDonough, his response was, "We can do all that, but it won't be enough."[74]

McDonough believed the organizational model that had proved so successful in Massachusetts wouldn't operate in the decentralized and face-to-face politics of West Virginia. The key to West Virginia politics, he argued, was the county unit and personal contact.[75]

O'Brien would later conclude that McDonough was right. The problem in West Virginia was that much of the real power lay in the counties, where a relatively small number—no more than 100 local politicians—influenced the votes of thousands. To be successful in these counties, Kennedy would need to be endorsed by one or more factions within a county and put on their public list or "slate."[76]

Moreover, the candidate needed to campaign extensively in a political culture that emphasized retail politics. It's not surprising that after the shock of Wisconsin, the Kennedy campaign announced that the candidate would be in West Virginia not for the one scheduled week, but for four weeks leading up to the vote.

A briefing memo from Ted Sorensen and Bob Wallace highlighted the importance of personal contact in West Virginia politics. "West Virginia delegation must be appealed to on a personal basis," the memo read, and the Kennedy camp needed to "create a favorable atmosphere for JFK among influential Democrats in the state."[77] To this end, the memo supplied a detailed review of Kennedy's status in the each of the state's six congressional districts. Featured in this section were the visits Kennedy had made or planned to make to each one.[78]

From April to October 1959, McDonough traveled the state gathering a file of those county Democrat politicians interested in Kennedy and established a formal organization. By January 5, 1960, three days after John Kennedy formally announced his candidacy, Bob Wallace reported that a political organization was in place in West Virginia with state senator Charles Love as the head, McDonough as secretary, and a chairman appointed for each of the six congressional districts.[79] After working for almost a year, Matthew Reese and McDonough had set up "Kennedy for President—West Virginia" organizations, each headed by a chairman in 39 of the state's 55 counties.[80]

The campaign initially hoped to link their organization with the leading gubernatorial candidate in the Democratic primary, Attorney General William Wallace "Wally" Barron. In public Barron claimed to be neutral, privately saying that he would work quietly for Kennedy.[81] But Barron's words were questionable, as he had also said the same thing to the Humphrey camp. As a result, the Kennedy campaign was deprived of organizational help from Wally Barron, who easily won the 1960 gubernatorial primary.

Setting up an organization in the Mountain State would start with an attempt to obtain the support of the strongest political faction in each county. This was especially important in the southern counties that would distribute slates.[82] If the county's dominant political faction would not back Kennedy, support from a rival faction would be solicited. This happened in Logan County when the dominant Chafin faction endorsed Humphrey. Just before the vote, Chafin secretly switched support, and on Election Day Kennedy's name was on the slates of two factions.[83]

If recruitment of existing political factions failed, or if a county didn't have factions, the Kennedy campaign would build their own group. Matt Reese, the executive director, said that when none of those options worked, he would go to the local diner and ask for names of prominent Catholics in the county—a cadre he knew he could rely on.[84]

Although Reese managed to set up organizations in 39 of the state's counties, many had not met the criteria laid out in O'Brien's manual. Those criteria included finding subordinate district chairmen, a primary day chairman to arrange voter transportation on election day, and two standby deputy chairmen available 24 hours a day for literature distribution.[85]

In contrast, the Humphrey campaign structure bordered on nonexistence. Starting late, there was no effort to establish a presence in a majority of West Virginia counties. Instead, Humphrey supporters divided the state into two parts and recruited two state cochairmen. William L. Jacobs of Parkersburg, a former Wood County Democratic chairman, organized the northern half of the state, while Marshall West of Oceana in Wyoming County was in charge of the southern half.

In addition to being hindered by a late start, the Humphrey effort lacked funding. Jacobs recollected that when he started his job, his only asset besides Humphrey's campaign skills was a telephone card. "I was supplied with no funds whatsoever to put on any kind of drive, but I did use my telephone card to call people across the northern half of the state, various lawyers with whom I had been associated, and various Democratic leaders that I'd come into contact with."[86]

The first and only organizational crisis the Kennedy team experienced in its yearlong buildup occurred in early 1960 when labor and liberals voiced concerns about the state chairman, state senator Charles Love, and the campaign manager, Bob McDonough. Love was viewed as "too reactionary" and McDonough as anti-union because his printing company was "open-shop"—it did not require union membership for employment.[87]

Kennedy acted swiftly on concerns about the former, replacing Love with state senator Ward Wylie of Pineville in Wyoming County, someone who was acceptable to the leadership of the AFL-CIO and United Mine Workers. Kennedy could not afford to alienate these two unions, who would stay neutral in the primary despite Humphrey's excellent record on unions and Kennedy's questionable record.[88]

More important than the replacement at the top of the organization, however, was what Kennedy didn't do with McDonough. He stayed in place—a decision that recognized his talent and reflected Kennedy's moderation on the labor front.

Another speed bump to the Kennedy campaign in West Virginia came in February from US senator Robert Byrd. The junior senator was Lyndon Johnson's most vocal supporter and John Kennedy's most visible critic in the Mountain State.[89] In February, the same month Kennedy registered to enter the West Virginia presidential primary, Byrd distributed a poll showing that Lyndon Johnson was the first choice and Kennedy was last choice of the Democratic local leaders. Like his other efforts to boost Lyndon Johnson, the Byrd poll was questionable in its methodology and counterproductive in its results. W. E. Chilton III, the editor of the *Gazette*, correctly charged that the poll was stacked, and his top political reporter, Harry Hoffman, reported that the poll surveyed only selective Democrats.[90] When the campaign heated up in April, there would be more efforts by Byrd. But like the discredited poll, none posed a serious attack on the Massachusetts senator, or provided major help to Humphrey.

Chapter 2

KENNEDY ADOPTS A RELIGIOUS CONFRONTATION STRATEGY

It's pretty hard to run against the Protestant Reformation.

—John F. Kennedy, handwritten note, April 23, 1960[1]

At 8:30 a.m. on September 12, 1960, a crowd of 300 spectators outside the Rice Hotel in Houston saw John Kennedy emerge dressed in a dark suit and white shirt. What they didn't see was that the candidate had mixed socks, one black and one brown. According to advisor Dave Powers, Kennedy discovered the mistake while on the elevator to the lobby and expressed concern, but Powers told him the audience wouldn't care.[2] He was correct. Kennedy's religion, not his wardrobe, was the focus when the Democratic nominee addressed the Houston Ministerial Association.

The ministers in Texas were not alone in their concerns. A Gallup Poll in 1959 showed that almost 20 percent of polled voters would not support a Catholic for president even if the person was "generally well qualified." In the South it was one voter out of three. (Ironically, in 1959 only 47 percent of polled voters knew that John Kennedy was a Catholic.)[3]

To that hostile audience of Baptist ministers in the hotel ballroom, the second Catholic presidential candidate nominated by a major political party gave the same pronouncement that he had delivered on television to West Virginia voters four months earlier: a strong declaration in the belief of separation of church and state and a promise to privatize his faith by not allowing his religion to influence his public policy.

At that Houston assemblage, Kennedy stated in stark terms his intention to separate his beliefs from his presidential policies: "I believe in an America where the separation of church and state is absolute. Where no Catholic fellow would tell the president should he be Catholic how to act, and no Protestant minister would tell his parishioners for whom to vote."[4]

Kennedy's proclamation of what Teddy White calls the "doctrine of the modern Catholic in a democratic society" had its Catholic critics. They saw the statement as a sellout. They argued that his entry into American presidential politics was bought at the cost of Catholic religious principles. To them it seemed the man who wanted to be the first Catholic president was not Catholic enough. Mark Massa later argued that Kennedy's Houston speech "represented a secularization of American politics: it removed religion as an appropriate topic from the Oval Office."[5]

But while some Catholics took issue with Kennedy's calculated effort to distance himself from his religion for electoral reasons, many saw it as a pragmatic avenue to an important victory. They saw it as a price to pay for admission to presidential politics, a practical concession to reassure concerned Protestants.

But while Kennedy championed separation of church and state, he also confronted his audience on the unfairness of anti-Catholic opinions, repeating the language he used so often on the campaign trail in West Virginia: "If this election is decided on the basis of 40 million Americans who lost their chance of being president on the day that they were baptized, then it is the whole nation that will be the loser in the eyes of Catholics and non-Catholics around the world, and in the eyes of history, and in the eyes of our people."[6]

Kennedy's confrontational strategy on the religious issue, seen in Houston in September, was rooted in the mountains of West Virginia in April, when the candidate spent weeks championing his belief in separation of church and state, and addressing the anti-Catholicism concerns that plagued Governor Al Smith 32 years earlier. But unlike that presidential candidate, John Kennedy's strategy was not confined to a single speech. Religion was the subject of multiple speeches on television and at venues across the Mountain State.

It was the specter of defeat in West Virginia that prompted the candidate to adopt this strategy.[7] The new approach represented a sharp break from the Wisconsin campaign, where he avoided any discussion of his religion. It also reflected a desperation in the Kennedy camp, which watched its presumed lead over Hubert Humphrey vanish after the Wisconsin primary.

The Unwritten Law and the Ghost of 1928

The biggest obstacle to getting John Kennedy the nomination in 1960 was the widespread belief that a segment of the majority Protestant electorate would not support a Catholic for president. Evidence to support that opinion was Al Smith's landslide loss over three decades prior. An article in *Time* magazine observed, "In the 1960 debate over a Roman Catholic's chances of winning the presidency, many an argument is cinched with a reference to Al Smith's campaign of 1928."[8]

Al Smith posed the first serious threat to Protestant control of the United States presidency when he captured the Democratic party's presidential nomination. But that fall, the majority of voters didn't accept him. While historians may offer many reasons for this, conventional wisdom at the time and afterward offered just one—his faith. His loss of five traditional Democratic states in the South was attributed to the reluctance of fundamentalists to support the Catholic nominee. Smith certainly believed it when he bemoaned that "the time hasn't come when a man can say his [rosary] beads in the White House."[9]

For decades afterward, Smith's loss in 1928 was cited as evidence that Catholicism was a liability in presidential politics. This idea hardened into an axiom, often called the "unwritten law" of US politics: no Roman Catholic can get elected president of the United States.

Facing a torrent of anti-Catholic words and publications, Smith adopted a policy of silence on the religious issue. Only once during the campaign did he meet the religious issue head-on in a public place, and when he did, it was dramatic in its location, confrontational in its tone, and national in its audience. Smith's campaign stop in Oklahoma City amounted to a single shot in hostile territory with no evidence of careful preparation beforehand and no plan for follow-through afterward.

The selection of Oklahoma City cast Smith as Daniel in the lions' den, as the Sooner State had a strong Ku Klux Klan presence. When the campaign train crossed from Kansas into Oklahoma, Smith saw a burning cross.[10]

His address was a bold speech, but not an effective one. One speech in Oklahoma could not turn back the tide against religious intolerance. Religion remained an important issue in the 1928 presidential campaign, and Smith's discourse did not change that situation.[11]

On the following night, an anti-Smith rally was held in the same coliseum, and thousands heard a speech titled Al Smith and the Forces of Hell.[12] On election night, the state that Smith chose for his attack on religious intolerance would support Herbert Hoover by a two-to-one margin.[13]

Like the ghost in Hamlet, Al Smith's defeat in 1928 haunted the Democratic Party for it confirmed the unwritten law that Catholicism was a liability in presidential politics. But while Hamlet's ghost pushed the young prince to act and take revenge, Smith's specter was a catalyst for inaction—a constant reminder that Democrats should avoid a presidential nominee who was Catholic. Smith's ghost needed to be exorcised before another Catholic could be considered to be the party's standard bearer.[14]

Only a Kennedy win in November of 1960 would negate the lesson that many took away from Smith's defeat in 1928. But to have that opportunity, Kennedy needed to get his party's nomination in July 1960, and Democrats needed to view the 1928 election through a different lens.

Fortunately for Kennedy, scholars during the 1950s reinterpreted the 1928 election in a way that would be beneficial to Catholic candidates in general and John Kennedy in particular. Their studies not only discounted the role of religion in Smith's 1928 defeat, but also unearthed in the ashes of his landslide loss the seeds of the New Deal coalition that would dominate the nation. Al Smith, the victim of religious bigotry in 1928, became Al Smith, the candidate who mobilized millions of his coreligionists and set the stage for the resurgence of the Democratic party.[15]

The next serious Catholic contender for president would not be so unprepared, 32 years later. Although anti-Catholicism in 1960 was not as rampant, public, or powerful as what Smith confronted in 1928, the issue remained the most serious obstacle to John Kennedy's nomination and his election to the White House.

The legacy of Smith's defeat was a heavy one, but the lessons that Kennedy would learn from it were instructive. His handling of the religious issue can be divided into two parts: before and after the Wisconsin primary.

The "Discuss and Dismiss" Strategy

Before the April 10 Wisconsin primary, Kennedy's approach to the religious issue was careful, calculated, and cautious. The candidate employed what could be called a "discuss and dismiss" strategy. He raised the issue only in controlled situations, such as a March 1959 *Look* article written by a family friend, Fletcher Knebel. In this article he allayed Protestant concerns by promoting separation of church and state in general, and separation of his private religion and public policy in particular. He followed a scripted two-step, discussing then dismissing the religious issue, by saying, "The American people are more concerned with a man's view and abilities than with the church to which he belongs."[16]

While the candidate would talk about his religion under certain conditions, he avoided any discussion of the topic in his campaign speeches. He never brought up the issue and would only discuss it if it came up during a question-and-answer opportunity. The strategy reflected the belief that championing the separation of church and state in print would be enough to reassure Protestant voters and wouldn't alienate Catholic supporters.

While Kennedy's strong stand on the separation of church and state did reassure many Protestants, it irritated some Catholics, including his father, who wondered if his son was too quick to dismiss his faith.[17] But to ease concerns of Protestant fundamentalists, Kennedy repeatedly told voters that his religion would not influence his presidential actions. He openly discussed his policy disagreements with his church's positions on public aid for parochial schools and sending an ambassador to the Vatican.[18] Such statements supported his pledge to keep his religious beliefs separate from his presidential policies and may have explained Minnesota senator Eugene McCarthy's quip in early 1960 that "I'm twice as Catholic as Kennedy and twice as liberal as Humphrey."[19]

The attacks on his devotion would be a small but constant counterpoint to Kennedy's effort to reassure worried Protestants. An example of this Catholic backlash came from the *Indiana Catholic and Record*, which wrote, "Young Senator Kennedy had better watch his language."[20] But Kennedy was watching his language. He was playing the electoral calculus of being a serious Catholic candidate running for the presidential nomination in a majority Protestant nation at a time when there were still serious concerns about having a Catholic in the White House, a time when the defeat of the Democrats' first Catholic candidate for president was still remembered in a nation that displayed a historic pattern of Catholic prejudice.

The key to the "discuss and dismiss" strategy was that John Kennedy, like Al Smith, would champion the separation of church and state. But while Al Smith had only announced his position in one article and one major speech, Kennedy highlighted his in a more pronounced and public manner.[21]

While some Catholics took issue with Kennedy's calculated effort to distance himself from his religion for electoral reasons, many saw it as pragmatic avenue to an important victory over the unwritten law that a Catholic could not occupy the presidency.[22]

To ease concerns of Protestant fundamentalists, Kennedy repeatedly told voters that his religion would not influence his presidential actions. In his comments, he appeared to distance himself from his religion by promising to keep his religious beliefs separate from his presidential policies. He openly discussed his policy disagreements with his church's positions on public aid for parochial schools and sending an ambassador to the Vatican.[23]

His campaign was also to avoid visual associations of the candidate and Catholicism. For example, the staff made sure that Protestant clergy gave the blessing at the campaign luncheons and dinners. Matt Reese recalled the time when an Episcopalian minister appeared at a Kennedy breakfast event in Parkersburg to give the invocation, and made some of the staff nervous. Apparently, his cleric collar had led them to assume he was a priest. After telling this story to Jackie Kennedy, she said, "Yes. I find we always run like hell when we see a priest or a nun these days."[24]

As long as Kennedy remained the front-runner for the 1960 Democratic presidential nomination, the religious question was "inseparable from the 1960 presidential election."[25] But at the end of March the Kennedy campaign appeared confident. Their careful strategy on the religious issue seemed to be working as the candidate navigated his way successfully "between the need to get Protestant votes without alienating Catholic voters."[26] But the Wisconsin primary sent a shock wave through the Kennedy campaign and prompted the initiation of a new strategy on his handling of the religious issue. The Mountain State would be the stage where that new strategy of confrontation would play. Now the candidate would directly raise the religious issue through a variety of venues, including TV commercials, a television program, and speeches on the campaign trail.

Religious Confrontational Strategy

The first part of the West Virginia strategy was to confront the religious issue directly. As columnist Doris Fleeson noted, Kennedy turned his minority religious status, a political liability, into an "underdog appeal." [27]

The decision to adopt a confrontational strategy had been discussed at the strategy meeting in Charleston, West Virginia, the day after the Wisconsin primary. [28] But it was not put into prominent play on the campaign trail until April 18, when Kennedy made a campaign swing through the north-central part of the state.[29] At a noon rally in Morgantown, the candidate addressed religion directly rather than wait until there was a question from the audience. Ken O'Donnell, who was with the candidate, recalled that "it was so unexpected, and such a strange experience for me to hear him talking about his Catholicism before a Protestant audience, that I felt like a bucket of cold water had been thrown at my face."[30]

The next day AP reporter Herb Little wrote about John Kennedy's open battle against anti-Catholic bias in West Virginia and noted the candidate's declaration that "we might as well settle this (religious) issue right here in West Virginia." To an applauding crowd in Fairmont Kennedy said that "I don't think that my religion is any one's business but my business."[31]

Four Advantages

While the confrontational strategy posed risks by bringing attention to his liability, it had four benefits, namely the chance to correct misinformation, use a shame dynamic, serve as a distraction, and label Kennedy an underdog.

Misinformation

First, it addressed what everyone knew was out there: voter concern and misinformation about Catholicism—for instance, rumors that the Pope could tell Kennedy what to do, or that all schools would become parochial. Kennedy told newsmen on his campaign bus that day in April 1960 that this switch in tactics stemmed from an awareness that his religion was "quite obviously on everybody's mind," adding that "I just thought that rather than wait, I'd bring it out into the open."[32]

It is difficult in the twenty-first century to understand the level of anti-Catholic sentiment that existed in the nation in the mid-twentieth century. But it was a fact and reflected a long history of Protestant distrust. In 1960, the prejudice was reflected in literature that circulated and even in the jokes that people told. "If Kennedy gets elected," began one joke, "we'll change the coinage from 'In God we trust,' to 'In the Pope we hope.'" Another was a direct replay of a 1928 joke with Kennedy's name inserted for Al Smith's: "If Kennedy loses this election, he will send a one-word telegram to the Pope saying, 'Unpack.'"[33]

These and other anti-Catholic statements reflected the belief that Catholics were un-American and different. They were "Papists" who were loyal to their Pope, devoted to their private school system, and blind followers of their dogma. And these fears about a Catholic president were not just expressed by fringe fundamentalists but also by mainline religious leaders, including both Martin Luther King Sr. and Norman Vincent Peale.[34]

Shame Dynamic

The second advantage of adopting a confrontational strategy was that it transformed the debate. By addressing the issue openly, Kennedy implied that anyone who was against him was a bigot. The only way voters could prove their tolerance was by giving him a victory. Kennedy foresaw this when asked by Oscar Hammerstein about the obstacles caused by anti-Catholicism. As Cleveland Amory recalls, Kennedy replied, "I'm going to make it so that the prejudice is if you vote for me for that reason."[35]

Columnist L. T. Anderson picked up on this when he reported on "the popular psychology which suggested that a West Virginia vote against Senator Kennedy is a vote for bigotry." Ironically, its victim would be the man who, "perhaps more than any other in public life, had been the champion of equality and tolerance, Hubert Humphrey."[36]

"Whether out of conviction or out of tactics," Theodore White observed, "no sounder Kennedy decision could have been made. Once the issue could be made one of tolerance or intolerance, Hubert Humphrey was hung. No one could prove to his own conscience that by voting for Humphrey he was displaying tolerance. Yet any man, indecisive in mind on the Presidency, could prove that he was at least tolerant by voting for Jack Kennedy. The shape of the problem made it impossible for Humphrey, himself the most tolerant of men, to run in favor of tolerance."[37]

It is not surprising that Kennedy's opponents believed that he raised the religious issue on purpose. A frustrated Senator Robert C. Byrd charged Kennedy with "trying to capitalize on the religious issue in order to shame us [to vote for him] or provide alibi for him [if he lost]."[38]

Kennedy's pollster Lou Harris witnessed this "shame dynamic" at work when he interviewed a Kanawha County voter before and after Kennedy's Sunday night program, just before the primary vote. Her hostility, Harris reported, followed a pattern. "You would meet a Madame LaFarge type all dressed black and she would say, 'I don't care about Humphrey, but I just don't want a Catholic.'" But when Harris returned to interview this particular voter after the Kennedy program, there was a change, "as she took me in, pulled down the blinds and said she was going to vote for Kennedy now. 'We have enough trouble in West Virginia, let alone to be called bigots, too.'"[39]

Distraction

Another benefit of the confrontational strategy was that it drew attention away from other subjects. As Humphrey's campaign manager, William Jacobs, noted, the focus on religion created a climate that made it appear unfair not to vote for Kennedy, "regardless of whether or not he is not qualified." It overshadowed Humphrey's charges that Kennedy was too young and inexperienced.[40]

Underdog

An additional benefit of Kennedy's confrontational stance is that it allowed the wealthy front-runner from Massachusetts to be seen as an underdog. In a state whose citizens were very much aware of how prejudices and stereotypes could harm a person, "Kennedy as a victim" had political clout.

Confrontations with the Press

Kennedy's adoption of the confrontational strategy reflected a concern that he was losing control of the primary contests. To change the story, the candidate needed to change the focus of the press. He did so in a Washington, DC, ballroom on the evening of April 21, 1960, in a speech to the American Society of Newspaper Editors, only days after his campaign first directly addressed the religious issue. While critics asserted that he was "fanning the controversy" to benefit his campaign, Kennedy claimed that he was only replying to bigots.[41]

In a speech that mixed criticism and humor, he scolded the press for concentrating on his religion. He blamed the press for arousing needless fears and not placing the religious issue in perspective. His words were a strong indictment that the press had not done a good job of gatekeeping. Instead they magnified the issue, oversimplified it, and overstated its importance on the national scene. In effect, the press played up the religious issue and played down the other issues.

After documenting and ridiculing the press for their coverage on religion in Wisconsin, Kennedy asserted that journalists were peddling the same story in the Mountain State: "As reported in yesterday's *Washington Post*, the great bulk of West Virginians paid very little attention to my religion—until they read repeatedly in the nation's press that this was the decisive issue in West Virginia."[42]

Kennedy ended his speech with a stirring call against bigotry. He announced that he would not withdraw in order to avoid a "nasty religious controversy." After the Wisconsin primary, Kennedy's campaign had attempted to get Humphrey to drop out of the West Virginia primary for that very reason—that a primary contest would spark a religious donnybrook that would cripple both candidates and hurt the Democratic Party. Humphrey resisted such calls from national labor leader Walter Reuther, New York labor leader Alex Rose, and an indirect appeal from California governor Pat Brown.[43]

Kennedy concluded that "if there is bigotry in the country, then so be it—there is bigotry. If that bigotry is too great to permit the fair consideration of a Catholic who has made clear his complete independence and his complete dedication to separation of church and state, then we ought to know it."[44]

Kennedy's speech was well received, but the next day some questioned his claim that the press had brought attention on the religious issue. *New York Times* reporter James Reston pointed out that at the 1956 convention, the Kennedy camp had raised the religious issue when it circulated the "Bailey" memo that noted the large number of Catholic voters living in big electoral states like Illinois and Pennsylvania.[45] Columnist Doris Fleeson made a similar argument, noting that the issue of Kennedy's religion hadn't started in West Virginia in 1960, but in Chicago in 1956 when the Kennedy camp circulated the "Bailey" memo to gather support for John Kennedy as the vice-presidential nominee.[46]

Ads on Religion

It was not surprising that the Kennedy campaign wasn't going to rely on the press to tell the story on religion. Nor was it a surprise that it would turn to television ads featuring the candidate and Franklin Roosevelt Jr. Such action reflected its adeptness in utilizing both technology and celebrity.

As the first serious Catholic contender for his party's presidential nomination since Al Smith, John Kennedy generated the same anti-Catholic concerns that plagued Smith. At the heart of the religious issue was a question of loyalty.

Kennedy's first television ad in the West Virginia primary focused on his dual loyalty as a Catholic candidate. "Would he," asks a young woman in a Q and A session, "be divided between two—between your church and your state if you were re-elected [*sic*] president of the United States?" It's an awkwardly asked question, but it addresses Kennedy's greatest handicap.

The candidate replies by restating the question and making a declaration. "The question is, If I were elected president, would I be divided between two loyalties: my church and my state. Let me say I would not."

Kennedy then provides what will be his standard three-part response to any question about his religion. In what can be described as the Catholic candidate three-step, he talks first about the Constitution, second about fairness, and third, patriotism.

In regard to the Constitution, he cites the two relevant sections: the First Amendment, which affirms separation of church and state, and Article 6, which prohibits religious tests for office. He then frames the religious issue in terms of fairness: "Now, you cannot tell me that the day I was born [Catholic] it was said that I could not run for president because I could not meet my oath of office."[47]

Kentucky governor Happy Chandler, a Kennedy supporter, would dramatically emphasize this link between military service and religious tolerance. When he told his audiences about a young Jack Kennedy in the Pacific Ocean pulling sailors into a lifeboat, he would be careful to mention every Protestant denomination: "He [Kennedy] didn't ask the sailor if he was a Southern Baptist when he extended his hand. . . . He didn't ask the next sailor if he was an Episcopalian . . . if he was Methodist . . . if he was Presbyterian."[48]

The message was simple: If religion did not matter in military service, why should it matter in the presidency? It was a powerful argument, but it was going against a powerful assumption—that Catholics had dual loyalty, one for their nation and one for their Pope.

That first Kennedy campaign ad on religion in West Virginia was filmed on the state capitol grounds and contained a defensive candidate, an awkward question from the audience, and a rambling response from the defensive candidate whose answer was too stilted, and too long.

Three weeks later the campaign produced a second commercial on the religious issue that featured a more concise answer to the most frequently asked question of Kennedy's campaign in the Mountain State. Filmed at Morris Harvey College on April 11, 1960, the ad reflected both the confrontation strategy adopted by the Kennedy campaign and the confidence the candidate had gained in discussing the religious issue.[49]

Like the earlier ad, this commercial features an audience member asking the senator how his religion will affect his duties as president. But while the format is the same, the audience is different—an overflow audience of students and townspeople at Morris Harvey College in Charleston. And the questioner is Walton Shepard, a notable Charleston lawyer and a prominent Kennedy supporter.[50]

Kennedy proceeds to give the standard three-part answer to the religious question asked by Shepard and summarized by the ad's narrator. He begins with the standard reference to the Constitution, declaring that "I wouldn't have come to West Virginia if I did not believe that the people of West Virginia believed in the Constitution." He then emphasizes the issues of fairness, noting that the oath that he would take as president, to defend the Constitution, was the same one he took as a member of Congress and a member of the military.[51]

He then plays the patriotism card. First he mentions his own military service ("Now, I have been in the service of the United States—I spent three years in a hospital"). Then he mentions the World War II combat deaths in his family ("My brother was killed in the war. My sister's husband was killed in the war. I'd like to know if there is some opinion that I cannot fulfill my office of citizenship.")

Having addressed the religious issue, he proceeds to dismiss it, saying, "I don't happen to believe that one of those serious issues is where I go to church on Sunday." The ad ends showing the audience on its feet clapping as the announcer says, "What better answer for West Virginians [of their approval], than their enthusiastic applause."[52]

The ad's power reflects the sentiments of the candidate who had abandoned his cautious handling of the religious issue. After refusing to discuss his religion in Wisconsin, Kennedy became passionate about the subject in West Virginia.

The other two ads on the religious issue feature not the candidate, but Franklin Delano Roosevelt Jr., the son of the state's most beloved president. In both, the son speaks directly to the camera. His words are strong, though undercut by his monotone delivery. In the first ad, Frank Roosevelt plays family historian, explaining that the Roosevelts immigrated in 1621 to escape religious persecution, and ends with a warning that prejudice and persecution have no place in "our American way of life," (implying that if it doesn't belong in America, it should certainly should not have place In West Virginia).[53]

In the second ad, he becomes a common scold: "My friends, I am shocked to find in this West Virginia primary campaign that the fact that Jack Kennedy is a Catholic has become a political issue." After noting that nobody asked John Kennedy when he went into the Navy "if he was a Protestant, a Jew, or a Catholic," he declares, "Let us not now allow religious prejudice to come into American politics to divide a nation when we need to be united."[54]

Sunday TV Program

After Roosevelt Jr.'s ads aired, Kennedy took the confrontation strategy to a new level. He addressed West Virginians in a half-hour TV broadcast on Sunday evening, May 8, 1960. Frank Roosevelt was with the candidate; this time his role was not to admonish state voters but to ask prepared questions, most of which were about religion.[55] This use of the medium represented the final effort of the Kennedy campaign to allay concerns about where the candidate went to church on Sunday. No copy of the broadcast has been found, but pollster Lou Harris credited it with influencing voters.

As with everything produced by the Kennedy campaign, the program was carefully prepared. Over the weekend Kennedy had asked Ted Sorensen to draw up questions on the key issues that worried Protestants most about Catholics. Sorensen stayed up all night pondering the problem and came up with the questions that reflected Protestant concerns.[56]

Would Kennedy's church influence him in the White House? Would the Pope tell him what to do? Would he, as president, have difficulty attending a funeral service in a Protestant church? Is Kennedy bound by the declarations of popes and bishops that differ from those he espouses?[57]

Kennedy argued that the failure of a president to follow the doctrine of separation of church and state constituted not only an impeachable offense but also a moral sin. He said it should lead not just to congressional action, but also moral condemnation. He then used body language to emphasize his point. Kennedy turned directly to the camera and said, "So when any man stands on the steps of the Capitol and takes the oath of office for president, he is swearing to support the separation of church and state." He raised his hand from an imaginary Bible, as if lifting it to God, and softly said that to break an oath was not just a crime but a sin, for "he has sworn on the Bible."[58]

As the results of the primary would reveal, the religious issue was not as important as the press had reported or many in the Kennedy staff believed. But the opportunity to break a political taboo, and to challenge the unwritten law of presidential politics, contributed to a siege mentality at the state headquarters that justified smearing Humphrey during the last week of the campaign. For some of his supporters, the primary wasn't just about the ambition of one candidate, but also about religious bigotry in the nation.

Conclusion

Jackie Kennedy reportedly told Arthur Krock that she was both mystified and bemused over non-Catholic fear of her husband becoming president: "I think it's so unfair of people to be against Jack because he is Catholic. He's such a poor Catholic. Now if it were Bobby, I could understand. He never misses Mass and prays all the time."[59]

Observers noticed that John Kennedy wore his religion lightly. Historian Arthur Schlesinger Jr. said that John took religion "with detachment."[60] Ted Sorensen wrote, "He cared not a whit for theology." Sorensen had never seen

Kennedy pray aloud in the presence of others.[61] Sorensen observed that Kennedy "felt neither self-conscious nor superior about his religion but simply accepted it as part of his life." While the senator faithfully attended Mass each Sunday (even when out of the country and during the Los Angeles nominating convention), he never once in eleven years discussed his personal views with Sorensen.

John Kennedy reflected an environment where religion is dominant in the church but not in politics. A cliché in Boston regarding religion was "We listen to the Pope on religion and to Boston for politics."[62]

But it was this part of his identity that posed the greatest threat to his presidential nomination. On the night of January 2, 1961, the date that Kennedy declared his candidacy, Arthur M. Schlesinger Jr. reported that the candidate "conveyed an intangible feeling of depression." Schlesinger noted, "I had the sense that he feels himself increasingly hemmed in as a result of a circumstance over which he has no control—his religion; and he inevitably tends toward gloom and irritation when he considers how the circumstance may deny him what he thinks his talent and efforts have earned."[63]

The fate of John Kennedy's nomination would come to rest in a state with only a 4 percent population of what he called his "coreligionists." With the exception of Utah, no other state in the nation had a smaller percentage of Catholics; the state was not just Protestant, it was fundamentalist. But it was in the Mountain State that he changed the way he handled the religious issue—and undermined the religious taboo that he'd faced since he started his career.

Chapter 3

KENNEDY PROMOTES
FOOD, FAMILY, AND THE FLAG

I came to West Virginia to run. West Virginia is suffering some of
the most serious problems of any of our states, but I don't think one
of them is religion.

—John Kennedy, *Morgantown Post*, April 19, 1960

To win the West Virginia presidential primary, John Kennedy needed to do
more than simply confront the religious issue. He needed to focus voters' attention on other parts of his identity, which he achieved through the three-F
strategy. The trifecta of issues he addressed—food, family, and flag—resonated
throughout West Virginia.[1]

Such a strategy enabled the candidate to acquire a new political persona.
In the remaining five weeks before the primary election, Kennedy the Catholic
became Kennedy the New Dealer, the second FDR promising economic aid to a
state; Kennedy the Family Man, the candidate who brought the Kennedy members to a state that valued family; and Kennedy the veteran, the decorated war
hero who courted votes in a state that honored military service. For each role
he provided supporting evidence that voters could see: a testimonial from FDR
Jr., a cluster of relatives campaigning in the state, and two medals he earned for
military service in the Pacific. These three identities allowed him to overcome
the suspicions of those who viewed him as a wealthy outsider with a Harvard
education, a Boston accent, and a Catholic religion.

The three themes arose from a campaign discussion at a meeting in Charleston just after the Wisconsin primary. At that gathering, some expressed the
need for Kennedy to connect with the voters as a new FDR[2] and to promote
issues that were relevant in the critical strongholds of southern West Virginia
where "It is simply food, family, and flag."[3] This troika of issues, initially associated with southern West Virginia only, would become the focus of the campaign throughout the state. As such, it provides insight not just into the strategy
of a besieged candidate but also of the region.

Food

The most important issue was the first F of the three-F strategy. An emphasis on food rang true in a state where 250,000 of West Virginia's 2 million citizens were dependent on government food supplies. In some counties, the percentage reached a full quarter of the population.[4]

Such facts explain the admonishment by Kennedy's state campaign director, Bob McDonough, that the focus in West Virginia should not be on the future challenges of the 1960s but on help for a state bypassed by the prosperity of the 1950s. "Down here," McDonough argued, "he's got to talk about the challenge of yesterday. A lot of these people haven't eaten since the day before yesterday."[5]

At a time when the nation was enjoying its greatest period of prosperity, Kennedy would focus attention on hunger in West Virginia and attack the Republican president Dwight Eisenhower for neglecting the state. On a visit to Welch, he taunted Eisenhower, saying that "Our President has traveled to Asia and Europe and South America—but never to McDowell County. He has seen the poor and hungry of foreign lands—but he has not seen the poor and hungry of McDowell County."[6] Kennedy's words were ironic. Until he campaigned in West Virginia, the senator, unlike Hubert Humphrey, had had little interaction with extreme poverty either.

Had Eisenhower come to McDowell, Kennedy continued, "he would have seen a once prosperous people—the people of the largest and most important coal mining county in the world—were now victims of poverty, want, and hunger." He noted that 50 percent of McDowell County residents "were forced to struggle for existence on a government surplus food diet of rice, flour, and cornmeal, and—on special occasions—a little lard, dried eggs, and milk."[7]

As portrayed by Kennedy, these were a proud, "once prosperous people" who through no fault of their own became victims and needed to be rescued immediately by Kennedy and federal intervention.[8]

Stung by the press criticism, President Eisenhower invited Governor Underwood to the White House on April 27, 1960, to assure him that he would urge all federal agencies "to do whatever they could to help West Virginia."[9] But such action only fed the campaign beast. Kennedy lambasted the governor, asking, "Why didn't Underwood have his conference with Eisenhower long before this? It's time the Republican governor and president begin to find out about West Virginia."[10]

John Kennedy himself knew little about extreme poverty before he came to West Virginia. The campaign educated the wealthy candidate, who became a quick student of food commodities. At a Mount Hope stop he easily rattled off the monthly provisions given to a West Virginia family with seven children:

five bags of flour, four cans of powdered eggs, three five-pound bags of corn-meal, eight pounds of shortening, four pounds of rice, and powdered milk. He expressed concern not just about the quantity, but also the quality of the food distributed, emphasizing that such a diet could lead only to malnutrition. "That diet is the cause of rotten teeth and shattered hopes," Kennedy said. He declared that it posed not only a health hazard to West Virginians, but also an embarrassment to the nation. He called it a "disgrace in a country that calls it-self the land of opportunity, the richest country on earth, the arsenal of the Free World."[11]

While there was not a television ad on the topic of food, Kennedy addressed it when he answered questions in a commercial he had filmed in a coal mine. After noting that much of the food "that comes down to West Virginia is badly distributed," Kennedy stated that "the diet is bad. They ought to get milk, eggs, butter, chickens, especially since the American government sends better food overseas."[12]

On the issue of nutrition, as with others in the West Virginia campaign, Humphrey had the better resumé and the more comprehensive policy. Kennedy had the better optics. For years Humphrey had advocated a food stamp plan to replace the present food distribution program. Senator Kennedy only advo-cated increases in the existing program, not replacement of it. Kennedy's refusal in 1959 to support the Minnesota senator's replacement proposal prompted Re-publican Governor Underwood to ask in 1960, "Couldn't Jack stomach Hubert's food stamp plan?"[13] The governor got his answer eight months later, in March of 1961, when President Kennedy implemented the Food Stamp Program that candidate Kennedy would not endorse.

Both primary candidates spoke about the food issue, but Kennedy illustrated it more effectively. Humphrey highlighted the issue via a "show and tell" ex-ercise at a Charleston grocery store where he purchased the actual items and amounts of food that the government distributed in West Virginia. Noting that the total retail cost for that monthly allotment was $3.89 ($34.50 in 2019 dollars), Humphrey noted sarcastically, "That is what the President calls 'very material assistance.'" Humphrey's effort resulted in a newspaper article on the topic.[14]

In contrast, Kennedy highlighted the issue to an audience of 500,000 people who watched the televised debate. First he read a letter from an unemployed Logan County coal miner with seven children and detailed what the family received each month. Then the candidate reached behind the nameplate on his desk and pulled out a can of powdered milk, providing a visual aid for the viewers.[15]

A state reporter following Kennedy in the southern counties described the audiences as "beaten people." There were unemployed older men who depended on the government for food. Historian Ian Hartman contends that John Kennedy "relied heavily on the imagined legacy of race and the mythology of the frontier to win West Virginia's Democratic primary." He used what Hartman calls the "rhetoric of fallen whites"—descendants of proud pioneers who fell victim to forces beyond their control. The images and the argument set the stage for federal legislation to help the Appalachian region.[16]

Kennedy and his audiences, however, recognized that a successful candidate needed to address more than the hunger problem in the state. The person also needed to provide a plan for viable economic growth. That's why Kennedy's promotion of the first F, food, went beyond an adequate diet. It also represented economic development in general, and jobs in particular.

When discussing West Virginia's economics and poverty, Kennedy carefully crafted a four-part narrative. He would first offer his audiences praise, then an explanation, followed by a plan and a promise of immediate government action if he became president.

Praise

The Massachusetts senator took time to praise the state in nearly every speech. He singled out its patriotism (a high rate of military service), its workforce (hardworking), and its values (of patriotism and family). He noted that McDowell County was the most important coal mining county in the world, and that Beckley had scenery rivaling Switzerland. When he spoke of a negative, such as unemployment in some southern counties, he would always balance it with something positive, such the prospering chemical plants in the Kanawha Valley.

Kennedy recognized that West Virginians received both an economic blow in the 1950s, when unemployment went up and people moved out, and a psychological beating. Kennedy's praise reflected an earlier insight of Humphrey's advisor, Louis Bean, who observed, "West Virginians are proud, decent, and conscientious people." Bean argued that they didn't like the image of their state "given in the faceless statistics of low income and persistent unemployment. Hard up they may be, but West Virginians objected to being pointed at." He emphasized that West Virginians wanted respect, not stereotypes from outsiders.[17]

Explanation

After reassuring West Virginia voters of their worth, Kennedy would offer an explanation for their woes. He told his audiences that their bad times were a result of larger economic trends of automation—the increasing mechanization of the American workforce: "If a machine comes along and takes the job of ten men, what happens to those ten men? In the coal industry here in West Virginia they have been left idle." The numbers were dramatic. Just 20 years previously, Logan County had 15,000 working miners, and by 1960, Kennedy pointed out, there were "only 5,500, but they turn out greater tonnage."[18]

He then predicted that their state's economic problem would soon become the nation's problem. "What has happened in West Virginia is going to happen in many states in the Union unless the federal government begins to recognize that this is a great national problem to which we have devoted very little attention."

Kennedy's discussion of automation in the Mountain State was enhanced by his experience with it in Massachusetts. He noted that both states had problems with their chief industry, coal and textiles, respectively. The candidate's history lesson of Massachusetts offered hope for the Mountain State. When the textile industries left Massachusetts after World War II, some old mill towns, Lawrence and Lowell, found new industries with government help. But it was obvious in West Virginia that the federal government had not played a role commensurate with its authority, responsibility, and opportunity.[19]

Plan

Kennedy believed that the key to an economic transition was the federal government. At the heart of his discussion of economic development was his conception of the office of the presidency. The chief executive, he said, is the center of action as he appoints officers who are in charge of the nation and who impact each state.[20]

During his swing through the towns of southern West Virginia, the press reported that at each stop, Kennedy addressed the theme that the administration in Washington is and has been indifferent to areas suffering from depressed economic conditions.

To the miners in his coal mine ad, Kennedy promoted four programs of government action: area redevelopment, unemployment compensation, defense contracts in areas of high unemployment, and a better diet of surplus commodities for the poor and unemployed.[21] But as the campaign evolved, the number of proposed programs increased. On April 18, 1960, he announced a six-point plan to help the state, and a week later he expanded it into a ten-point program to promote economic development in the state.[22]

When it came to coal mining, both candidates had plans to aid the ailing industry, and each assailed President Eisenhower for his vetoes of the coal research bills. As with the food issue, Humphrey had the most imaginative proposal for the coal mining industry. The Minnesota senator promoted "mine-mouth" electric power stations at mine sites. While it had been long believed that it was not economically viable to transmit electricity more than 200 miles,

Humphrey noted that both Sweden and Russia were transmitting 500,000 volts more than 500 miles in an effort to inspire change.[23]

"West Virginia," he declared, "is ideally located for such power stations. In time electrical power from your coal could hum steadily through the high lines stretching to America's great industrial and urban centers. The coal beneath your hills could then become the source of new wealth and economic security for West Virginians."[24]

Humphrey had more innovative proposals, but Kennedy won more publicity. His visit to a coal mine, and the commercial made from that visit, provided a powerful visual identification of Kennedy with the state's most important industry.

The ad begins with a declaration on the importance of coal to the West Virginia economy, as the announcer says in a sonorous tone, "when the mines are run full blast and the men are employed. But let the mines slow down and let the miners feel the pinch of unemployment, then people all over the state are affected by the repercussions." The narrator then highlights the candidate's interest in coal, saying, "That is why it is so important that Senator John F. Kennedy, front-running candidate for the Democratic nomination for the presidency, should visit the coal mining areas of West Virginia. There to learn firsthand from the miners some of their problems and there to answer their questions."[25]

The ad switches to Kennedy facing a group of coal miners who look like they just finished a shift. When asked about his plans for the coal mines, the candidate says that there are "at least four or five things the government can do." And then he proceeds to name them.[26]

Promise

Kennedy would end speeches with a promise of immediate help, if elected president. He offered the voters a political covenant that if West Virginia helped him in the primary, as president he would help the Mountain State.[27] The promise John Kennedy made to a small and slighted state was that West Virginia would be the center of attention at a Kennedy White House. In a letter to fellow West Virginia Democrats, Kennedy wrote, "Much more can and should be done. That is why West Virginia will be on the top of my agenda at the White House.[28]

To that promise of immediate executive attention, the candidate promised on election eve, "If I'm nominated and elected president, within sixty days of the start of my administration, I will introduce a program to the Congress for aid to West Virginia."[29] Of the 50 states in the union, the Mountain State would get priority.

As liberal Democrats, both Kennedy and Humphrey offered bold plans of direct federal help. Each promoted an aggressive agenda for the economic recovery of West Virginia, promising legislative and executive action on a number of fronts. Their model was Franklin Delano Roosevelt, a political saint in a state that remembered his aid efforts during the Great Depression.

At first glance, Humphrey had the better claim to being the second FDR. The Minnesota senator modeled his political career after the legendary president. On his first date with Muriel, he spent most of the night telling his future wife about his admiration for the president.[30] In the US Senate he took the lead in passing legislation for government action. In the early spring of 1960 he came to West Virginia ready to be identified with a second New Deal for the Mountain State. In his speech to the state legislature, he proposed an action agenda and argued that federal spending in the Mountain State was not an expenditure, but an investment.[31]

Humphrey's proposals for economic revival were more ambitious than Kennedy's program. The Minnesota senator who advocated for a food stamp program[32] also proposed a Youth Conservation Corps in West Virginia that would be a state-level version of the Civilian Conservation Corps implemented by President Roosevelt in the 1930s.[33]

Kennedy, however, proved successful in his effort to portray himself as the real heir of the New Deal legacy. He was certainly more aggressive. Through words and optics he encouraged voters to associate him with FDR rather than Humphrey.

On April 12, 1960, the fifteenth anniversary of President Roosevelt's death, Kennedy directly claimed the mantle of the popular president. Noting that Roosevelt did more in 100 days than Eisenhower, a campaign press release declared, "And now it is time for another 'New Deal'—a New Deal for West Virginia."[34]

In speech after speech, Kennedy promised action based on the Roosevelt model: "Help me now, and I will help you later when I am in the White House, just as FDR did three decades ago."[35] By offering an aggressive agenda for economic recovery, he was providing himself with one part of his new identity: "Kennedy the Catholic" became "Kennedy the second FDR."

To West Virginia Democrats, Kennedy offered his list of liberal promises in a campaign ad that detailed their impact, from raising the minimum wage to making federal aid to education more need based. After promising higher pay for some and more jobs and better education for all, the ad concludes with an appeal to self-interest: "It is to your interest to vote for a man dedicated to your welfare. May tenth, vote for you, vote Kennedy!"[36] This appeal was followed by the tagline "Vote for you and Kennedy!"

Kennedy used more than speeches and ads to identify himself with Franklin Roosevelt. He enlisted the namesake son of the president. As Peter Lisagor observed, recruiting FDR Jr. provided a valuable trump card in the West

Virginia primary. "While Kennedy went up through the valley, Roosevelt was with us," Lisagor recalled, "He would make remarks on the back of a truck. You could see in the people when he started hammering away that they were quite fascinated and intrigued, that this was the son of their great idol."[37]

Frank Roosevelt's endorsement was puzzling in light of his father's bitter feud with Joe Kennedy during World War II, his mother's distrust of the Kennedys, and his mother's open support for Adlai Stevenson.[38] But in the political climate of 1960, visuals were more important than history. Eleanor did not openly discuss her concerns about her son's involvement with John Kennedy, nor did the press focus on her husband's feud with Ambassador Joe Kennedy a generation earlier.

In speeches, newspapers, and television ads, Frank Roosevelt promoted Kennedy as the natural heir to his father. He assured voters that Kennedy would continue the job his father had started. JFK became the second FDR, and his economic plan would be the second New Deal.[39] One of Roosevelt's ads highlighted this linkage as the announcer declares that "the memory of Franklin Delano Roosevelt is being vividly brought back to West Virginia as the son of the late, great president travels throughout every section of the state in support of the candidacy of Senator John F. Kennedy."[40]

In his filmed remarks at Cabin Creek, FDR Jr. links his family to the state but fails to link his father to Kennedy. That is left up to the announcer, who says that "in other talks, FDR Jr. has said, 'John Kennedy has the same heart, the same feeling for the people as my father. He is picking up where my father left off.'" The ad ends with the announcer saying, "Remember this, when you vote on May tenth. Vote Kennedy."[41]

The association of the Massachusetts senator with the beloved president was sanctified by the FDR Jr. in a newspaper ad that appeared on election eve in the Charleston papers. The ad featured a sketch of President Roosevelt with a signed message from his son: "I am positive that John F. Kennedy is the only candidate for president who can do for West Virginia in the '60s what my father did for West Virginia in the '30s."[42]

Family

The second of the three Fs in Kennedy's West Virginia political strategy stood for family, an institution of particular importance to Appalachians. And one which John Kennedy was in an excellent position to exploit with his large, energetic, and photogenic family.

For the first time in American political history, a clan took center stage in presidential politics. At a Gridiron Club dinner at Statler-Hilton hotel, Senator

John Kennedy was introduced as "the first candidate to run for president on the family plan." With lyrics by Fletcher Knebel to tune of "All of Me," the enterprise was explained in song by "papa Joseph P. Kennedy."

> All of us
> Why not take all of us
> Fabulous
> You can't live without us
> My son Jack
> Heads the procession
> Then comes Bob
> Groomed for succession.
> We're the most
> We stretch from coast to coast
> Kennedys
> Just go on forever
> I've got the dough
> You might as well know
> With one—
> You get all of us.[43]

The Kennedy clan offered an important advantage to Appalachia. In a place and time where retail politics was mandatory, Kennedy family members offered a personal connection between the candidate and the voter. John Kennedy brought as many as 50 Kennedy family members and friends to West Virginia to campaign for him.

Family had been a standard ingredient in Kennedy campaigns since he first ran for office in 1946. In that campaign, and in subsequent Massachusetts races, Kennedy had the active involvement of his family. It's not surprising that the Kennedy clan would also be put to work in Wisconsin, his first contested presidential primary. In that contest the candidate employed his mother, Rose; brothers Bobby and Teddy; and sisters Eunice, Patricia, and Jean; as well as in-laws Sargent Shriver, Stephen E. Smith, and Peter Lawford, the Hollywood actor married to Patricia.[44]

The only missing sibling was Rosemary, who had been institutionalized after a failed lobotomy in 1941, and since 1949 resided in Jefferson, Wisconsin, on the grounds of St. Coletta's Sisters School for Exceptional Children.[45] Not until after John's election, when *National Enquirer* wrote that "the president-elect has a mentally retarded sister,"[46] would there be a clear statement about Rosemary's condition.

The Kennedys who campaigned for Jack that early spring in Wisconsin followed the "family plan." In the West Virginia primary campaign, Kennedy family members repeated the Wisconsin strategy, with some modifications.[47] At each appearance, a Kennedy would be accompanied by a local person who knew the names of townspeople. Afterward the Kennedy would send a personal letter from the Senate office to local Democratic leaders they met.

Columnist Doris Fleeson observed that the Kennedy celebrity enhanced rather than undermined the campaign in West Virginia. "The Kennedys do not condescend to a less well-off public by any change of dress or manner," Fleeson wrote. "They come from the great world and they carry it about with them. Some observers think it's a large part of their appeal."[48]

The campaign saturation of family in West Virginia differed from that of the Wisconsin primary in only two ways: the absence of his mother and a reduction in the role of his sisters.

Joe Kennedy was already kept away from his son's campaign. While John accepted and, in fact, depended on the ambassador's money, advice, and support, they both acknowledged the need for the father to distance himself from the candidate. Joe's feud with President Franklin Roosevelt, his association with isolationism, and his reputation as a Svengali controlling his son behind the scenes marked him as toxic. His absence inspired a couplet: "Jack and Bob will run the show / While Ted's in charge of hiding Joe."[49]

The mother, Rose Kennedy, was another story. The daughter of flamboyant and successful Boston mayor "Honey Fitz," she grew up in politics and had an intimate knowledge of campaigning. In Wisconsin she spent eight days traveling the state and drew rave reviews, but in West Virginia she was not asked to participate. Her sons told her that she needed rest after the grueling Wisconsin campaign, but in her autobiography she acknowledged that religion was the real reason. Her curtailed agenda reflected the Kennedy campaign's concern over the religious issue in the Mountain State.

A devout Roman Catholic, Rose Kennedy was closely identified with the church, and in 1951 she became only the sixth woman in America to be granted the rare title of "papal countess" by the Roman Catholic Church. Pope Pius XII bestowed the honor in recognition of her "exemplary motherhood and many charitable works." She realized that she would spend much of her time in West Virginia explaining her religion rather than promoting her son.[50]

Kennedy's sisters' role was less noticeable in West Virginia than it had been in Wisconsin because the campaign believed they were not a good fit for a poor state.[51] The attractiveness of Joan Kennedy proved to be a liability. When she visited a coal mine with her brother-in-law she set off a chorus of shouts and whistles that distracted attention from the candidate. And it proved to be the last time she traveled with John Kennedy.[52]

The exception, not surprisingly, was the oldest Kennedy sister, Eunice, who keep a busy schedule and traveled to communities across the state. Although the *Beckley Post-Herald* misspelled her name, it did correctly report her crowded itinerary for a visit through the southern part of the state. She started her day at 9:00 a.m. at the Knotty Pine Restaurant in Oceana, which seven women attended, followed by receptions in the private home of Mrs. Clarence Worrell at Pineville, which 35 women attended, and from 2:30 to 3:30 in Mullens in the home of Mrs. Ward Wylie, the wife of Kennedy's official campaign chair.[53]

The greatest family asset was Jackie Kennedy. *Washington Post* reporter Don Smith wrote that at first the members of the press who covered the Kennedy campaigns wondered at "how this very shy, very beautiful, very young woman would go down with voters as potential first lady."[54]Smith noted that by the time the West Virginia campaign ended, they were convinced of her benefit to the campaign.

Within the state organization of the Kennedy campaign, there was some initial concern that Jackie's style and manners might alienate voters. Charlie Peters, Kennedy organizer in Kanawha County, had, in fact, suggested that Jackie Kennedy stay away because she "would seem phony to West Virginians compared to the natural, down-to-earth Muriel Humphrey." She spoke French, wore high fashion, had a quiet demeanor, and allegedly had a French cook. Such traits stood in contrast to Muriel Humphrey, who made her own clothes and shared her beef soup recipe on the campaign trail.[55] Peters later recalled, "I was overruled unanimously and was fortunate not to be banished from the campaign." Peters notes that Jackie came to West Virginia, "where to my surprise she was seen as a princess who added glamour and excitement to the primary."[56]

Jackie proved to be an effective campaigner. Already a month pregnant and at risk of another miscarriage, she would disappear from the rest of the 1960 campaign, but in West Virginia she worked aggressively on behalf of her husband. Ken O'Donnell remembered her visiting miners' wives, shaking hands on the streets, passing out bumper stickers, and in one case, chatting with railroad workers during their lunch break.[57] O'Donnell recalled the time that Jackie spotted a group of women across a brook: "The only way to speak to them was to walk across a plank about ten feet long and six inches wide. She removed her shoes and walked across the sagging plank to chat with the women."[58]

On the campaign trail she spoke in her low voice, confessing to one audience her Republican roots: "I have to confess, I was born a Republican, but you have to be Republican to realize how nice it is to be a Democrat."[59] And told another about the increased vocabulary of her two-year-old daughter, Caroline. "Her first words were 'plane,' 'goodbye,' and 'New Hampshire,' and just this morning she said 'Wisconsin' and 'West Virginia.'"[60]

If Jackie Kennedy left an impression on West Virginians, the people of West Virginia left a lasting impression on her. After she became first lady, Jackie stated that "in all the places we campaigned . . . [West Virginians] are the people who touched me most. The poverty there hit me more than it did in India—maybe because I just didn't realize that existed in [the] US."[61] When it came time to purchase crystal for White House functions, she ordered six dozen sets of glassware from West Virginia's Morgantown Glassware Guild.[62]

As they had in Wisconsin, the Kennedy brothers played a key role in the West Virginia primary. While brother Bobby ran the campaign in West Virginia, brother Ted served as number one surrogate for his oldest brother. At the age of 28, Ted had just graduated from University of Virginia Law School and was 15 years younger than John.[63]

Ted stood in for his brother when Jack got laryngitis. This sibling handoff became standard procedure for the campaign in the final two weeks. As the nearest relative available, Ted would step up and take his place.

The same procedure applied to the candidate's spouse as well. When Jackie had to leave the campaign just before her husband's biggest campaign rally, her replacement at the Parkersburg event was Eunice Kennedy Shriver. Eunice was on the podium and in the reception line on that important day.

In West Virginia, Ted received instruction in campaigning from a master, A. James Manchin of Marion County. The future West Virginia secretary of state (1977–1985) and treasurer (1985–1989), Manchin was recognized as one of the best campaigners and orators in the state. He often accompanied the younger Kennedy and provided a workshop on electioneering.[64]

An itinerary for Ted's one-day visit to central West Virginia reveals his busy schedule as surrogate. That day "Young Ted Kennedy" visited three factories (the Westinghouse plant at Fairmont, the Hazel-Atlas plant of Continental Can, and the Eagle-Convex plant at Clarksburg), and one mine (States Mine in Marion County).[65] At each stop he stayed on message, explaining the importance of the primary. At a glass factory in Clarksburg he told a crowd of 100 that John Kennedy "believes that this is the most important primary and that his political future will be decided in communities like Clarksburg across the state."

In addition to family members, the candidate assembled an impressive campaign entourage of close friends who were willing to work without pay and live almost full time in the Mountain State until the primary vote. Kennedy's personal secretary, Evelyn Lincoln, noted the large number when she wrote two weeks before the primary election that "the Senator has brought all the people he can think of into the campaign. He has Lem Billing, Chuck Spalding, Ben Smith, Grant Stockdale, Bob Troutman, Sargent Shriver and many others down there working for him. Bobby is going all over making speeches and Teddy is too.

Larry O'Brien is in charge of the organization and Kenny O'Donnell arranges his speaking schedule. Ralph Dungan is handling the labor setup. Chuck Roche and Pierre Salinger handle the press release, TV, etc. Ted Reardon is in Wheeling."[66]

Celebrities

In a concerted effort not to miss any chance for votes, the Kennedy supporters sought out celebrities as well as family and friends to campaign in West Virginia. Such recruitment reflected the campaign's effort to use every available means to mobilize voters in the Mountain State. It also foreshadowed the future direction of political campaigns in their use of celebrities.

The celebrity recruitment also reflected Kennedy's lack of support within the state Democratic establishment. None of the six members of the US House delegation endorsed the Massachusetts senator, and, as noted previously, he was openly opposed by the state's junior US senator, Robert C. Byrd.[67]

The most prominent West Virginian enlisted was not a politician, but a football player. Sam Huff was the first football player to be on the cover of *Time* magazine just a year earlier, in 1959. The son of a coal miner, Huff grew up in the No. 9 coal mining camp in Edna Gas, West Virginia. He became a standout player at West Virginia University before becoming the star linebacker for the New York Giants.[68]

Huff's participation in the Kennedy campaign is instructive not just for what it reveals about the campaign's strategy, but also for the reaction of his prejudiced father. During the off-season, Sam worked for his father, who had a farm in Marion County. When Huff's father heard that his son had been asked to introduce Kennedy at a Marion County dinner, he objected and told him not to participate because Kennedy was a Catholic.[69]

Sam Huff was not the only football celebrity recruited by the Kennedy campaign in West Virginia. They also enlisted the help of standout "Big Joe" Stydahar, who was the first West Virginia University graduate to enter the Pro Football Hall of Fame. The Shinnston High School graduate was a first-round draft pick for the Chicago Bears and later coached professional football.[70] The Kennedy campaign asked him to come back to his native state "to shake a few hands and tell the folks of Harrison County [where Shinnston was located] to vote for Kennedy."[71]

Athletes such as Sam Huff and Joe Stydahar brought great publicity and offered no risk to the Kennedy campaign in West Virginia. But the recruitment of former governor William Marland did. The wunderkind of West Virginia politics in the 1950s, Marland was elected governor in 1952 at the age of 34. His political career, however, was soon undermined in part by a serious drinking problem.

Barred by the state constitution from seeking another term, Marland lost two statewide races.[72] In January 1960, Marland left West Virginia for a sales job in Chicago, but just three months later he was recruited by the Kennedy campaign to return. All went well for the first few days, but then Marland, who had been warned not to drink, was discovered drunk in the lobby of the Kanawha Hotel. The response of the Kennedy people was immediate. The former governor was put on a plane and sent back to Chicago.[73]

The Kennedy campaign's willingness to recruit Marland despite his history demonstrated their fear that victory was slipping away and their belief that they had to exhaust all efforts to get votes. Marland's quick departure reflected the campaign's concern with public relations.

With all the family and friends Kennedy enlisted to help in the Mountain State, it's not surprising that Hubert Humphrey felt once again overwhelmed. Campaigning in a political culture that valued personal contact and family, Humphrey was simply outmanned. His family support in West Virginia consisted of his wife; a sister, Mrs. Francis Howard; and his two teenage sons, Bob, 16, and Douglas, 12. Another son, Hubert III or Skipper, was in school in Minnesota, and Nancy, 21, was a student nurse in Northwestern Hospital in Minnesota who would be married the week after the primary.[74]

Muriel Humprhey constituted Hubert's most important electioneering asset. At a meeting of the Women's National Democratic Club, he paid extravagant and well-earned tribute to her role in the Wisconsin primary campaign, saying, "One dedicated woman is worth hundreds of people who are just sort of for you." His accolade was on the mark, as the press observed she was an extraordinary campaigner.[75]

In addition to her other talents, the wife of the Minnesota senator not only made her own dresses, but had her own color. A newspaper article noted that for the Charleston luncheon, Mrs. Humphrey wore "a French jersey sheath dress which she designed and made herself. The dress was a bright blue which has become known as 'Muriel blue,' since she has worn the color through most of the tour."[76]

During the 1960 Wisconsin primary, Muriel Humphrey held coffees across the state, but in West Virginia she became more well known for serving coffee out of a car rather than in a house. She would often strike out on her own, driving her station wagon filled with campaign literature and a coffee urn to meet workers at various factory gates. At each stop she handed out coffee mugs and passed out her recipe for homemade beef soup—a standard in all the Humphrey campaigns.[77]

On April 14, 1960, she embarked on a three-day drive from Charleston to Clarksburg in a station wagon. She stopped at filling stations, garages, country stores, and restaurants from Charleston to Clendenin to Sutton, to Buckhannon and then to Clarksburg, and almost everywhere she met optimistic supporters. The press reported that "At each stop she would pin badges on supporters and hand her beef soup recipe out to scores of people along the route."[78]

Her twelve-hour itinerary for the next day started with a breakfast meeting and press conference in Clarksburg at 8:00 a.m., then a Kiwanis Club dinner in Grafton at 6 p.m., and ended with a visit to Fire Hall in Morgantown at 8:45 p.m. In between she attended a luncheon and hosted a total of five coffee receptions in three different counties.[79]

As Hubert's spouse provided full-time assistance, his sister provided part-time support. Mrs. Frances Humphrey Howard of Baltimore served as the executive secretary of the Maryland Association for the United Nations. [80] When campaigning for her brother, she kept her informational talks on the UN—in which she was nonpartisan—separate from her promotion of her brother.[81]

Overwhelmed by his opponent's use of family, friends, and celebrities, Humphrey turned to political associates from Minnesota to be his surrogates. While Kennedy brought no politicians from his state, Humphrey would bring at least six Minnesota politicians to West Virginia.

The long list of Minnesota's top officeholders who came to West Virginia represented a show of support by state Democrats for the senator. In addition to Congressmen Jon Blatnik and Joe Karth, these politicians included Governor Orville Freeman, Lieutenant Governor Karl Rolvaag, Senator Gene McCarthy, and Mayor Joseph Dillon of St. Paul, Minnesota.[82]

The most effective surrogate for the senator from Minnesota was Freeman, the 41-year-old governor. He promoted Humphrey by highlighting the similarity of the economic hardships of West Virginia coal miners to the plight of iron ore miners in northern Minnesota—a connection Humphrey never made.[83] Freeman also demonstrated his campaign dexterity when he began his address to the Cabin Creek District Democratic Club by linking hometown hero basketball star Jerry West with Humphrey's home state of Minnesota. He told the audience that the people of Minnesota "are mighty proud" to have West playing for the Minneapolis Lakers.[84] He then pointed out that the "Lakers are at their best when they play the fast break and control the boards," and predicted that this was "the kind of government Hubert Humphrey would give this country, instead of watching helplessly as our enemies roll up the score."[85]

Lieutenant Governor Rolvaag visited at least seven cities during his week-long stay in the Mountain State.[86] Most of the time he was identified by his political title, but a Fairmont headline simply said, "Minn. Man to Campaign for Humphrey."[87]

Humphrey's reliance on several "Minn. Man" politician surrogates put him at a disadvantage in the West Virginia primary fight. At one point he exclaimed, "I don't seem to recall anybody giving the Kennedy family—father, mother, sons, or daughters—the privilege of deciding who should be our party's nominee."[88] The Kennedy family did not have, of course, the privilege of "deciding who should be" the nominee, but their participation in the campaign constituted an asset.

Flag

The third F of West Virginia politics is the "flag." On this issue Kennedy enjoyed a distinct advantage. In a state that had more Veterans of Foreign War posts than high schools, he had a war record. His opponent, on the other hand, wasn't one of the 12 million Americans who wore a military uniform in World War II. While Kennedy was in the South Pacific commanding PT-109, Hubert Humphrey was a government worker, a college teacher, and then the mayor of Minneapolis.

In Wisconsin the Kennedy campaign made only one effort to highlight his war record—a last-minute television program that featured a reunion of five of the crew members of PT-109.[89] But in West Virginia the campaign used letters, articles, and a documentary to highlight the candidate's military service.

Such action in the Mountain State was not surprising, for the state, born out of war, had an impressive record of military service by its citizens. In 1960 it could claim 12 congressional Medal of Honor recipients.[90] The state sent a greater proportion of men to World War II than any other state, and more West Virginians lost their lives in the Korean War than any state of its size in the Union. In commending the state's military service, John Kennedy even reached back to the American Revolution. In the introduction to his televised debate he quoted George Washington's praise of the men west of the Appalachian Mountains who served so gallantly.[91]

Such a history explains why Kennedy's service record resonated in West Virginia, and why his campaign exploited it so much. The focus on the flag provided three benefits. First, it offered an opportunity for Kennedy to be identified as a decorated veteran rather than a Roman Catholic. The rosary was replaced with a PT-109 pin.

Second, the flag highlighted the fairness issue. Having identified Kennedy as a war hero, one could ask why he should be denied the right to run for president. As Harry Ernst pointed out, the implied message was that "a man who almost died for his country certainly should not be denied its highest office because of his religion."[92] And the question became one of not just fairness to John Kennedy, but also to all the other Catholics who wore a uniform in World War II, a war that ended just 15 years earlier.

Former Kentucky governor Happy Chandler promoted this issue when campaigning for Kennedy. Chandler reminded the audience that no one asks a soldier's religion when they are being pulled into a lifeboat.[93]

Third, the promotion of Kennedy's war record offered a way to underscore Humphrey's lack of wartime experience. At the start of his first swing around the state, Kennedy told a reporter that his staff had prepared an all-out attack on the record of Senator Humphrey, including a review of his "possible" war record. The reporter noted the wisdom of such a strategy, since in West Virginia, "Veterans' posts are about as numerous as churches."

Kennedy assured the reporter that this "war-record angle" would be used only as a last resort and "employed in self-defense."[94] What he did not tell the reporter was that earlier in the year, his campaign had received "supposed copies" of correspondence between Humphrey and his draft board from an anonymous Minnesota source.[95] During the final days of the campaign, this information would come to cast a shadow over both candidates' time in West Virginia.

War Record

John Kennedy was a certified World War II hero. He was awarded US Navy and Marine Corps medals for bravery and the Purple Heart. But a particularly interesting side to his participation occurred in what can be described as the most famous small-craft engagement in naval history.

In the South Pacific on the morning of August 2, 1943, the PT boat commanded by Lieutenant John Kennedy was cut in half by a Japanese destroyer. It was the only time a PT boat was rammed by an enemy destroyer and the only time an American PT boat was lost in World War II.[96]

If the incident was unusual, the conduct Kennedy displayed in rescuing his men was heroic. In the aftermath of the 2:30 a.m. collision, Kennedy, who had been on the Harvard swim team, led the ten surviving sailors on a three-mile swim to a nearby island. For four hours he swam the backstroke while pulling a wounded sailor, Patrick McMahon, by a life jacket strap that Kennedy held in his teeth.

Ultimately Kennedy and his crew were rescued by natives who discovered them and brought a message from Kennedy carved on a green coconut husk to a New Zealand military commander. The commander arranged the recovery of the crew on the morning of August 8, a week after their boat had been sunk and four days after Kennedy's father had been notified that his son was missing in action.[97]

At a later date, when asked to explain how he had come to be a hero, John Kennedy, in a display of typical Kennedy wit, replied laconically, "It was involuntary. They sank my boat."[98] "Involuntary" may have been an overstatement, however, as Kennedy wasn't even medically fit to serve. His poor health would have disqualified him from service. He had to pull strings to get a military assignment in the first place.[99]

Of the million stories of valor and endurance in World War II, John F. Kennedy's became one of the most publicized. Three factors explain how the military exploits of this future American president achieved iconic status by 1946. First was Kennedy's celebrity standing at the time. His status as the son of a former ambassador prompted his naval superiors to notify both UPI and AP reporters, who rushed to the scene of the rescue. It also ensured that the story would be on the front page of the *New York Times*, where the young lieutenant was described as a hero.[100]

The second factor was John Hersey, whose writing talent enabled the story to gain an audience in the *New Yorker* magazine. Hersey had already written an article for *Life* on PT boats when a chance meeting with Kennedy prompted him to craft "Survival," a story about the young lieutenant's experiences.[101]

Finally, due to intervention on the part of Kennedy's father, the story that Hersey wrote for the highbrow *New Yorker* reached a wider audience by being reprinted in the more accessible *Reader's Digest*, which had the nation's largest magazine circulation.

After the war, Joe Kennedy engineered a publicity offensive that would highlight his son's military accomplishments, circulating copies of that article in each of the Kennedy campaigns. In West Virginia an estimated 40,000 copies of the *Reader's Digest* article "Survival" were distributed in the state, half of them in Kanawha County alone.[102]

During the West Virginia campaign, Kennedy did not initially dwell on his military experiences. When he mentioned them, he referred to the impact of the war rather than his action in it. He spoke of his hospitalization for injuries rather than how he got the injuries. He would discuss the deaths in World War II of his brother, Joe Jr., and his English brother-in-law, William Cavendish, but never about his own decorations.

His reticence was in part because he was uncomfortable speaking about the topic. Ted Sorensen observed that he never boasted of his military service, or even reminisced about it, and never complained about his injuries.[103] But his reserve also reflected the fact that his story was already known. And Kennedy knew that his campaign staff was busy promoting his military record. So ingrained was the story in public consciousness that his supporters handed out small metal pins with the image of a PT-109 boat.[104]

The campaign sent personalized letters to the leaders of all the 120 Veterans of Foreign War posts in the state. The letter stated, "We are not opposed to Hubert Humphrey because of his lack of any war record. But we believe that these facts show why Jack Kennedy has a better understanding of veterans' problems."[105]

Voters also learned about Kennedy's military record by watching rebroadcasts of "PT-109" which was taken from the television show "*Navy Log* and shown by his campaign on various television stations in the state."[106]

The most notable surrogate responsible for promoting Kennedy's military service was Frank Roosevelt, who once again played a key role in championing his identity in West Virginia as a war hero and fellow serviceman in the Pacific.[107] Roosevelt and Kennedy never met when they served in the Pacific theater, but one would not know that by listening to Franklin Roosevelt Jr. on the campaign stump. He made it appear as if they'd served together on the same ship, not just in the same ocean, telling his audiences, "We were in the Pacific together."[108]

Roosevelt played an integral role in the three-part flag strategy used in the West Virginia primary campaign. In the first stage, the press reported that "He (Senator Kennedy) is making sure his audiences know he lost a brother-one of the ten most decorated Navy fliers- during World War II and that he himself spent years in a veterans hospital."[109] In the second stage, two weeks before the election primary, surrogate Frank Roosevelt Jr. discussed Humphrey's lack of a military record as well as Kennedy's record. At that time the press reported, "Roosevelt has been touring the state pointing to Kennedy's war record. He then mentions that Humphrey, who had a hernia, never served in the war at all."[110] In the last days of the primary campaign, Roosevelt initiated stage three when he either implied or stated outright that Humphrey was a draft dodger. When asked by a *Gazette* reporter, "Did you call Sen. Humphrey a draft dodger," Roosevelt replied emphatically, "I've never said that and I never meant that. I did not use that phrase."[111] But the reporter observed that the substance was there if not the semantics: "It's not exactly clear now how far Roosevelt went. He insists he never went so far as to call Humphrey a draft dodger, but, however far it was, Humphrey says it was too far."[112]

The charge was based on a confidential file of letters between Humphrey and his draft board that the Kennedy campaign had received from an "anonymous Minnesota source." Initially the campaign tried to recruit reporters to publish a story based on the materials, but several refused to write about it. According to *New York Times* reporter Bill Lawrence, who became a player in this drama, the Kennedy forces decided to hold the materials in reserve, to be used only in retaliation against Humphrey for "some extremely low blow."[113]

When the "low blow" didn't come in the final week, Roosevelt raised the issue after intense pressure from Bobby Kennedy. On Friday, May 6, 1960, four days before the election, he asked at a public rally, "Where was Hubert in the war," and then declared that "I don't know where he was in World War II."[114]

The *Washington Star* called Roosevelt's words a "low blow in dirty politics," noting that Humphrey, as a married father, was first put in a deferred classification and later turned down when he tried to volunteer. "If Mr. Roosevelt does not think these really are the facts, that is one thing. But to simply say that 'I don't know where he was in World War II,'" the *Star* observed, "is a slur which all decent people will resent."[115]

Roosevelt denied calling Humphrey a draft dodger, but the damage was done. One can only guess at the political impact of the *Charleston Gazette* headline that placed the Minnesota senator next to the words "Draft Dodger."[116] Humphrey couldn't unring that bell. *Time* magazine joined the *Washington Star* in accusing Roosevelt of dirty politics,[117] but as Doris Kearns Goodwin later observed, "The deed was already done, the contrast had been drawn between a young decorated veteran and a politician who didn't even want to be a soldier."[118] The record, however, did not sustain such a charge or justify such a smear. At the start of the war, Humphrey was classified III-A because he was married and a father. During that time he served serval posts in the state associated with the war effort.[119] Later he was reclassified as II-A, an essential civilian, because in 1943 he was teaching Air Corps cadets at Macalester College in St. Paul. It was the closest he ever came to military service. In July 1944 he was reclassified I-A and sent to the Fort Snelling induction center, but he was sent home five days later when doctors found a double hernia.[120]

Humphrey conveyed this information to the Kennedy brothers, but neither censured or stopped Roosevelt's attack. In a 1971 interview, Humphrey stated, "It's a simple story—I simply wasn't accepted. Roosevelt knew that, I brought him into my office after the campaign and showed these draft records. I said to him, 'Frank, you know goddamn well that what you said isn't true.' And Frank said, 'I know that, but Bobby asked me to do it.'"[121]

According to Ken O'Donnell, Bobby's actions were not surprising—both in the apparent pressuring of Roosevelt and the refusal to tell him to stop the accusation. "Bobby was all about victory," O'Donnell would observe and he "would leave no weapon in their arsenal unused."[122]

Larry O'Brien, a close friend and advisor to John Kennedy, would label the incident as one of his "few regrets in campaigns." He concluded that "we should have destroyed the rubbish, not turned it over to Frank Roosevelt."[123] Kenny O'Donnell called it "one step too far."[124] The regret about the incident was well-founded, for the smear boomeranged. The public outrage over the attack lasted through the week and prompted both Frank Roosevelt and John Kennedy to apologize.[125] But each appeared to hedge, and neither exonerated Humphrey.

Nothing so dramatically reflects the change in the American electoral landscape than the reaction to that smear. In 1960, such a personal attack was not only unusual but also counterproductive. The public apparently wasn't ready to listen, and the press stood ready to condemn it.

On this issue, as on others, Frank Roosevelt cut political commercials that fulfilled the "hatchet role" he adopted. The ad provides insight into the strategy surrounding the third F during the closing days of the primary contest.[126] The ad, filmed at Cabin Creek, starts with the announcer saying, "Listen to Franklin Delano Roosevelt Jr." The President's son begins by noting that "Jack Kennedy has served his country with distinction and with great ability in times of peace and in time of war."[127] He then announces, "I know where Jack Kennedy . . . [and] fifteen million other Americans were [in World War II]." He then suggests that the audience "might just look into the record a little bit and see where some of these other candidates were, what they were doing." The quality of the film was poor—very dark, with talking among the audience—which suggests that the ad wasn't played or at least not widely viewed. It does, however, provide an audiovisual of the "smear" innuendo attack on Humphrey launched in the final week of the primary campaign.[128]

John Kennedy's Response

The blowback from the draft-dodger episode undermined the Kennedy campaign's reputation of competence and control, and threatened the campaign itself. A frustrated and apparently surprised John Kennedy tried to first distance, then deflect, and then dismiss the controversy.

On Saturday, May 7, 1960, when the *New York Times* printed Lawrence's article, Kennedy distanced himself, saying that he "disagreed with injection of this issue into the campaign."[129] But the candidate did not openly question the accusation or defend Humphrey. The next day he further distanced himself from Roosevelt by claiming that the criticism of Senator Humphrey was done by "someone who's supporting me." A hollow statement since, as the *Gazette* pointed out, FDR Jr. wasn't just a supporter but a "chief lieutenant" in the campaign.

When notified that Kennedy had disowned the Roosevelt statement, Humphrey told a reporter, "That's a lot of baloney." He noted that the two Kennedy brothers had adopted a good cop / bad cop stance. "One takes the high road and the other the low road, and they can't keep out of each other's ditches."[130]

Kennedy then attempted to deflect the issue by portraying himself as a victim of "personal abuse" by Humphrey, who used "inappropriate" language ("gutter politics") that was "unbecoming a presidential candidate."[131] When deflection failed, Kennedy tried dismissal by calling the incident a distraction that "is not of interest to anybody."[132]

The attack on Humphrey had important effects on all three key players. It proved devastating to Franklin Roosevelt Jr., the loyal water carrier for the Kennedy campaign in West Virginia. In response to public criticism, he apologized and offered to leave the campaign. John Kennedy decided not to disown him, although some had urged such action.[133] But according to Bobby Kennedy's biographer, Arthur Schlesinger Jr., "Roosevelt's political career did not survive this incident in West Virginia."[134] After the election, President Kennedy didn't appoint Roosevelt to the post he coveted and his father had held: assistant secretary of the navy. Although the decision may have reflected concern for Roosevelt's heavy drinking rather than his identification with the smear on Humphrey, the fact remained that the most important campaigner for John Kennedy in West Virginia ended his efforts in the Mountain State under a cloud from which he never escaped.

The attack also infuriated Senator Humphrey. He later wrote that he had confronted the Kennedy brothers and corrected the record, but they refused to take action. "They believed me, but never shut FDR Jr. up, as they easily could have."[135] The bitterness Humphrey felt was uncharacteristic and deep. Although he would later accept John's words that he had no prior knowledge of the attack, Humphrey never fully forgave either Frank Roosevelt or Bobby Kennedy.

John F. Kennedy's landslide win demonstrates why the smear was unnecessary. His military-hero status was enough of an asset that he didn't need to take down his opponent. The episode reveals both the ambition and the desperation of the Kennedy campaign in the final days before the West Virginia presidential primary. While the last-minute smear didn't undermine the campaign, it did reveal a siege mentality that condoned questionable means to further defensible ends. This "ends justifies means" mentality was fueled in part by a belief that at stake was not just the fate of a candidate, but also that of 40 million Catholics.

Aside from the backlash of the attempted smear, Kennedy was well-served by his focus on the flag—along with the other two Fs, food and family. His adoption of religious confrontation was also effective. In the end, this two-pronged strategy, not needed or used in Wisconsin, proved viable in the Mountain State.

John F. Kennedy with Jennings Randolph and Paul Watson, assistant general superintendent, U. S. Steel Cleaning Plant, Gary, McDowell County, May 9, 1959, Jennings Randolph Collection, West Virginia State Archives

John F. Kennedy with Jennings Randolph and unidentified miners, U. S. Steel Cleaning Plant, Gary, McDowell County, May 9, 1959, Jennings Randolph Collection, West Virginia State Archives

Senator John F. Kennedy at Secretary of State Joe Burdette's desk filing to run in the presidential primary, February 6, 1960, Emil Varney Collection, West Virginia State Archives

Hubert H. Humphrey talking to a miner in Cabin Creek, April 8, 1960, Frank Wilkin Collection, West Virginia State Archives

John Fitzgerald Kennedy campaigning in a crowd of what appears to be college students, possibly April 11, 1960, Charleston Newspapers Collection, West Virginia State Archives

John F. Kennedy giving a speech on the steps at the State Capitol during the West Virginia primary campaign, April 11, 1960, David Todd Carden Collection, West Virginia State Archives

John F. Kennedy standing in front
of the Post Office at Ona, probably
April 11, 1960, Purchased Items
Collection, West Virginia State
Archives

John F. Kennedy on camera at WBOY-TV, Clarksburg, possibly April 18, 1960,
Milton Furner Collection, West Virginia State Archives

John F. Kennedy outdoors with crowd at school, Gauley Bridge, probably April 20, 1960, Town of Gauley Bridge/Midge Crandall Collection, West Virginia State Archives

John F. Kennedy with nine young girls of the American Legion Children Junior Auxiliary, Town of Gauley Bridge/Midge Crandall Collection, West Virginia State Archives

After campaigning in the 1960 primary, John F. Kennedy joined reporters for steaks and beer in back room of the Smoke House. Logan, April 25, 1960, Herb Little Collection, West Virginia State Archives

Lyndon B. Johnson arriving at the Benedum Airport in Bridgeport, May 7, 1960, Clarksburg Engraving Company Collection, West Virginia State Archives

Lyndon B. Johnson talking with Hubert H. Humphrey in the banquet hall at the Masonic Temple, Clarksburg, May 7, 1960, Clarksburg Engraving Company Collection, West Virginia State Archives

Katy Doonan chatting with Senator John F. Kennedy on WSAZ broadcast, February 6, 1960, Emil Varney Collection, West Virginia State Archives

Jennings Randolph with John F. Kennedy and Lyndon B. Johnson, Jennings Randolph Collection, West Virginia State Archives

Crowd gathered for President John F. Kennedy's speech at the West Virginia Centennial in Charleston, June 20, 1963, Don Flesher Collection, West Virginia State Archives

John F. Kennedy delivering speech at West Virginia's Centennial Celebration in Charleston, June 20, 1963, Frank Wilkin Collection, West Virginia State Archives

Kennedy-Humphrey debate, showing Senator Kennedy, Charleston, West Virginia, May 1960, Harry Brawley Collection, West Virginia State Archives

Kennedy-Humphrey debate, showing Senator Kennedy, Ted Kennedy, and Hawthorne D. Battle, station president outside WCHS studio, Charleston, West Virginia, May 1960, Harry Brawley Collection, West Virginia State Archives

Kennedy-Humphrey debate, showing Senator Humphrey, Dale Schussler of WTRF-TV, Bill Ames of WCHS-TV, and Ned Chilton of the *Charleston Gazette*, Charleston, West Virginia, May 1960, Harry Brawley Collection, West Virginia State Archives

J. F. Kennedy, Sen. Ward Wylie, and Franklin D. Roosevelt Jr., n.d., Charleston Newspapers Collection, West Virginia State Archives

Tribute in downtown store following Kennedy assassination, Charleston, West Virginia, November 1963, George Holbrook Collection, West Virginia State Archives

Chapter 4

THE PRESS REPORTS

The 1960 West Virginia presidential primary featured an unequal duel between the old retail politics of Hubert Humphrey and the new wholesale politics of John Kennedy with its emphasis on money, organization, and television. The Kennedy camp overwhelmed Humphrey with unparalleled expenditures, an organizational blitzkrieg, an unprecedented use of television, and the support of prominent journalists. As such, the contest provides a unique window into the much-vaunted Kennedy machine.

Financial Disparity

Any exploration of the 1960 presidential primary in West Virginia must begin with money. John Kennedy started this campaign with many hurdles to overcome, but money would not be one. His father had set up a million-dollar trust fund for him when he was nine years old, as he did with all his children. When asked during the campaign about his wealth, John admitted he was worth "about a million, maybe only $900,000."[1]

In contrast, Humphrey said that his wealth was about average for a small-town druggist. He estimated his cash assets at a total of $10,000 in savings and mutual securities, plus a paid mortgage on his Washington home. In 1960 he still owed $17,000 on his house in Minnesota.[2]

John Kennedy could also count on campaign funds from his father, whose personal wealth was estimated to be at least $200 million.[3] At a family meeting in 1959, Joe Kennedy announced that they had come this far and were not going to let money be an obstacle.[4] He confided to James Landis, "What's a hundred million if it will help Jack?"[5]

In addition to family resources, John had the benefit of wealthy close friends. Some he knew from school, and some he knew from the war, like William Battle, whose father was the former governor of Virginia. They were among the many who volunteered their time for the Kennedy campaign in the Mountain State without compensation.

His legendary expenditures in West Virginia prompted jokes from his supporters. Claude Ellis, the Kennedy county chair in Logan County, remarked later that Kennedy "didn't want to buy West Virginia. He just rented it for the day."[6]

In uncomfortable situations, John Kennedy would make self-deprecating jokes about himself and his wealthy family. At the Gridiron Club in 1958, he made light of his father's fortune and told the audience that a recent telegram from his father had said: "Dear Jack: Don't buy a single vote more than is necessary. I'll help you win this election, but I'll be damned if I'm going to pay for a landslide!"[7]

He used the same joke two years later on the campaign trail in West Virginia. On his first visit to McDowell County, he arrived at Welch and had his sound truck pull outside the parking garage, despite a gathering windstorm. He then "hopped on top of his truck, reached in his suit pocket and pulled out what he said was a telegram from his father, tycoon Joseph P. Kennedy, who had been accused of trying to buy his son the election. 'Don't buy one more vote than necessary,' Kennedy read, 'Dammed if I'm going to pay for a landslide.'" According to the newspaper reporting on the event, "The candidate smiled; the crowd roared."[8]

There is no way to get an accurate financial report count by the Kennedy campaign as the reporting of legal expenditures was a flawed, farcical system. Candidates weren't required to report most of the money they spent. For example, campaign's expenditures didn't include Kennedy's airplane, or the efforts of friends who worked on the campaign without pay.

When a questionable pre-election expenditure came out on April 10 showing that Humphrey had spent $13,835 to Kennedy's $11,211, the Kennedy campaign made the questionable assertion that they were in debt and had been outspent by Humphrey in West Virginia. Their claim merited a front-page story in the *New York Times*. Bill Lawrence's headline read, "Kennedy Backers in Debt, They Say; Supporters Report Spending 20% Less Than Humphrey Forces in West Virginia."[9]

Yet investigation of advertising expenditures revealed that Kennedy consistently outspent his rival. A review of news outlets in the two largest cities, Huntington and Charleston, showed that Kennedy had spent $21,416 on radio, television, and newspapers a week before the election, while Humphrey spent only $2,750.[10]

Estimates of spending by the Kennedy campaign in West Virginia have ranged across the board from a low of $250,000 to high of $900,000. The latter number came from Matt Reese, a key campaign insider who shared the information with Charlie Peters a decade later. Since the estimate didn't include the friends who worked in the Mountain State without pay, or such expenses as the Kennedy aircraft, one can speak of a million-dollar primary at a time when a gubernatorial race in West Virginia cost a half-million dollars.[11]

Humphrey, who had no family access to campaign funds, was broke after the Wisconsin primary. He operated in West Virginia on what he called a "shoestring cut in half." He lamented, "My cupboard is bare, my treasury is red and the only thing running good will be Humphrey himself. We are operating on Humphrey's energy and Humphrey's ability to campaign—not on other people's money."[12]

Late in the campaign, on April 26, 1960, Humphrey attacked Kennedy's spending, pointing out that he didn't have the "unlimited financial resources of Kennedy."[13] He also spoke of black bags of money, but he never provided any evidence, nor did he elaborate on the charges.

Stories abound throughout the state about the unprecedented campaign money that year, including the one fictionalized in Denise Giardina's novel *The Unquiet Earth*, when the Kennedy campaign worker asked a county boss what he needed to slate Kennedy and remove all the Humphrey signs, the boss asked for "twenty-nine," meaning $2,900, but he got $29,000.[14]

Transportation

As a result of the unlimited financial resources of his family, Kennedy was able to use campaign tools, like his private airplane, that were not available to his opponent. As Humphrey exclaimed, "I hardly have the money to drive that bus down the road. Much less buy an airplane."[15] The period leading up to the Democratic convention illustrates the great divide in the two candidates' resources. While Kennedy could fly anywhere, Humphrey plodded along on the ground in the Wisconsin and West Virginia campaigns, traveling around (and sometimes sleeping) in an older bus. He recounted his frustration one night in Wisconsin when "I heard a plane overhead. On my cot, bundled in layers of uncomfortable clothes, both chilled and sweaty, I yelled, 'Come down here, Jack, and play fair.'"[16]

Fairness, however, was not part of the Kennedys' current game plan. The Kennedy camp thought that they had played fair in Wisconsin, and the result was a Pyrrhic victory, a tainted win that highlighted the religious issue and kept Humphrey in the race. With the stakes so high in West Virginia and the hill so seemingly steep, they pulled all the stops to get a victory that would not only undermine Humphrey, but also erase the religious issue.

In 1959 Joe Kennedy arranged for the family to buy a jet turboprop Convair and lease it to John at $1.75 a mile from the Ken-Air Corporation, which was owned by Jack's siblings and in-laws.[17] The plane was reconfigured from 44 seats to 18 and included a sofa, a hi-fi music system, and a private bedroom for the candidate. Between September 1959 and late summer of 1960, the candidate logged 110,000 miles on the plane, named *Caroline* in honor of his daughter.[18]

One reason the campaign gave for the purchase of the plane was that bumpy roads were hard on Jack's back. But the advantages added up to more than just the protection of his health. In West Virginia, a private plane allowed him to campaign in several regions of the state on the same day. On April 3, 1960, during his first full day of campaigning in West Virginia, he visited three cities in different regions: Parkersburg in the northwest, Charleston in the center, and Beckley in the south—all on the same day. Such a one day itinerary could not be easily duplicated without an airplane.[19]

Access to a private aircraft also enabled Kennedy to go back and forth to Washington, while Humphrey traveled via commercial airlines. Senator Eugene McCarthy recalled, "I remember poor Hubert out there . . . running to catch the North Central DC-3 and then looking out on the field to see the *Caroline* waiting on the apron with the soup bubbling in the kitchen."[20]

Another advantage, which the public was not aware of, was that Kennedy also used his plane to travel to Montego Bay in Jamaica for holidays before and during his extensive campaign in West Virginia.[21]

With access to unlimited funds, the Kennedy campaign could also take advantage of other aircraft. For example, when "faced with deadline for a series of newspapers ads, Kennedy aides hired two private planes to fly the mats from Cincinnati to daily papers throughout the state."[22]

But Kennedy understood that the plane, which was a campaign asset, could also be an electoral liability. The $385,000 aircraft could become a visual reminder of his wealth, especially if the public knew the plane had a full meal service with a stewardess serving food on china plates.[23] Such awareness explains why he wouldn't let Humphrey accompany him when both senators had to travel to Washington to vote on a bill. Humphrey learned why Kennedy was reluctant only after the convention. On a plane ride to Minnesota, Kennedy told Humphrey that he did not want his opponent to see the inside of his private plane and the luxury of the transportation he was enjoying. Humphrey recalled that Kennedy said, "I suppose the smartest thing that I did during the primary was to deny a ride on the plane the day both of us had to get back to Washington to vote. You would have painted me as a man enjoying the luxuries of life while the people down below were struggling. You would have torn me apart." He correctly realized that the comfort and extravagance of his airplane could be a campaign issue for Humphrey, who traveled the state in a bus that often broke down and had a bad heater.[24]

Kennedy's explanation would also explain why his brother Bobby turned down Humphrey's request for a ride on the night of the televised debate. That night the plane was going to Wheeling without Kennedy. When Humphrey missed the plane to Wheeling and made his request, Bobby's response was to use profanity. With reporters watching, he left the Minnesota senator stranded in Charleston and unable to come to Wheeling until four the next morning.[25]

The differences in transportation provided an advantage for Kennedy, who would invite reporters to be with him when he flew. Those fortunate enough to be asked could look forward to plane ride to their destination and a hot meal, while Kennedy, subject of a sensitive stomach, ate tomato soup.[26]

Later, Hubert Humphrey would learn of a more sinister use of Joe Kennedy's financial help. In his autobiography Humphrey relates how Cardinal Richard Cushing told him that he and Joe Kennedy influenced the outcome in West Virginia by dispersing payments to Protestant ministers, particularly to the smaller churches in black communities." [27]

After relating this story, however, Humphrey went on to write that he was "whipped not only by money and organization, but, more particularly, by an extraordinary man."[28]

Connections

Joe Kennedy brought more than funds to his son's quest for the 1960 presidential nomination. He also brought connections. One of them was Jim McCahey, a coal buyer in Chicago, who brought pressure on Island Creek Coal Company, one of the biggest mining outfits in the state and employed 1,000 people in Logan County. Island Creek influenced other coal companies in the area, including Massey Coal, which employed local political boss Raymond Chafin. Under pressure from his company, Chafin switched his support to Kennedy. He explained his action to the leaders in his faction by saying, "Boys, Kennedy's gotta come or I gotta go."[29]

A more public example occurred in Clarksburg, West Virginia, when corporate contacts allowed John Kennedy to campaign inside the Hazel-Atlas Glass Factory, a large producer of glass containers. The company had more than ten plants across the nation and a policy banning politicking. Earlier Humphrey had been denied entrance to the factory. But when Kennedy was turned away, he called the "right people" in Washington and got the ban lifted because his father was a large stockholder in the parent company.[30]

After the election, charges of fraud and corruption made headlines in several newspapers and prompted state, federal and media investigations. In West Virginia, the attorney general conducted a state investigation. The US Justice Department sent FBI agents to West Virginia, but after several weeks Attorney General William Rogers called off the investigation, which hadn't found hard evidence. The FBI Report of July 12, 1960, to the Assistant Attorney General Civil Rights Division at the Department of Justice, didn't substantiate any federal election law violations.[31]

A number of reporters came to the state after the vote. But as Edward Folliad noted in the *Washington Post*, none were able "to document a Kennedy money scandal." [32] While some of the investigations found evidence of political corruption such as vote buying on the local level, none uncovered any significant fraud in the presidential primary contest.

The *Wall Street Journal* conducted a five-week investigation that did find buying onto slates and political payoffs in West Virginia, but the paper never printed the story for lack of direct evidence of vote-buying by the Kennedy campaign.[33] An investigation of Logan County by reporter Jack Anderson also found no hard evidence.[34] Even Senator Barry Goldwater got involved by hiring a former FBI agent to investigate voter fraud.[35] On the state level, the *Charleston Gazette* sent Don Marsh and John C. Morgan to investigate vote buying and political corruption in nine counties. Their conclusion was that there was no substantial evidence to support the charge that Kennedy had bought the election.[36]

Per the possible role of the organized crime in West Virginia, there is no direct evidence of Mafia funds beyond "unsupported boasts by gangsters" and unsupported allegations.[37] As Kennedy operative Paul Corbin observed, Bobby Kennedy would never allow Mafia money in the campaign. [38]

Organization Disparity

Jimmy Wolford, the folk singer who served as a crowd warmup act on the Humphrey campaign, declared that "Kennedy's organization was like Harvard, while Humphrey's was like a state-sponsored school."[39] The analogy between the wealthiest college in the nation and a state university was appropriate, for in West Virginia Kennedy outspent and out-organized his opponent. A review of Kennedy's effort in the Mountain State reinforces an observation the Minnesota senator made during the Wisconsin primary: "I felt like an independent merchant competing against a chain store."[40]

In the West Virginia primary, John Kennedy benefited from unlimited resources, better connections, and an early start. By January of 1960, when he announced his candidacy for the Democratic presidential nomination, Kennedy polled West Virginia Democratic voters, visited several West Virginia cities, and set up a state organization.[41] By April 4, John Kennedy's presence in the political landscape of West Virginia seemed secure. He had an operation in 39 of the state's 55 counties, and his campaign manager was the talented Bob McDonough.[42]

In contrast to the Kennedy campaign, Humphrey lacked statewide organization. The Humphrey campaign in West Virginia had two cochairmen: William L. Jacobs of Parkersburg in Wood County and Marshall West of Oceana in Wyoming County. Jacobs was assigned to organize the northern and western parts of the state, and West organized the rest of the state. Expressing envy at the "tremendous advantage of the well-financed Kennedy organization," Jacobs noted with frustration that "I repeatedly ran across people who told me that they had already been contacted by the Kennedy people and had already committed themselves."[43]

The early involvement of the Kennedy camp in West Virginia provided the time to not only set up a statewide organization, but also to seek advice from a variety of sources. These included his own pollster, Lou Harris, who looked for the key issues in the state,[44] and three West Virginia congressmen, Ken Hechler, Cleve Bailey, and Harley Staggers, who offered suggestions.[45]

Indicative of the Kennedy organization's careful preparation was a briefing memo on Jerry West, star of the West Virginia University basketball team, who had just guided the Mountaineers to the 1959 NCAA championship game. A native of the Cabin Creek area near Charleston, his WVU jersey number "44" was recognized throughout the state.[46]

In the memo, Kennedy was advised that since many West Virginians have "an inferiority complex," he should "praise the exploits of Jerry West and West Virginia University." However, there were geographic limits to such action. The memo cautioned that such praise for West shouldn't be done in Huntington, the home of Marshall College, a heated rival of West Virginia University, as the citizens in Cabell County "usually felt slighted because much more publicity was given the larger school."[47]

If the West anecdote shows the dividends of research enjoyed by the Kennedy camp, the opposite was demonstrated by Humphrey, who was unprepared when reporters asked him to comment on West Virginia's most famous athlete. He had to admit that he didn't know who West was. The ability to identify basketball players was irrelevant to being president, but knowing what subjects voters were interested in was essential to being a candidate. This gap in Humphrey's knowledge seemed particularly glaring, as Jerry West was going to play for the Minnesota Lakers.[48]

Congressman Ken Hechler witnessed the disparity in organization firsthand when Kennedy invited him to fly back to Washington, DC, after a rally in Raleigh County. Before the plane left, the congressman observed a campaign staff meeting in the conference room at the Beckley airport.[49]

The meeting started promptly—almost on the dot at 8:00 p.m.—as relatives and organizers arrived. Bobby Kennedy came in one door, Ted Kennedy in another door, and through another came Sargent Shriver. Hechler noticed that without saying hello, they gave presentations on what was needed to be done, specifically in terms of issues and personalities in each area of the state. Hechler recalled that "it was almost like a well-oiled machine, like a well-rehearsed drama, the way that it unfolded."[50]

The very next night, Hechler was with Humphrey in Madison, West Virginia, and witnessed anything but organizational efficiency. Humphrey was concerned about having his campaign handouts in the ballroom where he would speak. Indicative of the senator's lack of a professional staff, Hechler remembers that in the elevator going up to the ballroom, Humphrey turned to one of his aides and asked, "Bob, do we have a table for our literature up there?"[51]

Meanwhile, the Kennedy campaign broke boundaries in West Virginia with its use of campaign literature. As of April 13, 1960, almost a month before the election, 754,475 items had been sent into a state that had a population of around two million, with some 400,000 Democrats expected to vote.

Campaign items included 75,000 bumper stickers, 200,000 buttons, 53,000 window stickers, and 1,100 window cards. Campaign literature included 75,000 labor brochures, 100,000 reprints of the *Reader's Digest* article about Kennedy's PT-109 experience during World War II, and 150,250 National Kennedy overviews, a newspaper format profile sheet on Kennedy and his family.[52] There were also targeted mailings to different constituencies. For example, after Kennedy spoke at the American Society of Newspaper Editors, ministers of certain denominations and all newspaper editors received a letter and a copy of Kennedy's speech on the separation of church and state.[53]

The Kennedy campaign excelled in sending out extensive personalized follow-up letters. A young woman with a stenographic notebook followed Kennedy when he was out shaking hands. As soon as he shook hands with somebody, the woman would get the voter's name, address, and some personal material. Within 24 hours, that voter would get a personally autographed letter from Kennedy that expressed pleasure at the opportunity to meet, and included enough personal material to appear much more than a form letter.[54]

For letters from Frank Roosevelt the return address would be Hyde Park, New York, the home of his famous father, President Roosevelt. Credit for that idea is given to Joe Kennedy.[55]

The large sums available to John Kennedy in West Virginia bought and paid for a large organization in the state as well as extensive use of television and other campaign tools. All of this not only overwhelmed Humphrey in West Virginia but also impacted future American presidential campaigns.

The unprecedented expenditures of the Kennedy campaign were a major factor in his winning the primary. But while the spending was both historic and plentiful, it did not guarantee or fully explain his landslide victory in West Virginia. For that, one needs to look at other factors, such as his strategy, his advertising, and his relations with the press.

Television

Ads

Joe Kennedy said that he would sell John Kennedy like soap flakes,[56] and in April and May of 1960, West Virginia television served as the medium for that transaction. The Massachusetts senator, who would have the first "televised presidency," used that medium extensively and successfully during that period.

As Henry Fairlie notes, John Kennedy "was the first politician in any nation to realize that television had given politics a new arena."[57] In the Mountain State, Kennedy used that new stage to reach voters in four ways: campaign ads, a documentary on PT-109, a television program, and a televised debate. His actions represented a full-court press to craft personas for the candidacy.

Kennedy had two advantages in this endeavor. First, he was on the field alone. His cash-strapped competitor couldn't raise the funds necessary to seek votes on the airwaves. Except for news interviews, the only times Hubert Humphrey was on television in West Virginia were during the May 4 candidate debate and a May 7 telethon.

Second, Kennedy went Hollywood in terms of personnel. Jack Denove, an experienced producer, directed the media campaign. His television credits included producing 22 episodes of the series *Cavalcade of America* (1954–1956) and seven episodes of *The Christophers* (1954–1958).[58] Before taking on full media responsibilities in the 1960 campaign, Denove had done work for Kennedy in 1958 on such campaign programs as "Coffee with the Kennedys," a call-in show that included footage from home movies. More importantly, Denove had produced *Navy Log*, a television dramatization that highlighted Kennedy's heroic action during World War II as commander of the PT-109.[59]

Kennedy's media efforts represented a step toward the alliance of Hollywood and politics; of California and Washington, DC; of using the media not to shape dreams, but to further political ambitions. It wasn't surprising that the Kennedy campaign reached out to Hollywood, for Joe Kennedy had been involved with the film industry in the 1920s and at one time was the de facto head of three studios in California.[60]

Denove produced at least 12 ads for the West Virginia primary campaign, each tailored to the state's voters. The time for the ads usually ranged from three to five minutes. The format for most of them was the same: a set speech or set answer to a question sandwiched by an announcer who introduced and closed the ad with the tagline "It is up to you . . . You and Kennedy . . . Vote Kennedy May tenth."

In West Virginia, as he had in other states, Denove liked to shoot on location instead of in the studio. This often allowed the viewer to see familiar landmarks rather than a studio backdrop. But such a process also required a local crew in each primary state.[61] Phil Smith of St. Albans headed the local film crew in West Virginia. He was working for the television station WCHS in Charleston (a cosponsor of the candidates' debate) when his boss, Mr. Tierney, called him about filming the Kennedy ads.

The weekly schedule began with Smith and Denove at the Ruffner Hotel in Charleston to meet the Kennedys and decide where the shoots would be and what footage they needed. During the week, he and Denove, along with a crew, would film the candidate and the setting on kinescope.[62]

On Fridays, Smith would collect the footage and meet Denove at the Charleston airport. They would fly then to Washington, DC, and process it at National Color—the company they used for all the film they shot during the West Virginia commercials. On Saturday nights, they edited film and flew back to Charleston. Smith remembered being so tired that on the flights back he slept three-fourths of the time. Upon arrival in Charleston, employees of Channel 8 (WCHS) would get the completed campaign commercials and distribute them to the different West Virginia television stations.[63]

Phil Smith not only got a salary for filming the Kennedy ads, but he also received a major gift. Smith had told Ted Kennedy that his wife complained about him working six days a week in the studio while she was at home with three young children and no washer or dryer. After hearing this, Ted Kennedy had his secretaries make arrangements to deliver a washer and dryer to the Smiths' house on 816 Hudson Street in Charleston.[64]

The television ads that Denove and Smith produced for the West Virginia voters were long, positive, and informative. Of the 12 campaign commercials at the West Virginia archives, six ads featured the candidate speaking. Four featured Franklin Roosevelt Jr., two with him in an office and two with him on the campaign stump.[65] Denove's procedure was to film entire speeches and then search them for usable material. A problem for him was Kennedy's tendency to increase his volume before large audiences, making a good deal of his remarks in large auditoriums too intense for TV. Denove had to find a section within the speech where Kennedy wasn't as forceful.[66]

The first two campaign commercials in the 1960 West Virginia presidential primary featured Kennedy in front of a crowd at the state capitol grounds. To get the overview shot of the candidate, Smith had to put a cameraman up on a metal rigging.[67] While he introduced himself in the first ad, he answered questions on religion in the second ad.[68]

In two ads Frank Roosevelt raised the religious issue directly. One ad featured the history of Roosevelt—not the candidate, but Franklin Delano Roosevelt Jr. In both, Roosevelt speaks directly to the camera while sitting behind a wooden desk in an office. His words are strong, though undercut by his mono-tone delivery. In the first ad on religion he explains that the Roosevelts escaped religious persecution in 1621 when they left England to come to America, and in the second ad he argued that religious prejudice should not exist in our nation.[69]

Three other Kennedy ads relate to economic development in West Virginia. The first features the candidate discussing his 14 years in Congress, addressing the issue, and noting that both Virginia and Massachusetts suffered the impact of automation.[70] In the second Kennedy gets into specifics, citing six proposals to reduce unemployment in the state. These included a program of coal research, redevelopment, and more government contracts for depressed areas. The com-mercial ends with an announcer telling the viewer, "It is to your interest to vote for a man dedicated to your welfare. May tenth, vote for you, vote Kennedy."[71]

The third and arguably most important political ad from the 1960 West Vir-ginia primary was filmed in a coal mine. The ad provides a visual linkage be-tween the earnest candidate and the state's most important industry. The juxta-position of the senator and the coal miners is awkward and the way the miners ask their questions seems staged and uncomfortable, but the five-minute com-mercial provides an opportunity for Kennedy to provide details of his economic plan for the state. The ad places him in a face-to-face question-and-answer sit-uation where he appears open and listening, even though the questions seem prepared.[72]

The ad closes with the announcer saying, "And there it is. Senator Kennedy bringing you issues of this presidential campaign as they affect West Virginia, as they affect you. Senator Kennedy, Democrat, can be our next president. The answer is here in West Virginia. It is up to you . . . You and Kennedy . . . Vote Kennedy . . . May tenth." In four short sentences, the announcer mentions Kennedy's name four times and West Virginia twice.[73]

No Kennedy campaign ad attacked his primary opponent directly. The clos-est to what one could call negative was the Gallup Poll ad stating that only 7 percent of Democrats prefer Humphrey. The ad went on to emphasize that Kennedy has a better chance to defeat Richard Nixon (Gallup poll had Kennedy leading 54 to 46 percent). The ad ends with the declaration that "time is run-ning out. You must say to yourself, to beat Nixon I must vote Kennedy."[74]

But if the Kennedy camp was reluctant to launch negative ads, it wasn't above playing the victim card.[75] A so-called gang-up ad portrayed John Kennedy as the target of a backroom deal. The commercial featured a cartoon of over-weight politicians in a smoke-filled room setting a trap for the voters of West Virginia. The announcer explains, "They ask you, you, and you, the people of West Virginia, to walk into their trap and support Humphrey. But will they themselves support Humphrey at the convention? Of course not. They'll drop

Humphrey like the hot potato he is, because everybody knows Humphrey couldn't possibly win the nomination, much less the election." The ad ends listing the states—New Hampshire, Wisconsin, Pennsylvania, Massachusetts, and Indiana—where the bosses tried to stop Kennedy. "But the people spoke up and Kennedy overwhelmingly won each primary. Make it an overwhelmingly people's vote, not a boss's vote here in West Virginia. May tenth, vote Kennedy." But the ad doesn't mention that in four of the five states invoked, Kennedy faced no serious opposition.[76]

In the end the Kennedy campaign ads may not have played a significant role in the outcome. The ads were not very sophisticated. They were mostly excerpts from his campaign stump speeches wedged in between an announcer reminding viewers, in a blatant appeal to self-interest, to "Vote Kennedy!" The ads often ended with the admonition that "when you vote Kennedy, remember, you are voting for a man who is constantly thinking of your welfare."[77]

One could argue that if Kennedy's television advertising in West Virginia had an impact, it was due in part to Humphrey's lack of it. The only television effort initiated by the Humphrey camp was a last-minute telethon that reached only Kanawha and surrounding counties. And that media effort lacked all the finesse of the Kennedy operation. It was not well-planned, well-structured, or well-scripted. The candidate simply sat at a table in front of a camera and answered unscreened incoming calls.[78] As Kennedy said later to Ken O'Donnell, "If I had known Hubert wasn't screening those calls, I would have called up and asked him a few embarrassing questions. Or, better still, I might have gotten Bobby to call him."[79]

But having his brother call would've been unnecessary; the lack of a screening process in and of itself made the telethon a disaster for Humphrey. Early on an elderly female caller had some harsh words for him ("You get out of West Virginia, Mr. Humphrey!"), another caller gave a long, rambling question, and then an operator informed Humphrey that he needed to clear the lines because of an emergency.[80]

TV Drama

The second opportunity for voters to see Kennedy on television came in the form of a dramatization of the candidate's heroic actions during World War II. The drama was based on the *New Yorker* and *Reader's Digest* article "Survival" by John Hersey. Produced for US Rubber, the program was initially broadcast over the ABC network on the show *Navy Log* on October 17, 1957. Its producer was Jack Denove, who would direct the Kennedy media effort three years later.[81] Rebroadcast on several stations in West Virginia, the program began with an announcer noting that "Kennedy is the only veteran in the West Virginia primary."[82]

Half-Hour Program

The most effective use of television programming by the Kennedy campaign was his half-hour television broadcast that aired on Sunday night, May 8, 1960. No transcript or tape of the program exists, but both Teddy White and Kennedy advisor Richard Donahue make the case that it was the finest TV broadcast by any political candidate that they heard.[83]

The program was a controlled media event that featured the candidate answering prepared questions from a friendly moderator, Frank Roosevelt.[84] At least half of the program centered on religion as the candidate carefully addressed a list of specific concerns, such as whether he would take orders from the pope and whether he could attend funerals in Protestant churches.

The program was the culmination of all the elements that would characterize Kennedy's election efforts in West Virginia and the general election in the fall. It featured celebrity (Franklin Delano Roosevelt Jr.), the new medium (television), and the money to buy television time. It was staged in a controlled environment (in a studio where a friendly anchor asked prepared questions). And it featured, of course, a performance that included a staged dramatic declaration (about impeachment), a dramatic gesture that demonstrated the candidate's visual flair (taking an oath on an imaginary Bible), and a dramatic assertion (calling a violation of church/state separation not only a legal crime but a sin against God).[85]

Debate

Kennedy's most historic use of television in West Virginia occurred four days earlier when he had his debate televised with Humphrey on May 4, 1960. Broadcast from WCHS studio in Charleston, the event was carried on four other television stations in the state: WHIS in Bluefield, WBOY in Clarksburg, WTRF in Wheeling, and WTAP in Parkersburg. The event reached an estimated audience of 600,000, which meant that more people saw John Kennedy on television that night than would see him in person during his weeks campaigning in the Mountain State.[86]

Americans in selected cities outside the state watched the event on the Westinghouse television network, which had outlets in San Francisco, Boston, Washington, Cleveland, and Pittsburgh. Millions also heard the debate on the radio through the Mutual Broadcasting Network. Excerpts of the event were shown later on Canadian television and some American network programs such as the *Today* show on NBC.[87]

Humphrey did not want to debate his opponent in West Virginia. But he failed to inform his campaign advisor, Rein J. Vander Zee, who was quick to accept the offer tendered in April from the Kennedy camp.[88] Humphrey's instincts were correct. John Kennedy successfully displayed an aptitude at communication in the new medium. He focused on state issues, spoke in plain language, and even employed a visual aid when he held up a can of surplus government food as he discussed the need for better nutrition. His performance foreshadowed his success in debating Richard Nixon in the fall, and in using television in his administration.

Even so, Kennedy's participation in the debate with Humphrey represented his most risky use of the new medium. The debate format offered several perils. First was the loss of control. A live debate contained elements of uncertainty that were not present in his scripted ads or his mock interview featuring a friendly host asking him questions that he knew in advance. The second risk involved the comparative skill and experience of the participants. Although Kennedy had debated in both his Senate campaigns, there was a perception that Humphrey would hold an advantage in any televised debate. Kennedy's talented, long-winded, opponent was the most vocal person in the US Senate and a respected debater.

Such risks prompted Kennedy to refuse to engage in a debate in Wisconsin, let alone a televised debate. His refusal also reflected conventional wisdom that any debate always helped a challenger and could hurt the frontrunner. But if a confident Kennedy dodged a debate in Wisconsin, a worried Kennedy had a change of heart in West Virginia. As a result, voters in West Virginia saw a different candidate and campaign than Wisconsin voters had. In the Badger State, the confident candidate was publicly cautious, while in the Mountain State he was a risk taker. The candidate who would not raise the issue of his religion now addressed it directly. The candidate who would not debate now initiated one.

Kennedy, of course, framed his reversal as a matter of personal courage rather than political calculation. The beleaguered candidate portrayed himself as a victim of outrageous personal attacks. Adopting the role of victim, he stated on April 19, "I can't accept the current attacks without fighting back."[89]

Whatever the reason for the senator's new stance on debates, the stage was set for history. Only once before in American presidential politics had there been a televised debate between two presidential contenders. In 1956, during the Florida presidential primary, ABC televised a debate between contenders for the Democratic nomination, Adlai Stevenson and Estes Kefauver. But the format was more a discussion than a debate. The event had no opening statements and involved only a couple of questions for the candidates.[90]

Now in Charleston, West Virginia, on May 4, 1960, six days before that state's primary election, there would be a second event reflecting the more traditional debate format that would be used in most of the succeeding presidential campaigns. More than half a million viewers watched the two Democratic contenders, Kennedy and Humphrey, square off in Charleston. Later in September, 30 million would watch the major party nominees, Kennedy and Nixon, participate in the first of four presidential debates.[91]

The debate in West Virginia was a collaboration in voter education between the state's leading newspaper and the capital's newest, largest, and most popular television station, WCHS-TV. W. E. (Ned) Chilton III, assistant to the publisher of the *Charleston Gazette*, and John T. Gelder Jr., vice president and general manager of WCHS-TV in Charleston, came up with the idea.[92] Although the debate marked a symbolic milestone in the use of American television, the printed press dominated its implementation. *Gazette* promotion manager James E. Dent contacted the campaign managers and arranged the format, and *Gazette* readers submitted questions.

The *Gazette* encouraged reader participation by running ads in the paper with a coupon that readers could complete and return. The ads read, "PRESIDENTIAL PRIMARY DEBATE QUESTIONS: Do you have a question you'd like to ask Sen. Hubert Humphrey or Sen. John F. Kennedy in their WCHS television debate May 4? If so fill in this coupon."[93]

Besides the two candidates, there were three journalists in the studio that night, but their roles were limited. Bill Ames, news director of WCHS-TV, served as the moderator, and the two-member panel asking the questions consisted of Ned Chilton and Charles Schussler, a television reporter for WTRF-TV in Wheeling.[94]

The debate represented one more signpost in the ascension of television as the dominant media, but few recognized the historic importance of the broadcast at the time. Charles Schussler later recalled that his station sent him only because no one else on the staff wanted the assignment and the long drive to Charleston that went with it.[95]

But television came out the champion, as the medium was able to transmit instantly the event to more than a half million West Virginians. Even the *Gazette* acknowledged its advantages. An editorial on the day after the debate noted, "Television has a responsible role to play in the political campaigns, for no other medium can attract so vast an audience or have so immediate impact."[96]

The primitive status of the new medium was evident in the studio set. Because the cameras didn't have a zoom lens, the identification cards for the reporters and the candidates were printed in very large type. The only graphics were drawings of Minnesota and Massachusetts.[97]

On the night of the debate, John Kennedy arrived at the WCHS studio just minutes before the event started at 7:30 p.m. The television station was in a converted downtown mansion on Kanawha Boulevard. Kennedy won a coin toss by moderator Bill Ames and chose to give his opening statement second.[98] It was the first of many wise choices the Massachusetts senator made that night. The debate, while not that substantive or heated, proved to be a success for Kennedy in terms of style. The man who would have the first "televised presidency" demonstrated his skill in that medium.

While Humphrey led off with a statement more suited for a national audience, Kennedy made no such mistake. His priority was West Virginia voters. His appeal was provincial. The cities of New York and Chicago received no attention from the Massachusetts senator who focused on the audiences watching on one of six Mountaineer television stations. The candidate who entered the West Virginia primary as an outsider used the debate to help transform himself into an articulate and effective promoter of the Appalachian state that would impact his political future.

His performance surprised *New York Times* reporter James Reston, who noted that it was usually Senator Humphrey who made a connection with the audience. At the Charleston debate, however, it was Kennedy "who concentrated on the specific illustrations, and who avoided the jargon of Washington for the simple language of the average voter."[99] But it was more than just words Kennedy used that night to win over viewers, it was nuance. *Gazette* reporter Tom Stafford noted that Kennedy appealed to the injured pride of West Virginia. For an Appalachian audience, Kennedy sounded all the right themes, starting with praise.[100]

In his opening statement, Kennedy offered admiration for the courage of West Virginians, singling out not just those who worked in the mines, but also those who served their country. He personalized the latter by remarking, "I was in Hinton this morning, which is the home of the navigator who flew with my brother before he was killed."

He cited the number of West Virginians who lived on surplus commodities (250,000) and the number unemployed (100,000). He then personalized the problem by mentioning his visit the night before to McDowell County, "where there are more people on relief in that county than in any county in the country."

On the issue of food commodities, he personalized the statistic on the 250,000 recipients by reading a letter sent to him by McDowell County resident A. F. Johnston, who wrote about what he received every month from the government: "I'm a man with TB and I have to get surplus food. I have seven children. This is what I receive, 5 bags of flour, 4 cans of eggs, 3 5-pound bags of meal, 8 pounds of shortening, 4 pounds of rice, which you can't use if you don't get it clean, and 4 of milk. We do not get any butter, cheese, or beans."[101]

Then, to underscore the information, Kennedy, in a dramatic visual statement, pulled out a can of powdered eggs hidden behind his nameplate. "These are the powdered eggs. For a family of four, you get three of these for a month. . . . 250,000 people in West Virginia are getting this kind of assistance every month. It is an inadequate diet. There are a good many children who get their only good meal when they go to school and bring some of it home to share with their brothers and sisters."

The videotape and transcript of the debate itself confirm the assessment of the contemporary press that, like most campaign debates, it was a dull affair. "The most exceptional thing about the debate, was the lack of debate," reported Tom Stafford, who said that "Hubert Humphrey and John F. Kennedy threw away their brass knuckles here Wednesday night when they faced each other on TV camera, and discussed the nation's gravest issues with senatorial dignity."[102]

George Lawless noted the disappointment in the press quarters at 210 Hale Street, where a battery of newsmen sat in front of a TV set during the debate. He observed "20 male correspondents chewing cigars and pencils—probably the most expensive newspaper talent assigned to review a TV program in history."[103]

Indicative of the lack of fireworks, little time was spent on the most controversial issue in the West Virginia primary: Kennedy's religion. That issue was raised early in only two questions and quickly dispatched during the rest of the hour-long debate.[104] What the public didn't know was that managers from both campaigns had cautioned the candidates against personal attacks. In the weeks leading up to the debate, Humphrey's Herb Waters and Kennedy's Larry O'Brien met at the Charleston Press Club late at night. Their goal was to figure how to "keep our two tigers from tearing each other apart. The men successfully convinced the candidates to agree to not attack each other."[105] According to Waters, "Both principals agreed to this, but it was a tense moment when they came face to face because each didn't know if the other was going to break the rules."[106]

The lack of conflict also reflected the ideological similarity of both candidates in the 1960 Democratic primary. The Republican-leaning newspaper, the *Charleston Daily Mail*, described the debate in terms of Tweedledee and Tweedledum, the ridiculous, mediocre twins from *Alice in Wonderland*, describing the May confrontation as: "'Humphreydum and Kennedyee' talk it over for an hour without striking a spark."[107] It isn't surprising that the candidates spent more time attacking Republicans than each other. They both favored an active federal government in principle and promised to take such a role in the Mountain State.

The complaints about the tameness of such confrontations ignore the real value of such an event: it permits more voter examination than a candidate confrontation. As the *Morgantown Post* observed, "That night the newsmen wanted blood and grime—and they were disappointed. But the people wanted to see what the candidates looked like."[108]

The Kennedy-Humphrey debate was more important to history in general than for its impact on the outcome of that state's presidential primary. While the event wasn't what the press anticipated or wanted, James Reston of the *New York Times* understood that its importance lay in what it "set for the future, not the fireworks it did not display when the candidates faced off in the Charleston television studio on the night of May 4, 1960." The most significant outcome, he argued, was that the winner was "not the man but technique of using modern communication."[109]

West Virginia had an impact on the famous 1960 Kennedy-Nixon debates. Both Kennedy and Humphrey believed that its success contributed to the national networks' decision to initiate the Kennedy-Nixon debates in September.[110] Kennedy's strong performance exceeded expectations, and his success may have made him more willing to engage Nixon, who was considered, like Humphrey, to be a strong debater. Ironically, the reverse could also be true. Nixon, who watched a tape of the Charleston debate, may have considered Kennedy a weak debater, and therefore have been more open to participation in the fall debates.

The West Virginia campaign demonstrated Kennedy's use and mastery of the newest medium in American politics—television. But in 1960 the printed press still wielded the most power, and Kennedy had to show that he could impress them.

Press

The acknowledged importance of the 1960 West Virginia presidential primary drew the press to the Mountain State in record numbers. As Congressman Ken Hechler recalled in the *Congressional Record*, "When the early morning fog had lifted from the mountaintop airports, planeloads of news commentators, political experts, and curious visitors debarked and headed for the hills and hollows."[111] But the intersection of the national media and West Virginia in the spring of 1960 was not a happy one. A combination of biased reporters and sensitive citizens resulted in a bad experience for both groups.

In the spring of 1960, most Americans at the time knew little of West Virginia, and what they learned was not favorable. Negative coverage that year began with a hostile depiction of the state, published in the *Saturday Evening Post* on February 6, 1960. Titled "The Strange Case of West Virginia," the article disparaged the state as "remote, provincial and backward"—a hillbilly hell on earth.[112] For West Virginians, already sensitive to national ridicule, it exemplified the bias of the national media against them.

Describing the state as more like Afghanistan than Switzerland, the contributing editor Roul Tunley listed "a few unpleasant but unassailable factors." Despite being the fourth-richest state in natural resource production, West Virginia had the highest unemployment in the country, three times the national average. The state had a high illiteracy rate, and its schools ranked among the lowest in the nation. And "its young people . . . are deserting the ship in alarming numbers. . . . The state had a population loss of 3%—the highest in the nation."[113]

While Tunley's facts were correct, what angered many West Virginians was the article's uniformly negative tone. The article studiously avoided anything that might be seen as positive. Things were made worse when the *Post* editors decided to paste stickers reading "West Virginia: A Dying State" on the covers of many copies of the magazine.

The response across the state was quick, with many arguing that the poverty Tunley described was not just confined to West Virginia. It is interesting to note that the Advertising Club of Huntington invited Tunley to come in March and defend his article. On the night of the dinner, the city's mayor, Robert Ellis, presented Tunley with a key to the city and a new pair of glasses so the writer could "get a better view of things."[114] Although the magazine went out of business nine years later, the article still rankles some West Virginians today.

A low point for journalism in the West Virginia primary campaign occurred when a satire about bigotry was used as an example of bigotry. *New York Herald Tribune* reporter Rowland Evans went looking for an example of prejudice and found it in a headline from the *West Virginia Hillbilly* which read, "Pa Ain't Going to Sell His Vote to No Catholic."[115] Written by James F. Comstock, this front-page satire told of a father's unwillingness to vote for Kennedy because of his religion. "Why, I'd give my vote to a Republican," declared the father, "before I'd sell it to a Catholic." According to the parody, bigotry was generational. The son in the spoof remarked that "Pa said his pa told him and when I am a pa I certainly want to tell my son about not selling his vote to any Catholic." The piece went on to say, "Pa said his pa told him that the devil had his own ways of getting the Pope in the White House."[116]

One would think that a reporter would investigate the article rather than relying on the headline. If he had, for example, he might have noticed that the satire discussed how the election of Kennedy would result in running hot and cold holy water in the White House. But *Charleston Gazette* reporter L.T. Anderson stated that at least two metropolitan newspapers, the *Washington Post* and the *New York Herald Tribune*, picked up the Evans story. While the *Post* apologized to its readers for using it, the *Herald Tribune* did not.[117]

Many West Virginians believed that the intense scrutiny of their state by out-of-state reporters played a crucial role in perpetuating and magnifying stereotypes. "West Virginia was badly portrayed to the nation," pointed out Charleston reporter L. T. Anderson. "It was pictured as a kingdom of defiant, vulgar, gross and stupid bigotry." Ken Kurtz, a reporter at the time for WSAZ in Charleston, remembered the condescending attitude of the reporters who came to the state and assumed, as Kurtz recalled that "we were ignorant hillbillies and prejudiced Protestants."[118]

Bad Prediction

For the national press who covered the primary, the contest ended with what one could consider to be one of the biggest media embarrassments of twentieth-century American political journalism. Never have so many of the national reporters been so wrong about a primary election. No newspaper or pundit came close to anticipating the results. As *Gazette* reporter L. T. Anderson observed on the day after the primary vote, "Like Sen. Humphrey, the Washington press corps lost in Tuesday's election. No matter how many shrewd analyses are written today, no matter how many hitherto undisclosed pre-election signs are now produced, the fact that the nation's readers were misinformed about West Virginia and West Virginians cannot be altered."[119]

The embarrassment was made worse by the public taunting of the press corps by President Dwight Eisenhower. At his May 11, 1960, press conference he said that after reading the reporting on West Virginia, he was a "bit astonished" at the primary result. His remark generated laughter from the press, but his gentle jab was a public reminder that no major reporter had forecast the Kennedy landslide.[120]

But the misreading of the Democratic electorate wasn't confined to the outside press. A week before the primary, Carroll Kilpatrick of the *Washington Post* concluded that "with one or two exceptions, every West Virginia political newspaper writer that this reporter has interviewed has predicted a victory for Senator Humphrey" and that the reason for Kennedy's impending defeat was the "issue of religion."[121]

Don Marsh, *Gazette* political editor at the time, later suggested that the hesitancy of some state reporters to anticipate a Kennedy win could be traced to intimidation. He observed that they were "in awe of the big time reporters and unwilling to venture a contrary assessment to that which became the powerful template of campaign coverage."[122]

Ralph McGill was one of two reporters Carroll Kilpatrick found who held a contrary opinion. A Charleston columnist, McGill pushed back against the media stereotype of the state. He argued against painting it as a land of religious bigots, snake handlers, and Bible-thumpers, pointing out that a focus on the state's four percent Catholic population ignored the fact that 59 percent of its citizens had no formal religious affiliation.[123]

Ralph McGill believed that the national press was predisposed to accept that religion would be a strong issue.[124] A staffer who worked with Ken Kurtz of WSAZ in Charleston told him of an incident that she observed in Cabin Creek while Kennedy was campaigning. A reporter from a national news magazine was interviewing a hillbilly-type person. "Do you have any problem voting for a Catholic?" asked the reporter. "I vote Democrat," answered the voter. "Does Mr. Kennedy being a Catholic bother you?" continued the reporter. "I vote straight Democratic, son," answered the voter. "Well, does it disturb you that a Catholic is running for president? Do you have any ill feelings toward Catholics?" "Nope never met one."[125]

While the press didn't anticipate a Kennedy victory, many politicians did. These included Virginia senator Harry Byrd and West Virginia senator Jennings Randolph, as well as state Democratic chairman Hulett Smith. Also not surprised by a Kennedy primary victory were Richard Nixon and Lyndon Johnson.[126]

The West Virginia primary presented an opportunity for that one reporter who could have made journalism history by predicting a Kennedy victory. One West Virginia native who failed to write that story was Peter Lisagor, who at the time was the Washington bureau chief for the *Chicago Daily News*. Lisagor had been raised in the town of Keystone in McDowell County and later moved to Chicago. When he came to report on the campaign in West Virginia, Sid Christie, the local political boss of McDowell County, convinced him that Kennedy was going to win not only McDowell, but statewide. Lisagor prepared the story for his paper, predicting a Kennedy victory, but at the last moment he got cold feet.[127] Christie said that Lisagor later told him it was "the biggest blunder he had ever made since he had been a newspaper reporter, that he had a scoop and didn't recognize it."[128]

One explanation for the journalists' failure centers on the reporters themselves. Anne Hearst, a Kennedy county chair from Morgantown, criticized the press for being lazy.[129] A standing joke among the local correspondents was that too many outsiders "spent most of their time at the press club reading their own press releases."[130] According to Hearst, the national press "usually just talked to themselves—when they did ask us a question or two they would look at us as if were just stupid West Virginians, and we resented it. We knew Kennedy was going to win, because we had contacts in grassroots and press did not."[131]

Another explanation for the prediction embarrassment was voiced by the *Gazette* editor Ned Chilton who argued that reporters magnified and overplayed the religious issue. Following the wrong story from the start, they made the primary election a "referendum on religion."[132] While Kennedy did face a serious religious liability in West Virginia, it was overplayed by reporters in order to keep the narrative going.[133]

Kennedy's easy and unexpected victory suggests that the anti-Catholic feelings were indeed exaggerated. While such sentiments did exist, they were not apparently as bad as either the press or the Kennedy supporters believed. In this case the uncertainty of the religious issue overcame the normal instincts of many reporters.

Three Journalists

Three prominent journalists—Bill Lawrence of the *New York Times*, Ben Bradlee of *Newsweek*, and national columnist Joe Alsop—were friends of Kennedy when they covered his pursuit of the Democratic presidential nomination. Their close relationship with the candidate raises questions about their reporting of the West Virginia primary in particular, and of the relationship between reporters and their subjects in general.

Bill Lawrence

Bill Lawrence, the political editor of the *New York Times*, wrote more stories on the presidential primary than any other national reporter. His almost daily reports made him the most visible member of the national press corps covering the 1960 West Virginia primary. He was also the most embarrassed reporter on election night, as his front-page story on the primary stated that all signs pointed to a Humphrey victory.[134] In his assessment of the southern counties, he incorrectly reported that Humphrey's regional strength was in Kanawha Valley and the coalfields. Humphrey lost Kanawha County by a small margin, and all of the southern coalfields by large margins. He lost Mercer County by a two-to-one margin (5,174/11, 292), Wyoming County by a 3-to-1 margin vote (1,789/6,600), and McDowell by a 5-to-1 margin (2,708/14,336).[135]

Lawrence explained his mistake by asserting, "There was a feeling, I don't know where we got it, that he would lose south of the [Kanawha] river." As the reporter closest to the Kennedy campaign, he probably would have received such misinformation from the candidate's campaign staff. It's likely that he was played by the staff, who wanted Kennedy to be portrayed as the underdog.

Lawrence argued that Kennedy's unexpectedly strong performance south of the Kanawha River was a result of last-minute alliances with some of the local machines made in the last 24 or 48 hours of the campaign.[136] While it's true that a few counties like Logan made a late switch from Humphrey to Kennedy, Lawrence's theory fails to account for Kennedy's sweep of the south. In McDowell County, for example, Kennedy's careful two-year courting of Sid Christie yielded a public endorsement in the final week, not the final hours of the campaign. More importantly, Lawrence's explanation ignores the breadth of Kennedy's victory.[137]

What is disturbing is that Lawrence had contrary evidence, but he chose not to use it. A team of *New York Times* reporters had traveled throughout the state during the last ten days of the campaign. They identified "clear signs of a counter-reaction to wide publicity to anti-Catholic sentiments." And most importantly, they found a strong surge to Kennedy in the last week.[138] While Lawrence used information from their report, he did not accept their conclusion—an action he regretted on election night when he confided to Ned Chilton of the *Charleston Gazette* that he'd rewritten the story to discount a Kennedy victory. Lawrence told Chilton, "Son of a bitch, if we had only gone with the *Times* team." When asked to explain, Lawrence revealed that the *Times* had called the election as a Kennedy landslide, but *"we* didn't have the guts to use it" (italics mine).[139]

To understand Lawrence's actions, one must first appreciate the attraction of John Kennedy to the press. Unlike presidents Harry Truman and Dwight Eisenhower, who tolerated reporters, Kennedy courted them. As a candidate he would pay attention to them, and later as president he would invite them to White House dinners as guests—not as observers.

And Lawrence was courtable. In his tenure at the *Times* he focused on get-ting the scoop, the inside story, by getting close to his subjects. Russell Baker, who would replace Lawrence in 1961 at the *Times*, noted that Lawrence "cher-ished the scoop, and was willing to deal to get it."[140] As a result he was often a player rather than an observer. In his memoir *Six Presidents, Too Many Wars*, Lawrence, in fact, boasted about his "really close" relationship with Kennedy during the 1960 presidential campaign. He found Kennedy to be a delightful traveling companion and was proud that after the convention he and Kennedy became golfing companions at Hyannis Port.[141]

The risk of getting too close to the subject should have been apparent to a seasoned reporter like Lawrence. He didn't heed the advice that Baker had learned at the *Baltimore Sun*: reporters were to keep politicians at arm's length, stay alert for monkey business, and play the adversary. In his West Virginia coverage, he often appeared to reflect the Kennedy campaign line. Rather than investigate the political landscape of the Mountain State, Lawrence did little to challenge that Kennedy narrative of its primary. Lawrence promoted the un-derdog image of Kennedy by parroting the list of his campaign talking points. In doing so Lawrence overestimated the religious bigotry in the state and un-derestimated Kennedy's strengths.

Lawrence also inflated the alleged gang-up activities of Kennedy foes. While it's true that Senator Robert Byrd, a supporter of Lyndon Johnson, championed

Humphrey as a way to stop Kennedy, there's little evidence that Kennedy was a victim of coordinated gang-up by his rivals.[142] The closest effort at such a gang-up occurred in the final days, when some money was funneled into Humphrey's campaign by Sam Rowe, a Johnson supporter, but it was too little and too late. There's no evidence of any effective coordinated gang-up.[143] As Humphrey correctly observed at the Clarksburg dinner where Lyndon Johnson spoke, "I got little help."[144]

After Kennedy's victory in West Virginia, people asked how the nation's premier political reporter missed something as big as a landslide. The management at the *Times* became edgy as an explanation circulated that "Jack Kennedy had Bill Lawrence in his pocket."[145] Lawrence's questionable actions raised questions, but he was not alone in reporters who failed to gauge accurately the dynamics of the West Virginia contest. Writing years later, Chalmers Roberts observed that "I think the press was considerably conned by the Kennedy tactic (to highlight the religious issue) and that Humphrey had more than a point in his complaints about the emphasis on this single issue." [146]

Lawrence also played an instrumental role in highlighting Humphrey's military draft status—an example of not maintaining distance between the reporter and the reported.[147] People in the Kennedy organization gave Lawrence a file of letters from Humphrey's draft board, "but told him that he could not use them until Frank Roosevelt had gone public with them."[148] When Roosevelt did act in the final days of the campaign, Lawrence was ready to write about it.

Also not widely known was that during the spring of 1960, the twice-divorced 44-year-old reporter had fallen in love with a woman working in the Kennedy campaign.[149]

While Bill Lawrence's failure to predict a landslide damaged his own reputation, his focus on bigotry in the Mountain State damaged the state's reputation. *Charleston Gazette* editorial writer and columnist L.T. Anderson singled out Lawrence as one of the national reporters who magnified religious bigotry: "They did find bigotry here, of course. But it was obviously magnified in their pre-election stories."[150]

Anderson was probably writing about Lawrence when he reported that a New York political writer was astonished to find West Virginians who spoke so openly of their mistrust in Roman Catholicism. According to Anderson, the reporter assumed that those who were critical of the church would be unable to vote for Senator Kennedy. He couldn't believe that "persons who discussed religion so frankly could vote for a man with whose religion they disagreed."[151] Yet that was the basis of the Kennedy strategy in West Virginia: first to reassure those who had had doubts, and then advance several identities, each of which would provide reasons for voters to support him.

Lawrence was already in trouble with the *Times* management when the general election campaign started in the fall of 1960. The closeness of the journalist to a presidential candidate was becoming a liability to his paper. Evidence of that concern came in the form of a surprising decision later that fall to have Russell Baker, not Lawrence, cover the four televised debates between Kennedy and Vice President Richard Nixon.

Six months into the Kennedy administration, by the spring of 1961, Lawrence was no longer the top political editor at the *New York Times*. His departure came almost a year after he covered the West Virginia primary, misjudging the political situation because of poor reporting, bias, or both.[152]

Ben Bradlee

The second major journalist to report on the 1960 West Virginia presidential primary was Ben Bradlee, a Georgetown neighbor and a good friend of Kennedy's. The future editor of the *Washington Post* in the 1970s was the head of the Washington bureau for *Newsweek* in the early 1960s. As Bradlee would recall, the relationship had implications for both men. When asked, Bradlee said, "Did he use me? Of course he used me. Did I use him? Of course I used him. Are those the ground rules down here in Washington? Hell, yes."[153]

While Ben Bradlee did not appear in print to be as biased toward Kennedy as Bill Lawrence, the question remains as to whether he crossed a line when his friend ran for president. The Bradlee/Kennedy friendship started in early 1959 after both men and their wives bought houses in the Georgetown area of Washington, DC. That year the Bradlees took their first trip with the Kennedys, flying to a political meeting in Maryland and then taking their first trip to Hyannis Port.[154]

In the fall of 1959, Bradlee would usually be the only reporter invited to fly with Kennedy on campaign trips. After Kennedy's Wisconsin primary win, *Newsweek* bureau assigned Bradlee full time to his campaign. On the night of the West Virginia primary election, Bradlee and his wife were at the Kennedy house in Georgetown for dinner.[155] Later that night they drank champagne, then flew with him to Charleston for the victory celebration.

Bradlee had brought champagne to the Kennedy house, but during the campaign Kennedy apparently brought the talking points. Bradlee didn't have any coordination with the campaign as Bill Lawrence did, nor did he attack West Virginians as Joe Alsop's columns appeared to do. But like his colleagues, he overestimated the prejudice Kennedy faced and underestimated Kennedy's chances.[156] In one *Newsweek* article he wrote that "the deck looks to be hopelessly stacked against John Kennedy in both West Virginia—the boom-town northern half and the ghost-town southern half."[157] His articles highlighted both the religious prejudice Kennedy faced and his underdog status, both parts of the Kennedy narrative in the Mountain State.

Humphrey believed that Bradlee crossed the line when he reported questionable financial statements in the final weeks that showed Humphrey outspending Kennedy. A check of advertising expenditures would have revealed that the Kennedy campaign had outspent the opposition by ten to one in two key markets. But Bradlee chose to write a parody. In an article titled "Best Underdog in Show," he argued that both candidates were claiming underdog status.

A livid Humphrey argued that campaign expenditures should not be a laughing matter, especially if they were so lopsided. He accurately responded by declaring, "I'm a running against tremendous odds. Kennedy looks as much like an underdog as Man Mountain Dean looks like a pygmy," a reference to a large-sized professional wrestler who had a long beard.[158] But no column by Bradlee, Lawrence, or Alsop would focus on Kennedy's large expenditures. In fact, Lawrence would discuss a questionable pre-election expenditure report on the front page of the *Times* without a thorough questioning of its reliability.[159]

More important than Hubert Humphrey's response to Bradlee's article was the accusation by Humphrey's campaign cochair, Bill Jacobs, that Bradlee had violated journalism ethics. At issue was Bradlee's use of remarks that Jacobs thought were off the record. Bradlee had written that the chairman preferred Stevenson or Symington to Humphrey and quoted him as saying that Humphrey was "a wonderful, intelligent man," but "he's tough to sell."[160] When Jacobs learned a year later that Bradlee was a neighbor and a good friend of Kennedy's, Jacobs thought he had been taken.[161]

While Bill Lawrence's conduct with Kennedy would become a factor in losing his job six months after the inauguration, Bradlee's relationship with Kennedy before and during his presidency didn't raise concerns. But his coverage of the West Virginia presidential primary does raise questions about the proper relationship between journalist and a politician when that reporter is a friend.

Certainly Bradlee crossed the line several times after Kennedy became president. For example, he tipped Kennedy off about upcoming stories in the magazine. He also consulted with the president on which reporters he should hire for the *Newsweek* bureau. When Bradlee later examined the relationship, he asked, "What, in fact, was I? A friend, or a journalist? I wanted to be both."[162]

Joe Alsop

Another Georgetown neighbor and close friend of John Kennedy was Joe Alsop, a syndicated columnist whose work appeared in nearly 200 newspapers and reached 25 million readers. The celebrated political pundit had a reputation for being a hard worker with an affected British accent and aristocratic tastes.

Related to both Teddy Roosevelt and Eleanor Roosevelt, he was the quintessential establishment person who, like his brother, Stewart, became a powerful and respected journalist.[163]

But unlike his brother, Joe Alsop was, according to his biographer, "smitten by the entire Kennedy clan."[164] While Stewart maintained a reporter's distance from the Massachusetts senator, Joe included the Kennedys among his closest friends. In fact, after Kennedy's election, he wrote the senator, saying, "I feel that I've lost a friend while gaining a President."[165]

The Kennedys were frequent dinner guests at Alsop's home in the Dumbarton neighborhood of DC, and Alsop was often invited to their Georgetown home on N Street.[166] During Kennedy's quest for the Democratic presidential nomination, Alsop played a supportive role.[167] He helped write Kennedy's speech on the so-called missile gap and then praised it in two consecutive columns. His action prompted a thank-you note from Kennedy: "I want to thank you for your very fine columns and your original suggestion."[168]

Because Joe Alsop didn't want his support for John Kennedy known, he established his independence by announcing that he was a registered Republican, adding that he would most likely support Lyndon Johnson among the Democrats. While the former was true, the latter was a lie. He had only declared for Johnson to mislead his readers. Ned Chilton, publisher of the *Charleston Gazette*, accused Alsop of "being obviously for Kennedy" and working "the religious issue miserably to build up an underdog image of Kennedy" in the Mountain State.[169]

In more than one column Alsop openly suggested that it was bigotry to vote for Humphrey. The columnist played the role of a Kennedy cheerleader when he argued that "Sen. Hubert Humphrey owes at least half of his present voter-support in West Virginia to straight religious prejudice against Sen. John F. Kennedy's Catholic faith."[170]

Alsop's controversial column on his visit to the mining camp of Slab Fork began: "You wind down a deep-pocked road into a cramped and pit-like hollow in the hills. And there is Slab Fork, the hundred or so decrepit looking houses, the tipples of the two mines, the bare, unornamented minimum of little schools and churches and the company store and office, all bleak, graceless and scurfy with coal dust."[171]

Slab Fork, West Virginia, was a long way from the streets of Georgetown when Alsop and Kennedy's pollster Lou Harris polled a sample of 80 voters in the middle of April. The result, Alsop acknowledged, looked "very good for Kennedy—on the surface," as the Massachusetts senator had 30 votes to Humphrey's 27 votes, with 23 undecided or not registered. But Alsop wasn't interested in highlighting support for Kennedy. Instead the pundit looked below the surface and found bigotry, as the title of his column indicates ("Anti-Catholic Trend in Slab Fork Termed Humphrey Windfall").[172] The result of the election in Slab Fork proved Alsop wrong. The "Humphrey windfall" of Alsop's headline wasn't there on Election Day. Kennedy carried the town by a three-to-one margin, defeating Humphrey by a vote of 100 to 36.[173]

Even though Alsop did admit that Kennedy lost some votes because "he's a rich man, and Humphrey was born a working man like us," he remained confident that bigotry was the only reason to support Humphrey. His critics included the *New Republic*, which observed, "A very large number of voters are not going to accept the proposition that only by voting for Kennedy can they certify their lack of bias," and that support for Humphrey was evidence of religious prejudice.[174]

Ned Chilton offered an interesting interpretation of Alsop's rigid support of Kennedy and his disdain for Humphrey supporters. Chilton argued that in Joe Alsop's Manichean world of only black and white, nuance wasn't evident, and the majority of West Virginia voters were impossible to understand. Appalled by bigotry, the columnist couldn't comprehend how a voter could have questions about Catholicism but still be able to vote for Kennedy.[175]

Alsop's constant drumbeat was that "Humphrey could win only through religious prejudice; and a Kennedy win would represent triumph over that prejudice." He drew a stark line between the majority of Kennedy voters and the majority of Humphrey voters. The former were "serious citizens, who had studied their choice and chosen without prejudice" while the latter "were influenced by religious prejudices."[176]

Alsop was probably the unidentified columnist whom *Gazette* columnist L.T. Anderson wrote "declared before the election that he placed all who expressed anti-Catholic sentiment—whether based on honest inquiry, historical research or sheer distaste for liturgy—in the category of bigots."[177]

Alsop differentiated between "Catholic preference" and "Protestant bigotry" when discussing religion and voting. He condoned the former because "Catholics who vote for Kennedy because he is a fellow Catholic" were trying to break down the "ugly" WASP rule that only Protestants can be president. He saw such action as understandable and even, in part, excusable. But he condemned the latter: "Senator Humphrey's anti-Catholic support is both deplorable and inexcusable."

Joe Alsop's contempt for West Virginians was reflected in a piece about confronting a Humphrey supporter in Slab Fork, whom he described as a "coal-grimed, slatternly, barefoot wife" of a miner. [178] Later, to an audience that included Bobby Kennedy, Alsop elaborated his written description of the woman by saying that she had disheveled hair, was holding a broom, and was accompanied by a child with mud on his feet and snot in his nose. Alsop told his listeners that he felt that he had been reduced to "polling a slab of pork."[179] Given Alsop's own biases, it isn't surprising that Ned Chilton described his efforts to highlight the state's bigotry as "shabby."[180]

Alsop's visit to Slab Fork, West Virginia, provoked a harsh response from Humphrey who considered it an insult to both the people of West Virginia and to him. "It boiled down to one thing," Humphrey wrote in a letter to a *Washington Post* reporter, Chalmers Roberts, "that the decent, intelligent, educated people, according to the Alsop formula, were for Kennedy; that the poor illiterate, ignorant and prejudiced people were for Humphrey." Describing Alsop as a snob, Humphrey wrote that "he has deconstrued the unbelievable kind of class consciousness trying to promote class struggles and a religious struggle at the same time." [181]

The irony of Alsop's biased April 15, 1960 column on Slab Fork was that it was inaccurate. For on election day that supposed repository of bigotry supported John Kennedy by a wide margin. The *Charleston Gazette* would post the results on its front page under the headline "Un-American Slab Fork Floods Jack." The article noted that the Raleigh County mining camp where Alsop discovered "a great deal of 'un-American prejudice" voted 100 to 36 for John Kennedy.[182]

Alsop credited the remarkable victory of John Kennedy in West Virginia, a landslide unforeseen in any of his columns, to undecided voters going for John Kennedy. The national columnist would not acknowledge that some of the voters he found in southern West Virginia could, for a number of reasons, have a change of heart.[183]

John Kennedy's itinerary on his inauguration day reveals the close relationship between the politician and the powerful political pundit. After visiting the five inaugural balls, Kennedy stopped at his friend Joseph Alsop's house after midnight. He was the last person the new president visited on that important day.

During their meeting, the Secret Service detail waited in the snowy Georgetown Street and reporters paced out in front. Hugh Sidey reported that finally from "a side door of Alsop's came the President. Only the glowing end of a cigar showed in the night. He walked alone to his car. The caravan moved slowly back to the White House and finally the day was over."[184]

A few days later, Alsop was invited to the first social occasion of the Kennedy presidency. The Kennedys had just moved into the White House when they invited Alsop, along with Franklin Roosevelt Jr. and his wife, to an intimate Sunday night dinner. That night they ate ten pounds of caviar, drank champagne, and toured the family quarters. The only irritation that evening was Alsop's displeasure with Frank Roosevelt for addressing John Kennedy as "Jack" instead of "Mr. President."[185]

It is noteworthy that the new president would be entertaining two men who played a key role in his West Virginia primary win; Roosevelt lent his famous name, and Alsop his powerful pen. That Kennedy recognized both men's power attests to the political aptitude of the 35th American president.

John Kennedy displayed his skill in gaining allies in the traditional media, the press, by cultivating friendships and associations with prominent journalists. But he also had success with the tools of modern campaigning that would dominate presidential politics for the rest of the twentieth century—an unprecedented use of expenditure and organization, and the new medium of television.

Chapter 5

ON THE CAMPAIGN TRAIL

Senators Humphrey and Kennedy have been so active and so prominent on the West Virginia scene for several weeks that we sort of
recognize them as home-folk—and could properly address them in
Mountaineer style as Hubert and Jack.

—Editorial, "West Va. Will Be Winner," *Beckley Raleigh Register*,
May 6, 1960.

Both (Kennedy and Humphrey) are stumping in the state vigor-
ously and seemingly endlessly They shake hands all day and most of
the night, address meetings of from three people on up, and hold a
press conference at every opportunity.

—Henry Cathcart, "Bitterness Develops in W.V. Primary," in
Inside Washington: March of Events, Clarksburg *Exponent*,
May 3, 1960.

In the five weeks between the Wisconsin and West Virginia primaries, the candidates traveled extensively throughout West Virginia. For 26 of those days, at
least one candidate was in the state, and on the days either candidate was absent, at least one surrogate campaigned in his stead. John Kennedy visited more
than 100 towns and made multiple trips to larger cities in the state. Hubert
Humphrey visited more than 120 towns and also made several visits to cities
across West Virginia.

For Kennedy, the West Virginia journey started with the bittersweet victory
in Wisconsin on Tuesday, April 5. Despite winning the majority of the votes
and delegates in that contest, his success didn't boost his image as frontrunner
in the race for the 1960 Democratic presidential nomination. Instead it heightened his biggest liability—his Catholicism. This set him on the defensive as he
began his West Virginia campaign in earnest.

First Week, April 5–10

While the Massachusetts senator did not come to West Virginia until April 11, Hubert Humphrey arrived on Friday, April 8. After only three hours of sleep, the Minnesota senator started out at 6:30 a.m. on a two-day swing through southern West Virginia. An area rich in Democratic votes, the counties he visited were supposedly open to his populist message and folksy appeal.

Humphrey's first-day itinerary was typical of him: extensive, intensive, and exhausting for all but the candidate himself. At his first stop at the Libbey-Owens-Ford Glass Co. plant in Kanawha City, the tireless candidate shook an estimated 500 hands. Behind him were "aides with bundles of campaign literature they scattered like seeds."[1] He went to Marmet for breakfast, then made a series of short stops at communities along the coal-producing Cabin Creek section before making a major speech in Beckley, the last of 16 stops on his first day.[2]

Humphrey made the same "man-killing schedule" on the second day of his bus tour. On Saturday, April 9, he carried his campaign deeper into southern West Virginia, visiting Summers and Mercer Counties, before returning north to Charleston by way of Madison in Boone County. On Monday, April 11, he headed south again this time visiting the cities of Logan, Williamson, Welch, and Bluefield, as well as small towns in between.[3]

At the start of his first campaign tour in West Virginia, he declared that time was on his side.[4] At the end of his initial tour of southern West Virginia, he told his wife that he felt like "a triumphant Caesar."[5] But the question remained: would Humphrey's early start in campaigning and his compatible campaign persona be enough to offset his opponent's advantages—unlimited resources and earlier organization? The day after the Wisconsin primary, key advisors in the Kennedy campaign flew to Charleston, West Virginia, for strategy meetings. At a gathering of 70 workers from 28 southern counties, Bobby learned the bad news. The careful, confident, and organized Kennedy campaign in the Mountain State was in apparent free fall now that West Virginia voters were aware of Kennedy's religion.

Also present in the Mountain State that week was the campaign trump card. Franklin Delano Roosevelt Jr. had been used sparingly in Wisconsin, but in West Virginia he would spend almost five weeks touting Kennedy as the second FDR. The linkage was important, as President Roosevelt was idolized for bringing both aid and support for the labor unions to the Mountain State during the Great Depression.[6]

Arriving in the state on Friday April 8, 1960, Frank Roosevelt embarked on a busy itinerary that had him going to Clarksburg and Monongah, then south to Madison and Logan the next day. He often followed Humphrey's route into the southern coalfields, visiting the same counties.[7] By being Humphrey's shadow, the famous son helped undercut Humphrey's visit by diverting some of Humphrey's press attention.

Second Week, April 11–April 17

The second week after the Wisconsin primary began with John Kennedy's arrival in West Virginia for a three-day campaign swing across the state. He started along the Ohio River in Parkersburg discussing economic development before nearly 600 people at a breakfast coffee at the Elks Club. In his first prepared speech in West Virginia since the Wisconsin primary, the candidate promised a New Deal for the state. Franklin D. Roosevelt Jr. was scheduled to give visual support to Kennedy's adoption of the FDR mantle, but his scheduled stop was cancelled. Nevertheless, Kennedy promised the large crowd that "Franklin Roosevelt gave the American people a New Deal: social security, unemployment compensation, REA, minimum wages, protection to unions and farmers, and child labor and all the rest." He declared, "And now it is time for another 'New Deal'—a New Deal for West Virginia."[8]

However, it was not Kennedy's speech on economic development in Parkersburg that drew public attention, but his remarks on religion when he traveled to Charleston later that day.

At Morris Harvey College in the capital city, the press reported that Kennedy met "the so-called religious question head on."[9] Although his address that day focused on the worth of primaries, it was his remarks on the religious issue at the start of the speech and his answer to a question on the topic afterward that attracted the attention of the press. Footage from this event was later used for a TV campaign ad.

While Kennedy had an enthusiastic reception at Morris Harvey College, his other appearances that day in Charleston were disconcerting. When the candidate visited the Kanawha County courthouse, Ken O'Donnell, a close advisor, noticed an unusual phenomenon, namely that the Massachusetts senator drew large, but not enthusiastic crowds: "It was the first crowd I had seen around Kennedy that stayed away from him, watching him quietly from the sidewalk on the opposite side of the street." O'Donnell recalled that only two men approached the candidate to shake his hand. The situation prompted Kennedy to later quip, "Those two guys must have been a couple of visiting Catholics from Pennsylvania." O'Donnell observed that by the time Kennedy returned to his Charleston hotel, he said, "Well, I guess you guys were not exaggerating.[10]

It would become a common theme in the early weeks of April. The Massachusetts senator provoked curiosity but not enthusiasm; while crowds came, excitement did not follow. Such reserve reflected a traditional Appalachian skepticism about outsiders.[11] But *New York Times* reporter W. H. "Bill" Lawrence attributed it to that "undertone of anti-Catholic feeling never absent" even as the candidate "drew big crowds everywhere.[12] This focus on religious prejudice permeated many of Lawrence's articles on the West Virginia campaign and prompted continued concern within the Kennedy camp.

After Charleston, Kennedy spoke that Monday to a crowd at Marshall College in Huntington. Standing on the hood of a car, the candidate took the advice of Congressman Ken Hechler and gave support for the proposal to change Marshall College to Marshall University. Such a name change and incorporation of a graduate program would upgrade the college and make it semantically equal to the state's flagship institution, West Virginia University. Kennedy ended his first day by flying to Beckley, where he addressed a crowd of 500 at the Raleigh County courthouse. It had been a spirited 14 hours for the Massachusetts senator—four major cities in three regions of the state, all in one day. It was an itinerary that couldn't have been possible without his access to a private airplane.

While Kennedy spent the second day of his tour in the southern part of the state, two issues surfaced that threatened the campaign. But like flares in the night, each incident illuminated the political landscape without having an immediate or long-range impact on the eventual outcome.

The first occurred when America's most popular minister, Reverend Norman Vincent Peale, expressed concerns about Kennedy's religion at a press conference in Charleston, West Virginia. The ominous headline in the *Raleigh Register* read "Dr. Peale Raises Catholic 'Ghost.'" Reverend Peale had earlier in private raised such concerns about Kennedy's religion. But now the author of the bestselling book *The Power of Positive Thinking* went public with his reservations, asking if Kennedy's "first loyalty is to the United States." [13] He asserted that only Pope John XXIII could answer the questions Peale had raised about the senator's loyalty.[14]

While ominous, Peale's remarks were not detrimental. He may have been America's most publicly known minister, but his remarks were rebutted in the national press, and his concerns weren't supported by other mainline churches. In fact, in the final weeks of the campaign, the Methodist General Conference rebuked resolutions expressing the kinds of reservations Peale raised about a Catholic president.[15]

The second issue was the report that former United Mine Workers president John L. Lewis wanted Kennedy defeated. Lewis and other labor leaders had doubts about the senator's commitment to organized labor in general and concerns about his support for the 1959 Landrum-Griffin labor reform bill in particular. The senator's association with that law, which was considered anti-union, had prompted the *UMW Journal* to refer to the law as the Kennedy-Landrum-Griffin bill. [16]

Word of Lewis's hostility to Kennedy rekindled fears in the campaign that organized labor would help Humphrey in the West Virginia primary. To the disappointment of Humphrey, however, such aid would not be forthcoming, neither in terms of endorsements nor funding.

But these two stories weren't the main concerns of Kennedy campaign staffers that first week. They were more worried of the possible repercussions of Humphrey's head start in the Mountain State—that the Minnesota senator's tour of the voter-rich and coal-abundant southern region of the state had found friendly crowds in Logan, Mingo, McDowell, and Mercer Counties.[17]

However, Humphrey, the "natural campaigner," soon discovered that he didn't have sufficient organizational capacity in the Mountain State. The day after returning from his "triumphant" tour, Humphrey learned that his campaign was bankrupt and his organization was imploding. His campaign already had a debt from the Wisconsin primary, where it had spent $100,000 in a losing effort. Now, with four weeks before the West Virginia primary, Humphrey told the press he was operating on an "empty cupboard." [18] As a result, he was forced to take a $2,000 personal loan and cut his staff in half to continue the campaign. The personal loan was especially distressing, as the money had been set aside for his daughter's wedding in the fall.

Herb Waters, a Humphrey advisor, tried to tone down the bankruptcy story by telling the press that the immediate cash shortage wouldn't prevent Humphrey from campaigning in West Virginia, and that the Wisconsin deficit would be covered by friends in Minnesota. Waters told reporters the $2,000 personal loan to the campaign was just an advance until more fundraising occurred. Moreover, the staff changes didn't constitute reductions, but were reassignments of the Washington office to the Mountain State. In all, only a few stenographers were fired.[19] But Humphrey's "empty cupboard" quote highlighted the central fact of the 1960 primary: the resource divide between candidates. His funds were scarce, while those of his opponent were unlimited. Humphrey's state cochairman, William L. Jacobs, recalled that, except for a telephone card, the only asset with he began his job with was the "the tremendous ability of Senator Humphrey."[20]

The second week of the campaign closed with both senators returning to Washington to vote on key legislation for the area. Their mutual vote for the Area Redevelopment Act illustrated how close the candidates were on ideology. Their agreement on the issues meant that the outcome of the election would rest on personality, resources, and campaigning.

Nothing better illustrates the chasm in resources between the two candidates than their travel plans for the second weekend of the five-week campaign. Humphrey returned to his home in Bethesda, Maryland. Kennedy took the weekend off and flew on his private airplane to a resort in Jamaica for a vacation.[21]

Second Week Poll

The week that John Kennedy started his campaign in the Mountain State was also the week that a *Charleston Daily Mail* poll confirmed the candidate's worst fears. The headline of the newspaper's article read, "W. Va. Poll Rocks Kennedy's Hopes / Catholic Faith Swaying Many." The paper's political editor, Bob Mellace, pointed out that the large undecided vote (20 percent), accompanied by strong anti-Catholic support for Humphrey, had "the Kennedy camp shaking."[22] For example, of the 35 Humphrey voters in the Huntington Fifth Ward, 17 freely admitted that they were for the Minnesotan because Senator Kennedy was a Catholic.[23]

Noting the dominance of the religious issue, Mellace wrote that "it overshadows all else. Kennedy knows it now, and he is going to have to make a radical change in his state campaign plans if he is to have a chance in what, at best, is a tough, uphill fight."[24]

The headline the next day in the *Daily Mail* was even worse for Kennedy supporters: "Humphrey Has Big Lead in State Poll." The article described Humphrey's lead as "impressive." The survey results of 299 voters from the four targeted communities were 134 for Kennedy, 165 for Humphrey, and 41 undecided.[25]

The paper mentioned not just the large sample of the poll but also the credentials of the pollsters—Lou Harris, "who was retained by Senator Kennedy," and Joe Alsop, who was an "experienced pollster and the first member of the Washington press corps to employ the door-knocking technique."[26]

However, the limitations of their efforts are obvious. Unlike the December 1959 statewide poll Harris conducted for Kennedy, the polls commissioned by the *Daily Mail* targeted voters in only four communities in the state. And the sampling process was primitive and the efforts at getting a representative sample fell far short of modern polling techniques.[27]

However, the importance of the *Daily Mail* poll didn't rest on its scientific validity. While the methodology was flawed, the findings were accepted by both the public and the candidates' staff, and this acceptance prompted action. The press used it to support a focus on the religious issue. The Kennedy camp viewed it as a wake-up call.

The poll findings prompted Mellace to offer two suggestions to Kennedy staffers: first, their candidate should spend more time in the state, and second, he should confront the religious issue. The Kennedy camp had already dealt with the first suggestion. On the day that Mellace's article was published, the chairman of Kennedy's state organization, State Senator Ward Wylie, announced that the candidate would start a three-day campaign tour across the state on Monday, marking "the opening of an intensive drive to win."[28] Regarding his second suggestion, a reporter pointed out that "the pollsters, and now Sen. Kennedy, have down in writing all the fears and prejudices of non-Catholics for a Catholic in the highest public office. Kennedy must try to answer, and to explain what he has said before: That in good conscience he can take the oath, which he has taken many times, to support the Constitution of the United States."[29]

On this topic the Kennedy camp had already implemented the strategy of confrontation. The candidate had raised the issue directly at Morris Harvey College on Monday, April 11, 1960. But a week later on Monday, April 18, Kennedy took the strategy to a new level.

Third Week, April 18–24

Kennedy returned to the Mountain State from Jamaica "refreshed and tanned," according to the *Charleston Gazette*, and "more determined than ever to bring the 'subterranean' religious issue into the open."[30]

The "gloves-off" strategy was reflected in the *Charleston Daily Mail* headline "Change of Tactics—Angry Sen. Kennedy Brings Up Religion." Writing for the Associated Press, Herb Little reported that Kennedy "in an abrupt change of tactics," had discussed his religion saying that "we might as well settle this (religious) issue right here in West Virginia." In his appearances the candidate took the initiative and talked about his religion rather than wait for someone in the audience to ask the inevitable question of how his religion would impact the duties of his presidency. To a crowd at Fairmont he said that "I don't think that my religion is any one's business but my business."[31]

Kennedy told reporters on his campaign bus that this switch in tactics stemmed from an awareness that his religion was on everybody's mind. He just thought that rather than wait, "I'd bring it out into the open."[32]

Columnist L.T. Anderson of the *Charleston Sunday Gazette-Mail*, however, proposed another reason: Kennedy's discussion about his religion had prompted a new dynamic. "The popular psychology which suggests that a West Virginia vote against Senator Kennedy is a vote for bigotry" was apparently taking hold.[33] Ironically, its victim would be the man who, perhaps more than any other in public life, had been the champion of equality and tolerance, Hubert Humphrey.[34]

Monday, April 18

Kennedy initiated his new strategy on the first day of his three-day "gloves off" tour, first at a coffee in Clarksburg in the morning, then at a speech in downtown Fairmont in the afternoon, and finally at a reception in Morgantown at the Hotel Morgan that evening.[35]

In Clarksburg, speaking to a large crowd at the Stonewall Jackson Hotel, the candidate declared, "The real issues in West Virginia are unemployed coal miners and jobless glass workers, not where I go to church on Sunday."[36] He reframed the issue as one of fairness, pointing out that "nobody asked if I was Catholic when I joined the US Navy. Nobody asked my bother if he was a Catholic or Protestant before he climbed into an American bomber to fly his last mission."[37]

That afternoon in Fairmont, he repeated the "discuss and dismiss" two-step, first discussing then dismissing the religious issue. "One of the issues in this campaign is my religion," he told the crowd of 3,000 in front of the downtown theater. "I don't think that my religion is anyone's business but my business." After declaring his faith, he again highlighted the fairness issue. "Is anyone," he asked, "going to tell me that I lost this primary the day that I was born and baptized forty-two years ago? I don't believe it."[38]

Kennedy ended the historic day in Morgantown, where he again lashed out against religious bigotry. At a reception at the Hotel Morgan, a full crowd heard him ask for support at the polls while saying that the "religious issue can be settled right here in West Virginia." As he had at earlier stops, he raised and rejected the issue: "West Virginia is suffering some of the most serious problems of any of our states, but I don't think one of them is religion." And he repeated his refrain on fairness.[39]

Tuesday, April 19

On Tuesday April 19, Kennedy brought his "new look" to the Northern Panhandle when he spent the day in Wheeling. His more aggressive stance involved not just employing the confrontational strategy, but also accepting the invitation to debate face-to-face with Humphrey. Both actions allowed the candidate to adopt the stance of a victim, as the public saw him fighting against religious prejudice and unwarranted personal attacks. The press reported that "the aroused Kennedy got his Irish up and promised to 'fight back' against what he called 'the current attacks' against him."[40]

Kennedy made ten stops in the Wheeling area, including West Liberty College where 700 students applauded his vigorous defense of religious freedom. In addition to applause, the quick-thinking candidate also got laughs during the speech. When a student asked him if he would "sign an Act of Congress dealing with birth control," the senator asked the student "if he meant Congress might make birth control compulsory." But Kennedy added, "I may be opposed to birth control as a member of my church, but I have no desire to impose my views on others."[41]

That night Kennedy flew from Wheeling to Beckley, and the press noted the contrast in religious demographics of the regions he visited. The *Huntington Herald-Dispatch* pointed out that Kennedy's flight the day before from Wheeling in Ohio County to Beckley in Raleigh County, brought the senator from the most Catholic region in West Virginia to the most overwhelmingly Protestant. Catholics accounted for 30 percent of the population of Ohio County and 48 percent of the church members, while they constituted only 1 percent in Raleigh County.[42]

Wednesday April 20

On Wednesday, Kennedy began his last day of his three-day tour in Beckley and ended the night in Huntington. During his "long whistle-stop tour of a dozen unemployment-plagued towns along the way from Beckley to Huntington," in an area that had "more poverty and fewer Catholics than any region in the state," the candidate "took the initiative in bringing up the religious issue, insisting his faith would not hamper him in living up to the president's oath of office."[43] An April 21 article in the *Clarksburg Exponent*, "Religion Gets Stressed During Kennedy Stops; Southern County Swing Features that Issue," spoke of conducting a "gloves off" campaign against those who would make his Roman Catholic religion a factor in the state's primary, saying he would be "just as free to carry out the duties [of president] as anyone in West Virginia, a heavily Protestant state."[44]

But the candidate that day also addressed the food issue at his visit to Mount Hope, which followed his morning visit to Beckley. Speaking from a car roof, Kennedy addressed food quality more than religious fairness. His focus on food, the first F of his three-F strategy, was understandable in a region where many subsisted on government-issued surplus foods.

Wednesday's schedule continued with a news conference at WOAY-TV in Oak Hill and visit to Collins High School, where cheerleaders led the crowd in chanting, "Hey, hey, what do you say? We're for Kennedy all the way!"[45]

From there, he proceeded to the Fayette County Courthouse and Gauley Bridge High School, then finished with a brief stop along Route 60 at Cedar Grove and Cabin Creek Junction, where he spoke at a supermarket about his four years in the navy during World War II.

Kennedy ended his three-day tour of the state in Huntington at a packed ballroom in the Hotel Prichard.[46] The crowd, estimated at up to 1,000, was the biggest in the history of the hotel. There wasn't even elbow room by the time the senator arrived more than a half hour late. In deference to their waiting, Kennedy cast aside his prepared address on a seven-point proposal for West Virginia economic development. Instead he spoke extemporaneously, highlighting three principles, the first of which was "his insistence that religion should not be injected into the present campaign."[47]

It was a more aroused and energetic candidate who spoke that night in Huntington, certainly more so than during his previous visit nine days earlier. The change might have been the result of his public adoption of the new confrontation strategy, or of having already made dozens of speeches addressing the religious issue. Whatever the reason, John Kennedy was in top form as he addressed the overflowing crowd at the Prichard Hotel.[48]

Thursday, April 21

The next day, April 21, Kennedy escalated the religious issue by taking it to a national stage. Scheduled to address the meeting of the American Society of Newspaper Editors in Washington, DC, he discarded his original speech topic and instead addressed the religious issue, accusing the press of both magnifying and simplifying it at the expense of real issues.[49]

By the end of the third week of campaigning in West Virginia, Kennedy lost his voice. As the campaign entered the final stretch, the juxtaposition of the contestants was ironic. Humphrey, whom critics chastised for talking too much (his stump speeches lasted anywhere from 20 to 70 minutes), faced an opponent who could barely talk during seven of the last ten days.

"It was something like watching a ballet star trying to dance with a broken leg in a plaster cast," Arthur Edson observed, "Kennedy had the occupational disease of politicians; he had lost his voice." But Edson noted that Kennedy suffers "less in such a situation than other politicians. As they say in sports, he has a powerful bench." The family factor once again came into play as Teddy and FDR Jr. were in the wings. "Since other Kennedys' and numerous hired help, are eager to leap into the game," Edson noted, "it's no wonder Humphrey has complained that he sometimes feels he's matched against a small army."[50]

To preserve his voice, Kennedy communicated with written words. On a flight from Charleston to Parkersburg on April 23, 1960, Kennedy resorted to note cards during a conversation with reporter and longtime friend Charles Bartlett, who was with him on the campaign trail that day. Bartlett, a noted Washington reporter for *The Chattanooga Times*, recalled, "He seemed almost certain to be beaten in the West Va. primary then, his voice was gone, the day was gloomy, and the week ahead promised to be tough. He communicated by writing at a furious rate. . . . The cards were written as we sat facing each other across a table in the airplane."[51] Bartlett saved the cards, the contents of which reflected a worried candidate who still had a sense of humor. His first card read, "It's pretty hard to run against the Protestant Reformation."[52]

During the next weeks, the candidate often had to rely on others to address the crowd at campaign stops. He would address the audience for five or ten minutes and then turn it over to someone else, usually his younger brother Ted, but also to Ted Sorensen, Matt Reese, or his wife Jackie.[53]

Third-Week Polls

Kennedy's pessimistic notes to Bartlett reflect the fact that there was not any statewide scientific polling conducted during the contest. In fact the only such statewide poll was taken by Kennedy's pollster, Lou Harris in December 1959. During the five-week campaign in the Mountain State, Harris only polled selected precincts.[54]

The lack of scientific polling for the West Virginia primary resulted in a press obsession with anything that could be called a poll. As an example, reporter John Wicklein even included in his *New York Times* analysis the results of an unscientific survey in a Mullens supermarket that found one shopper for Humphrey, one for Kennedy, and ten undecided.[55]

Over the weekend, on Sunday, April 24, the *New York Times* published two sets of what can be called anecdotal polls that suggested trouble for Kennedy. The so-called surveys weren't scientific but theme based. In 1960, such specific targeted surveys were common. In this case, the groups were 24 editors of weekly papers in the state and a collection of West Virginia clergy.[56] Of the editors, only four predicted a Kennedy win. (Eleven predicted Humphrey, and nine rated the race as a toss-up.) The clergy poll of 61 Protestant ministers found a slight lead for Humphrey, and half were undecided just two weeks before the primary. In terms of motivation, the survey found that 16 of the 17 pro-Humphrey clergy were not for Humphrey, but against Kennedy because of his religion.[57]

Fourth Week, April 25–29

The fourth week witnessed both candidates once again starting out on the campaign trail.

Humphrey started a two-day, 400-mile bus tour that took him through the north-central region of the state on Monday, and then to the Eastern Panhandle on Tuesday. After spending Thursday in Charleston, Humphrey made a two-day campaign swing over the weekend visiting Richwood on Saturday and then Huntington and Logan on Sunday.

Kennedy returned to the state on Monday to begin a three-day bus tour through the southern coal regions. It was Kennedy's second trip in five days to the voter-rich, but economically poor coal region of the state. The previous Wednesday, Kennedy had been in the hard-hit counties of Fayette and Raleigh. Now he would travel on the Ohio border across the southern coalfields to Blue-field on the Virginia border, and then northeast through the Greenbrier Valley, ending up in Charles Town in the Eastern Panhandle.[58]

Monday, April 25

Kennedy's bus tour started in Huntington after he flew in from Oregon, where he also was entered in the Democratic presidential primary. Although his plane was late, the senator managed to work in a number of appearances, including breakfast with Democratic leaders, a tour of a dress factory, and a TV address. After leaving Huntington, he made a hasty inspection of the US Veterans Hospital in Wayne County[59] before leaving for a series of stops in southern West Virginia.[60]

The Kennedy caravan then toured the economically depressed counties along the Big Sandy and Tug Rivers, which divide Kentucky and West Virginia. The candidate, who usually traveled by car rather than in the campaign bus, stopped for short visits at five towns (Lavalette, Crum, Kermit, Williamson, and Omar), gave a speech in Wayne, and held an evening rally in Logan.[61]

It was "shirtsleeve campaigning," with the temperature edging over the 90-degree mark through much of the day as Kennedy visited the hot and dusty coal mining and railroad towns of southern West Virginia. In the heat the voters saw an unusual sight: John F. Kennedy in shirtsleeves. Unlike his brother Bobby, John was rarely without a suit coat. Even in a coal mine the candidate kept it on. But on this Monday, voters saw a perspiring Senator Kennedy hammering at the theme of federal neglect of the depressed economic conditions in this region of the state.[62]

Kennedy's theme changed little in the last two weeks of the campaign as he flayed the Eisenhower administration during the many quick stops on the often "shirt-clinging ride" from Huntington to Bluefield. Kennedy told groups gathered on courthouse lawns and in town squares of what he had learned about the state. He realized that they had been neglected by Eisenhower.

This neglect was a timely subject as far as his listeners were concerned. A reporter described the area as a "region of rock hills and barren soil, [where] stringent diets are more the rule than the exception, according to local observers. Coal mines of the region have been shut down and new industry has been slow in appearing and most of the people support themselves by part-time jobs."[63] The people were "depressed, hungry and angry," a local citizen told a reporter who noted that "unemployment and economic stagnation appeared to override questions of religious faith."

After taking the initiative the previous week in discussing his religion, Kennedy appeared to be soft-pedaling the issue during this trip.[64] At his first stop in Wayne County, Kennedy spoke to 250 people standing in warm sunshine on the courthouse lawn. In his speech Kennedy said, "There is really only one issue in this state, and that one is jobs." He observed that West Virginia had about 70,000 people out of work, one of the highest relative figures in the country, and that a quarter million of its residents received free food from the government.[65]

From Wayne, Kennedy went to Princeton in Mercer County, where he was greeted by a crowd of about 1,000 people who gathered around the courthouse square and in adjacent streets. Just as important as the size of the audience was the "large welcoming committee that greeted the candidate when he arrived, including representatives of the two Democratic factions here."[66]

On his way to Logan County he traveled along a highway dotted with "Kennedy for President" signs and small groups of citizens gathered at various points to get a glimpse of the candidate as he stopped several times along the way.

One of his stops that Monday in Logan County was at Rossmore, a mining camp just outside Logan. A few years earlier it had been thriving, but now only three or four families remained. The other dozen dwellings had boarded windows and were falling into decay. "This is as distressed an area as I've ever seen," Kennedy said of Rossmore.[67] Logan County had been devastated by automation. There were 15,000 working miners 20 years earlier. In 1960, there were only 5,500 working miners, but their output of coal tonnage was greater due to automation.[68]

That Monday night, a crowd estimated at 600 (in a town of 5,000) stood in a roped-off street in front of the courthouse to hear the candidate speak from inside the courtroom over a public address system. After some brief remarks, Kennedy went outside and stepped into the crowd to meet and shake hands with his well-wishers. Then he and his party walked over to the famous Smoke House Restaurant where he broadcast over both local radio stations.[69]

Humphrey started the fourth week of the campaign heading north on a two-day tour that would take him to Charles Town a day prior to Kennedy's visit. On the first day Humphrey traveled through the north-central region where he visited a half-dozen communities before ending up at Fairmont for an evening rally on April 25.[70] The procedure at each of the communities on the route was the same. Humphrey would greet local Democratic leaders and speak briefly on issues of the campaign. At his first stop in Summersville, he had breakfast with 30 residents. Humphrey then went on to the Nicholas County Courthouse where he gave a "stirring, fiery speech to a crowd of about 150 persons who stood on the sidewalk or sat on nearby park benches, listening to him."[71]

The speech that morning was positive. "I come here to speak for good, and I come to praise and not to condemn," said the candidate. At no time did he refer to his opponent, let alone criticize him. He stayed true to his promise to "use my time in West Virginia constructively."[72] During the rest of the day Humphrey only made one reference to Kennedy, stating at Webster Springs that in the so-called underdog fight, "I'm further behind than he is."[73]

Tuesday, April 26

The intended focus of Humphrey's two-day tour was supposed to be on his proposed food stamp plan, which, unlike Kennedy's proposals on hunger, offered a new strategy. But on the second day, April 26, Humphrey's tone changed and the focus shifted from the proposed program to his opponent's expenditures.[74] As AP reporter Arthur Edson observed, Humphrey toured the poorer sections of the state with a plea of a Kennedy-is-too-rich-and-I'm-poor-like-you theme. He argued that being born rich like Kennedy was actually a handicap. "I've been poor," he said "The people who haven't been have missed something." He then added, "I'm one of you."[75]

For the rest of the day, Humphrey hammered on the issue of expenditures. In Kingwood he ridiculed the claim by Kennedy supporters that Kennedy was the underdog. According to Humphrey the real gang-up victim was himself: he was being ganged up on by wealth.[76]

Later at Keyser, Humphrey specifically talked about "black bags of cash," a term he would use repeatedly when discussing Kennedy's expenditures. He declared that "this is a government of the people, by the people, and not of the checkbook." And he worried that "if only the wealthy can run, if politics has reached the place where only the rich and the pets of the political bosses can run, then God bless America."[77]

At the heart of Humphrey's remarks was the question of wealth in American elections. He was concerned that the new politics of big money had placed politics beyond reach of the common man. At Keyser, he recalled his earlier days as a druggist and said he knew "what it meant to compete against bigness in business as well as in politics."[78]

Although Humphrey never provided details or raised the issue during the televised debate, the attacks on Kennedy's wealth that started that day continued sporadically through the remainder of the campaign. Humphrey's frustration was, in part, fueled by a *Newsweek* article by Kennedy friend and neighbor Ben Bradlee, which suggested that Kennedy was an underdog.[79]

Humphrey's visit to West Virginia's Eastern Panhandle would become important not just for his strong rhetoric, but also for his weak organizational support. His effort there began poorly on Tuesday when no one in his campaign seemed to know that the Mountain State had an eastern daylight as well as an eastern standard time zone.

Discussing the two-day tour, a reporter noted for anyone "without Humphrey's eternal optimism, this journey would have been written off as a disaster." Up at 4:30 a.m. to shake hands at a plant, the candidate ended the day after giving seven speeches addressing fewer than 700 persons. The only good news that day was that a Humphrey campaign driver convinced basketball star Jerry West not to give a nomination speech for Kennedy at a student convention. The driver, who was from West's hometown of Cabin Creek, reasoned with West that his future employer, the Minneapolis Lakers, might not appreciate the speech. [80] As a local Martinsburg paper reported, "Somewhere along the line his crewmen failed to realize that Daylight Saving Time is observed here."[81]

Before his arrival in Berkeley Springs, it was uncertain as to whether he would arrive on daylight or standard time. Due at 3:30 p.m., the candidate arrived about 4:30 p.m. In Martinsburg, the story was the same. Scheduled to speak at the public square at 4:00 p.m., he was already an hour behind and added another hour because of his tight schedule. As a result, the candidate didn't arrive until 6:00 p.m. and "only a handful of people, 150 at the most, were on hand to hear him."[82]

At each stop, however, the local press observed that the audience was larger than would be expected given the lack of an organization and competent scheduling.[83] Humphrey certainly didn't let the scheduling error bother him. During his brief 35-minute stop at Berkeley Springs, he spoke before a quickly assembled crowd of 75 to 100, drank from the famous George Washington warm springs, and visited a local drugstore.[84]

Humphrey's remarks at Martinsburg were described by the local press as "an arm-waving speech" to a small audience. More ominous than the small crowd that greeted him was the lack of local Democratic political leaders. Only the Democratic mayor and two members of the Democratic executive committee attended.[85]

By the time Humphrey arrived in Charles Town, it was 7:00 p.m. He was far behind schedule, but a crowd of several hundred assembled.[86] It was far less than the estimated 3,000 citizens Kennedy would address the next night at the Charles Town rally. Thus, the candidates' visits to the Eastern Panhandle revealed that Humphrey's rhetoric was no match for Kennedy's resources. The Minnesota senator could outtalk his opponent, but Kennedy could outspend, outorganize, and outpromote him.

The expenditures in advertising in the Eastern Panhandle provide another example of the resource disparity between the candidates. Humphrey didn't have the funds to advertise in the region, while the Kennedy camp spent heavily on marketing. When a local paper published a poll of 100 local Democrats in Berkeley County showing Kennedy ahead (60 percent), it noted, "It also seemed obvious that Kennedy's heavy advertising by newspaper and radio in contrast to practically none by Humphrey is having its effect in swinging support to the Massachusetts man."[87]

Given this disparity, it wasn't surprising that Humphrey would raise the issue at this point in the campaign. For the rest of the campaign, Humphrey would bring up Kennedy's expenditures, but his argument was undercut by his reluctance to provide specifics. He gave neither examples nor explanations. The Minnesota senator backed off instead of going for the jugular. He weakened his own attack by saying, "But then if you can't vote for me, vote for my opponent—stay in the Democratic column."[88]

In the Massachusetts senator's camp on Tuesday was his "chief campaign lieutenant, Franklin D. Roosevelt Jr.," who according to the press, was ready to launch a frontal assault into the southernmost reaches of West Virginia.[89] Two weeks earlier, Humphrey had gone on a similar swing through the coalfields and received a response so positive that he declared that he felt like "a triumphant Caesar."[90] Now his opponent would get a similar response, as seen in the headline of an April 27 article in the *New York Times*: "Kennedy Hailed in Mining Regions: Crowds in West Virginia Are Large and Enthusiastic."[91]

Kennedy's largest receptions were in the sister mining towns of Pineville and Mullens in Wyoming County, a county he would eventually win in May by a three-to-one margin. At Pineville, a crowd of about 600 greeted his caravan of eight to ten cars, while at Mullens, hundreds lined the main street to get a look at Kennedy and his campaign partner, Franklin D. Roosevelt Jr. An estimated 1,000 stood on the sun-drenched courthouse lawn to hear Kennedy label the Republicans a do-nothing party.[92]

One reason for the large turnout was that Wyoming County was the home of State Senator Ward Wylie, the titular head of Kennedy's campaign. The press, however, attributed the crowd enthusiasm to his campaign partner, Franklin D. Roosevelt Jr. The press reported that that the residents seemed as taken with Kennedy's "campaign companion as the candidate himself." [93]

Roosevelt did more than just draw crowds; he also played the role of hatchet man. While Kennedy usually treated Humphrey with kid gloves, at least until the last two weeks, the younger Roosevelt did not. As a result, Kennedy could remain the good guy while his companion struck out and did the heavy damage. In Mullens, the press reported that Roosevelt "didn't treat Kennedy's opponent with the kid gloves that Kennedy himself usually did." Frank Roosevelt warned the crowd that a "vote for Hubert Humphrey would be a vote down the drain."[94]

That afternoon Kennedy visited a West Virginia coal mine, the iconic symbol of the state. But the visit almost ended in a tragedy when Kennedy had a close call with a high-voltage line. He was mingling with a gang of miners during a change of shifts, when in unison the 200 miners yelled, "Look out for the wire!" Kennedy ducked and disaster was averted. Afterward one miner joked, "That wire sure would have lit up your lights."[95] The youthful senator didn't let the incident faze him. He sat down on the mine tracks, leaned up against one of the mine cars, and reportedly "became almost as grimy as the miners while chewing the fat."[96] It was the most informal campaigning Kennedy had done in West Virginia. The press mentioned that when Kennedy left the mine, his face and hands were as black as if he had been digging coal.[97] Inside the mine, the candidate answered questions from miners, which was filmed and used in a television commercial.

Wednesday, April 27

If Tuesday, April 26, was the best day in West Virginia for the Kennedy camp, the next was its worst as an afternoon scheduling fiasco proved to be a public relations disaster.

The Massachusetts senator started the day at Bluefield State College, an historically black college founded in 1895. The talk would be the only time in the West Virginia primary campaign that he addressed a majority African American audience. Ironically, his speech to an audience that morning never mentioned civil rights. Instead, Kennedy talked about foreign policy, specifically disarmament, which he had not focused on for much of the primary. He spoke of the difficulty of disarmament and the introduction of a bill to establish an Arms Control Research Institute. According to the press, Kennedy's only mention of civil rights that morning was a declaration that "everybody should have an equal chance to develop his talents," then adding, "What we are will speak far louder that what we say."[98]

Although the candidate didn't address the issue of civil rights in his speeches, his campaign was active in seeking black support. The number of African Americans in West Virginia had peaked in 1940 at six percent (117,700) and dropped by 1960 to under five percent of the state's population (89,393). [99] Efforts to target those voters were led by Charleston lawyers William Lonesome and C. W. Dickerson. Lonesome was in charge of field operations, while Dickerson served as the black coordinator for the state headquarters. The campaign also brought in a DC judge, Marjorie Lawson, to help organize.[100]

After his start at Bluefield College, Kennedy was supposed to go by bus to Princeton before attending a noon rally at the railroad center of Hinton. The rest of the day he was slated to travel along the state border, giving a series of speeches at high schools in Alderson, Ronceverte, and Lewisburg.[101] The day was to end in the Eastern Panhandle at a large rally at the Charles Town fairgrounds.

But plans were changed when he was called to Washington to vote on a mine safety bill. The press reported the Kennedy's departure "set off a chain of misadventures that added up to perhaps the unhappiest day of his campaign." The Hinton visit became a debacle after the staff failed to alert supporters in the town of the change. When the "Kennedy for President" bus arrived in front of the Hinton Post Office, they were met by the Hinton High School band blaring away as a crowd of 700 wet, but enthusiastic, supporters waited in the rain expecting to see a candidate who wasn't on board.[102]

The contrasts between Humphrey's visit to the Eastern Panhandle on Tuesday, April 26 and Kennedy's visit the next day highlight the differences between the two campaigns. In terms of travel, while Humphrey arrived by bus on Tuesday Kennedy came on Wednesday by plane. And in terms of organization, Humphrey didn't have an organization in either of the panhandle's two largest counties, while the Massachusetts senator had Kennedy-for-President committees in both Berkeley and Jefferson Counties. In terms of audiences, Humphrey addressed no more than 500 during the entire day, while Kennedy spoke to a crowd of 3,000 at just one site—the Charles Town race track.

Thursday, April 28

After casting his vote on mine safety in the morning, the Massachusetts senator flew from Washington, DC, to the Martinsburg airport in Jefferson County. There he was joined by his wife, who had flown in from Bluefield where the candidate began that morning.

The few hours the senator spent in the Eastern Panhandle were busy ones. After Kennedy landed at the airport shortly after 6:30 p.m., he was whisked by police escort to radio station WEPM where he had a half-hour broadcast answering questions submitted by the public via telephone.[103] While the religious issue didn't come up during the program, it was the reason Kennedy took a detour when he left the station on his way to a big night rally at Charles Town. He had a secret meeting with Robert Strider, the former West Virginia Episcopal bishop. The purpose for the unannounced visit was to get an endorsement from him in hopes of offsetting the remarks of the current Episcopal bishop, Wilburn Campbell, who had openly questioned the prospect of a Catholic president.[104]

In this so-called Battle of Bishops, Kennedy got Strider's endorsement and a statement that he had "no hesitancy in voting for Kennedy, a Roman Catholic." Kennedy expressed his gratitude and said he hoped that "we can move to a discussion of the real issues facing West Virginia and the nation."[105]

Kennedy had a chance to discuss those "real issues" that night when he faced a large audience at the Charles Town racetrack. The event was historic. The Massachusetts senator was the first presidential candidate in modern times to have a major political rally in Jefferson County. And his audience of 3,000 was the largest of the campaign so far.[106]

The rally was well planned. The entertainment portion included the Charles Town High School band, a local quartet (Key Kings Quartet of Charles Town), and a group sing. Following the rally there was a dance featuring music by the Metronomes.[107] The planners even considered the possibility of bad weather conditions, which they'd failed to do for the public-relations disaster at Hinton. "It's all free," said Shirley Hunt, the chair of Jefferson County's Kennedy for President Committee, "and everything is under cover so we'll expect a big crowd, rain or shine."[108]

The irony was that Kennedy could barely talk in front of the largest crowd to date of the campaign. The senator began his remarks by telling the crowd that he was about to be rendered speechless from too much recent speech-making. His brief speech touched a number of topics: he praised presidents like Theodore Roosevelt and FDR, declared the importance of the upcoming election, and praised the state's patriotism, saying that the "fires of patriotism burn strongly" in West Virginia. He also had time to promote the state's self-image, saying that he didn't think the state had reached "high noon," and he was unwilling to accept the stories about the state's decline.[109]

If the candidate couldn't talk long with his audience, he could meet them face-to-face. After his remarks, a reception line began. When it quickly bottle-necked, a new line was started on the floor below. Meanwhile Mrs. Kennedy "strolled through the crowd, stopping here and there to chat."[110] The senator's day wouldn't end until he and Mrs. Kennedy returned to Martinsburg at about midnight and took off by plane for Washington.[111]

After the Charles Town rally, Kennedy left the campaign trail in West Virginia for the next two days, returning Saturday for what would be a sprint to Election Day in the last leg of the primary campaign.[112]

After a day's rest, Humphrey spent all day in Charleston. In addition to two televised news conferences in the capital city, he made two speeches, one at a noon rally from the Federal Building steps on Capitol Street and the other at 2:00 p.m. at Morris Harvey College. His well-known wit was on display in both speeches. When his public address system broke down during the outdoor address on Capitol Street, he quipped, "I wonder if the Republicans arranged that." He grabbed a portable, battery-operated loudspeaker and added, "See, we Democrats won't let any temporary setback throw us. We'll improvise some-how."[113] Later, when a Morris Harvey College student accidentally called him Senator Kennedy, Humphrey replied, "That's all right—100,000 voters in Wisconsin made the same mistake."[114]

In Charleston, Humphrey returned to the issue of food commodities, promoting his legislative efforts and ridiculing the Eisenhower administration's claims of assistance. But foreign policy, not food, was the major topic when the Minnesota senator addressed the students at Morris Harvey College. This topic was also an area of expertise for Humphrey, who preferred to use the term "international policy." The word "foreign," he explained, indicated "a lag in thinking, because nothing is foreign anymore."[115]

His extensive interest in international affairs was evident when he entered the college auditorium and was greeted by a large banner over a door declaring, "Defender of Korea Freedom at its Darkest Hour—Thanks, Sen. Humphrey!" Four Korean students at the college had erected the banner because of Humphrey's past support for restoration of civil liberties in South Korea. The banner prompted one of the rare times either candidate spoke about a current world event during the five-week campaign. In the hundreds of speeches by both candidates, foreign policy was generally ignored except for a few references to the Cold War. In his speech, Humphrey referred to the sign and his opposition to the authoritarian rule of strongman Syngman Rhee. Two days earlier, Rhee had stepped down and was flown out of South Korea by the CIA.[116]

Humphrey's speech on foreign affairs at Morris Harvey stood in contrast to his opponent's speech at the same auditorium 16 days earlier. In that address, Kennedy made no mention of foreign policy, while Humphrey offered a wider perspective, arguing that America could best stop the expansion of communism by helping other nations solve their problems with food, medicine, education, and so on.[117] He argued, "We've got to stop thinking of massive retaliation as a way of life, and think instead of massive doses of health, science, education."[118]

Friday, April 29

Kennedy's Wednesday fiasco was compounded on Friday when Franklin D. Roosevelt Jr. failed to show up at schedule appearance at Hotel McCreery in Hinton. The situation became worse when Senator Robert C. Byrd showed up at the hotel and promoted himself as a delegate candidate and explained why he favored the candidacy of Hubert Humphrey.

To make up for his as well as Frank Roosevelt's failure to appear in Hinton, Senator Kennedy promised to come the next Wednesday morning "rain or shine," He sent a telegram apologizing and expressing the hope that his "Hinton friends" would turn out to greet him the following week.

After three weeks on the campaign trail, the Minnesota senator seemed more than willing to continue his fast pace, this time to the southern cities and towns. Unlike previous campaign stops when he looked worn and strained, the press reported that he was "tanned, fit and rested and free of campaign fatigue."[119] When Humphrey boarded his campaign bus in Charleston on Friday, he warned the media that they were in for it. "I got a full night's sleep last night," he said, grinning.[120]

He wasn't exaggerating. That day took Humphrey to seven towns. He started in St. Albans, then went to Hurricane at 9:30 a.m, Milton at 10:00 a.m., and Barboursville at 11 a.m. After a 12:20 public reception in Huntington and a private luncheon with staffers, he headed south to Hamlin at 2:30 p.m., Chapmanville at 4:30 p.m., and Logan for an 8 p.m. speech. His day ended in Beckley where he stayed the night.[121]

But his full schedule didn't always imply a large audience. At his first stop, the press reported that "Sen. Hubert H. Humphrey was legging it down a St. Albans street today almost before the city had stirred."[122] He first ran into a dozen or so children on their way to school. After asking them about their homework, he told them, "We're going to have to run somebody to beat Mr. Nixon. Tell your mommies and poppies I want your help." Then he handed out Humphrey buttons.[123]

At an insurance company office, Humphrey got permission from Mrs. Elizabeth Hutchinson, the assistant bookkeeper, to go back and meet the employees. "'Girls,' the senator said as he marched from desk to desk with a fistful of campaign buttons, 'I'd like to pin these on. It gives me a little more time with you.'"[124]

Saturday April 30

Such small-group encounters stood in stark contrast to Kennedy's presentation the next day on Saturday, April 30, in front of a large crowd at the St. Albans Middle School. The rally, one of two that day in Kanawha County, was well organized and well attended. The school band played, Jackie Kennedy came, and the candidate spoke to an audience of more than 150 people.[125]

Humphrey's two-hour visit to Huntington (his third) witnessed more of his characteristic "hobnobbing and hand-pumping" style of personal-contact campaigning. It was this brand of retail politics that he repeated throughout the state.[126] At Marshall College, his first stop at the school, he shook hands with many students and pinned Humphrey buttons on them. His total audience was much smaller than the gathering Kennedy had addressed weeks earlier during his campus visit. At that time, Kennedy was ensured a large audience because his appearance coincided with the shift change at a nearby plant.

Humphrey's mastery of retail politics was evident that Friday in front of his headquarters at 1025 Third Avenue. He made a point of shaking hands with every boy in the Vinson High School band who'd played for him when he arrived. Seeing the band's majorettes, Humphrey then proceeded to shake hands with the majorettes and bestow a button upon each of them.[127]

During his six daytime stops, the candidate made only one formal address, and that was inside his Huntington campaign headquarters. In that speech he blasted the Republican administration in Washington for sins of omission and commission concerning the state of West Virginia.[128]

Humphrey gave a major campaign speech at 8:00 p.m. at the Logan County Courthouse. As important as the size of the audience were the personnel who organized the event. In Logan County, unlike many other southern counties in the state, Humphrey had the official support of the majority faction of the local Democratic Party. Chafin had secretly deserted Humphrey, but on this night his faction stood by Humphrey and publicly supported him.

At Courthouse Square, Senator Humphrey leveled his attack at the GOP, charging that their slogan should be "No, No, Go Slow, Not Now, Veto." And he generated large applause from the crowd of 600 when he attacked the Eisenhower administration's insufficient allowance of surplus commodities for the unemployed of the state.[129]

But the fireworks that Friday night weren't at the courthouse. They occurred at the radio station, WLOG, when Humphrey responded to the first personal assault of the campaign. In the Wisconsin primary contest Kennedy never mentioned his opponent by name, let alone singled him out for attack. But the truce had been broken that day when Kennedy accused his opponent of smear tactics and conducting a "gutter campaign."[130]

Whether an act of desperation, as charged by the Humphrey camp, or an act of calculation, the attack ushered in a new stage of the primary campaign. The kid gloves came off when a statement went out under the name of Senator John F. Kennedy, declaring that Humphrey had "distorted my record, attacked my integrity and played fast and loose with smears and innuendoes." Kennedy warned the other side that he did not "intend to take this kind of abuse indefinitely" and added, "Mr. Humphrey could not win the nomination."[131] Kennedy went on the attack for the same reason that he had earlier accepted the invitation to debate Humphrey: he perceived that his campaign in West Virginia was in trouble and running out of time.

Humphrey's initial reaction to Kennedy's accusation was one of humor. When he was told of the attack, Humphrey spread his hands in amazement and said, "What brought that on? What have I said about him? I haven't mentioned his name twice all day. I don't see what reason he had to say a thing like that." He went on to tease his opponent: "Keep your shirt on, Jack. Maintain a sense of humor and don't expect to win them all."[132]

But at the station, Humphrey's remarks were stronger. During a radio interview with the editor of the *Logan Banner*, Charlie Hylton, Humphrey swung what Hylton would describe as "a haymaker at his opponent." The next day the headline in the *Logan Banner* read, "Sen. Humphrey Takes Off Gloves, Hits Back at Kennedy Accusation."[133]

In his interview, Humphrey observed, "I think that what's happening is that for the first time my opponent is finding the going a little rough, like he's peeved, like he's not capable of taking competition in a political campaign." After declaring, "We're both grown men, and let's act that way," the candidate issued a warning. "When all this is over I would like to be able to support a Democratic nominee. A few more statements like that, and I'll not be able to do it."[134]

Later, Humphrey issued an even stronger statement, charging that Kennedy hadn't even authored the statement of attack; rather, it was the work of his brother Bobby, who that day was in Charleston headquarters to take charge of the campaign. Humphrey stated that "Jack will have plenty of chances to speak for himself without handouts through his brother, Bobby," and, "Politics is a serious business, not a boy's game where you can pick up the ball and run home if things don't go according to your idea of who should win."[135]

John Kennedy declined to comment, saying, "I don't want to get into a mud-slinging battle." But as the reporter observed, Kennedy "couldn't keep from throwing a few daubs of mud himself." Given the stakes in the primary and the uncertainty surrounding its outcome, it's almost surprising that such attacks hadn't surfaced earlier. Time was running out for Kennedy at a point when the *Washington Post* reported that local politicians rated Humphrey "the favorite largely because of what they believe is an anti-Catholic sentiment directed against Senator Kennedy."[136] Thus, "No holds were barred as Kennedy fought to retain his frontrunner position for the Democratic presidential nomination."[137]

A sign of the increased hostility was the "garbage" newspaper ad that belittled Hubert Humphrey, showing him standing beside a garbage can with a too-small derby perched on his head. Next to him was a glamourized John Kennedy standing next to the White House. The large ad suggested that votes for Humphrey would end up in a garbage can beside a road back to Minnesota, while votes for Senator Kennedy would drop through the roof of the White House.[138]

The damaging ad prompted Lieutenant Governor Carl Rolvaag of Minnesota to issue a press release challenging "the divine right of the Kennedys to determine who should be the Democratic nominee."[139] But in this case the

Kennedy campaign had the cash to place the ad in several newspapers, while the cash-strapped Humphrey camp couldn't afford to place any ad in response. It was one more example of the Kennedy campaign's one-sided use of paid media in the state.

While his opponent rested, Humphrey ended April in a flurry of campaign activities. His frantic pace reflected an effort to invest his time in a contest where he couldn't invest comparable resources.

Kennedy resumed his campaign on Saturday with a round of visits to ten communities in the Charleston area, and Humphrey continued his tour of the southern counties.

After a warm welcome in Rainelle, Humphrey traveled to Summit Lake, where some 4,000 fishermen arrived at 6 a.m. for the opening of trout season.[140] He then traveled to Richwood for the annual Ramp Festival, which attracted thousands to Nicholas County to consume a springtime onion-like plant native to Appalachia. Known more for its smell than its taste, West Virginians have a special affection for ramps.[141] Ramps also represent a potential campaign trap for awkward and unsuspecting candidates. Hubert Humphrey, however, was comfortable at such iconic small-town events. Ever the natural campaigner, Humphrey, like any good candidate in Appalachia, was willing to eat the obligatory ramps as a concession to local pride. After taking his first mouthful, Humphrey declared they were fine, but then added that he did not think it was as necessary as water.[142]

Franklin D. Roosevelt Jr. was also in Richwood that day—unsurprising, as he often shadowed Humphrey. Their paths crossed as Humphrey entered the grade school where the event was taking place, FDR Jr. "made a grand bow, threw open his arms, said, 'Good afternoon, Senator,' then asked how everything was coming along. 'Wonderfully, wonderfully,' Humphrey answered—his two words ended the conversation until Mrs. Humphrey asked Roosevelt sarcastically who made him the greeter."[143]

Unlike Humphrey, Franklin D. Roosevelt Jr. was unwilling to participate in the ramp tradition. According to *Hillbilly* editor Jim Comstock, when the younger Roosevelt stopped, he "took one sniff of the cooking ramps [and] the big city resident left."[144] Comstock noticed that Roosevelt also failed to understand his now-famous satire about religious bigotry, "Pa Ain't Sellin' His Vote to No Catholic," thinking the article was a slam against Kennedy. But Humphrey understood the satire, and at the Ramp Festival, he and Comstock exchanged wisecracks about it.

While Humphrey and Roosevelt were in Richwood on Saturday, Kennedy went to ten communities in the Charleston region. After visiting a crowd of 200 people on the front lawn of the Boone County Courthouse in Madison, he visited Eskdale in the Cabin Creek region, then traveled to Marmet, Kanawha City, downtown Charleston, the Mound in South Charleston, Upton's Creek, Wolf Pen, and the Unitarian church in North Charleston, followed by evening rallies at Dunbar and St. Albans.[145]

Kennedy was still suffering from a sore throat infection that left him without much voice. The candidate "went through the motions of filling his West Virginia campaign engagements Saturday, despite being barely able to speak."[146] Jacqueline Kennedy, who joined her husband that evening at the St. Albans Junior High School rally, told the audience that she'd been giving her husband "lots of gargles and pills."[147]

The treatment apparently hadn't worked, so once again Kennedy had to let others do the speaking for him. At the start, Matt Reese, executive secretary of West Virginians for Kennedy, delivered speeches while Kennedy limited himself to handshaking and a few weakly voiced words to each audience. Reese made approximately the same short speech at each stop: he reviewed Kennedy's record as a navy PT boat officer in the South Pacific and pointed out, "He's the only veteran running." Then he stressed what would become a daily theme in the Kennedy campaign: a vote for Humphrey on May 10 would be wasted because, as Reese put it, "Hubert Humphrey cannot win the nomination."[148]

The Saturday Kennedy spent in Kanawha County was important because it featured his first venture to Cabin Creek, a region of chronic unemployment that Humphrey had visited earlier and often. One of the poorest sections in that county, the area was the site of one of the deadliest and longest labor conflicts in American history, which occurred in 1912–1913.[149]

When Kennedy visited the region in 1960 it had numerous drab mining settlements, some of them now almost ghost towns, strung out along the creek. Kennedy went to Eskdale, a small mining community on the creek east of Charleston. There he and Reese spoke in front of a Quonset hut–type general store to a crowd of miners, many of them out of work.[150]

The day was also historic because it featured Kennedy's only campaign appearance at a church. His short address at the Unitarian church in North Charleston didn't focus on religion but rather repeated standard campaign fare. While religion may have been seen as the key issue in the primary, neither candidate used the pulpit during the four weeks of crisscrossing the state, except for this one instance.[151]

Sunday, May 1

On Sunday, Humphrey was in Washington and Kennedy was in the Parkersburg area ready to have the biggest day of his campaign. The day, however, found the candidate without a voice or a spouse. The press reported that the "twenty-nine-year-old" and "attractive" Jackie Kennedy returned to Washington Saturday night because of her three-year-old daughter's illness.[152] Since highlighting his family was an important part of his campaign strategy, Kennedy invited his sister, Eunice Kennedy Shriver of Chicago, to accompany him to Parkersburg.[153]

With regard to his own illness, John Kennedy's continuing throat infection rendered him voiceless. As such, he followed the brother-stand-in format he used at the Charles Town rally on Wednesday. At his first Sunday stop at Ravenswood, John Kennedy made brief remarks, and then Ted spoke on his behalf. Afterward John mingled with the hundreds of visitors and spoke in a whisper to them individually.[154]

The response at Ravenswood to the voiceless candidate gave testimony to his charisma. The local newspaper reported that "many dyed-in-the-wool Republicans who haven't spoken to a Democrat for years shook Kennedy's hand, and were quite obviously impressed and pleased." Moreover, "The county's Democrats—even those stumping for Adlai Stevenson and Stuart Symington— were in their glory."[155]

From the Ravenswood reception of 1,200, John Kennedy went to a Parkersburg ox roast. The Wood County sheriff, O. C. Boles, estimated that 4,000 people greeted the presidential contender that afternoon at the city park; others suggested there were more in the audience. A campaign spokesmen said the supply of buns at the ox roast ran out after some 3,600 were served, the beef supply was exhausted, and approximately 4,000 cups of Coca-Cola soda were served.[156] Whatever the true number, it was the largest live audience Kennedy would face in West Virginia.

The record-breaking crowd heard little from the candidate, who apologized for the "infection which at this crucial stage of my life has made it rather difficult for me to speak." In his brief remarks, he spoke about his motivation, contending that he was running for president for the same reason he ran for Congress and entered the navy: "That is, I was brought up to have a strong devotion to my country."[157] He assured his listeners that a majority in the May 10 primary would ensure his nomination. And he promised, "I assure you I will defeat Dick Nixon."[158]

His twenty-eight-year-old brother, Ted, then took the podium. In his speech, he stressed the importance of West Virginia's primary and disparaged Humphrey as someone who had "not the slightest chance of being elected president of the United States."[159] Ted didn't need to speak about his brother's military experience, since the audience was reminded of it by the Big Red Band of Parkersburg High School. In honor of the senator's service with the US Navy, the band members played "Anchors Aweigh" when he entered and exited the stage.[160]

Teamster Endorsement

In the final full week of the campaign, the state Teamsters Council endorsed Humphrey. The long-delayed action should have been a turning point for the candidate, as it was the only open endorsement by a large union of any candidate in the presidential primary.

But the action was followed by a sustained effort of the Kennedy camp to taint the endorsement by linking it to Jimmy Hoffa, the president of the national Teamsters International Union. This attempt to turn an opponent's asset into a liability was common in Kennedy campaigns. It was certainly not unexpected, given the bad press about the union president and the bad blood between Hoffa and the Kennedy brothers dating back to Bobby's tenure as the chief counsel of the Senate Select Committee on labor activities.[161]

The Kennedy campaign asserted that the West Virginia Teamster endorsement was generated not by the state organization, but ordered by the national president. As such, they argued, the action should be viewed as interference in the state by Hoffa. The campaign claimed that state leader, E. A. Carter, was following orders from Hoffa.

In Weirton on Sunday, May 1, Kennedy called on West Virginians to reject Hoffa's intervention in their Democratic preference primary. "I think people do not want Jimmy Hoffa to determine who is to be the nominee," Kennedy said. He noted that the Teamsters, through Hoffa, had intervened in Wisconsin, and the people of Wisconsin had rejected that intervention.[162]

Marshall West, co-chair of the Humphrey campaign, tried to break the linkage encouraged by the Kennedy camp. West argued that the state Teamsters' choice was "strictly a local decision by local people as to whom they favor in the local primary—and has nothing to do with Hoffa, regardless of how the Kennedy forces try to distort it."[163]

West also asserted that Kennedy's spokesmen "apparently in desperation are indicting themselves through flagrant 'guilt by association' tactics reminiscent of the McCarthy era."[164] West also condemned the linkage effort as an attempt at "guilt by association" with the late Joseph McCarthy, a controversial Republican senator from Wisconsin who'd been censured by the US Senate six years earlier for his anticommunist hearings.

Bringing up the image of McCarthy was a well-placed jab, for it touched a nerve in both Kennedy brothers. Bobby had served as counsel of the Senate investigations subcommittee headed by McCarthy at the time.[165] And it was a reminder of John Kennedy's reluctance to criticize the heavy-handed senator. Kennedy's silence on the censure of McCarthy prompted concern among liberal Democrats, including Eleanor Roosevelt. Commenting on the senator who

wrote *Profiles in Courage* she said, "I feel that I would hesitate to place the difficult decisions that the next President will have to make with someone who un-
derstands what courage is and admires it, but has not quite the independence
to have it." [166] The topic became so toxic that the Kennedy campaign prepared
an answer sheet on the issue for volunteers. [167]

Behind this back-and-forth of the Teamsters' endorsement, there was a
bigger story. The narrative of labor and the 1960 West Virginia presidential
primary wasn't about what happened, but what did not. Humphrey, with a
pro-union legislative record, didn't get the expected full union support of a
pro-union state. The late endorsement by the state Teamsters only heightened
the silence of the other unions in the Mountain State, who wouldn't support
Humphrey despite his compiling the most pro-labor record of any of the Democratic contenders for the presidential nomination in 1960.

During the West Virginia campaign, Humphrey met at least three times
with union leaders, but in the end the Teamsters were the only major union to
endorse him. The reluctance of the other unions reflected a belief that he would
not get the presidential nomination, and that Kennedy, with the weaker legislative record, was better than Lyndon Johnson and the other contenders. [168]

Fifth Week, May 2–8

Monday, May 2

The day after Kennedy's impressive rally in Parkersburg, Humphrey came to the
city. His effort that Monday stood in contrast with his opponent's campaign the
in three ways. First, Humphrey's plane arrived an hour late so that his already
tight schedule was made even more crowded. [169] Second, he handled a campaign
itinerary that would have tired a person half his age—his visit included a tour
of the downtown, a visit to two factories, and two speeches, one at a noon rally
downtown and the other at the VFW hall in the evening. Third, he couldn't
match Kennedy's audience numbers.

A large crowd assembled on the steps of the Wood County Courthouse for
the noon rally, and that night an audience heard him speak at the VFW hall, but
the several hundred in attendance paled when compared to the 4,000 people
who'd heard his opponent at the city park on the previous day. [170]

On Monday, Humphrey showed himself to be the handshake king of retail
politics. As evidence of his "fine reception" in Wood County, his campaign co-
chair, William L. Jacobs, noted that the senator had shaken 2,000 hands in one
day. [171] But again, Kennedy had spoken to twice that many people the day before.

Another troubling sign was Humphrey's meeting that morning with local
labor leaders at the Labor Temple on Thirteenth Street, the same place where

Kennedy had made his appearance at a federal employees rally. The juxtaposition of Kennedy one day addressing a crowd outside the labor building and Humphrey the next day inside pleading with union leaders for support illustrated how far Kennedy had come in neutralizing what many thought would be a strong advantage for Humphrey in West Virginia. On that day, as earlier, the chief advocate of organized labor in the senate would not get support from organized labor in the West Virginia primary.[172]

Tuesday, May 3

After conducting a whirlwind campaign in Parkersburg on Monday, Humphrey moved on to Huntington on Tuesday for another crowded schedule. In the morning he had breakfast with Democratic leaders (9:00 a.m.), gave a radio and television press conference (11:00 a.m.), and delivered an address on nuclear disarmament to the Huntington Kiwanis Club at noon. This was followed by a tour of downtown businesses and visits to three factories.

Humphrey finished the day by going to the Camden Amusement Park in Huntington. The event was attended by 10,000 people, the largest crowd either candidate drew. If the attraction for the Sunday ox roast was free food, the attraction Tuesday was free rides for children at the park.[173] Where the Humphrey campaign got the funds for the free rides was at the time a mystery. William A. Beckett, a Huntington attorney, said he arranged the rides at the park "for a client," whom he declined to identify.[174] The funds apparently came from Texans who backed Lyndon Johnson—one of the few times that the Humphrey campaign benefited from outside help.[175]

But not many of the thousands who came to the park actually heard the candidate. Humphrey mingled in the crowd, took a ride on a miniature train, and spoke briefly from the roof of an ice cream stand to an audience of mostly children. His speech was short—only eight minutes from a candidate whose speeches could last over an hour. In his brief remarks, he talked of the neglect from Washington and the need to change administrations in Charleston and Washington.[176]

That Tuesday in Huntington also featured Humphrey holding a provocative but confusing press conference where he once again hinted at Kennedy's expenditures, in the end pulling his punches. After suggesting that Kennedy's spending could be explosive, the Minnesota senator didn't elaborate. His restraint surprised the press. A reporter observed that Senator Humphrey "refused to be led in to derogatory remarks about this opponent."[177]

While Humphrey visited Huntington, Kennedy, who had taken Monday off, went for one last time to the southern coalfields. Not surprisingly, he spoke in Welch, the county seat of McDowell and the home of Sidney L. Christie.

Kennedy had first met Christie on May 9, 1959. He and Jackie had flown to Bluefield and were driven to Welch, where he spoke to 600 people for a Harry S. Truman birthday dinner at the town's elementary school.[178] Now, at the county courthouse, Kennedy addressed an audience estimated at 700, with another 300 listening to a public address system outside.

There was little that night for the large audience to hear directly from the candidate. Despite taking a two-day break from campaigning to rest, Kennedy's voice still wasn't strong. His remarks were brief before his youngest brother stepped in to speak.[179] In those remarks, Kennedy reminded the overflowing crowd that "I have been in Welch three times. I'm the only presidential candidate who can make that statement." It was a declaration that reminded the voters of the attention he had paid to them during the campaign and, with it, implied that he wouldn't forget them after the election. It also carried the implication that Humphrey had neglected that area.[180]

Just as important as that reminder was Sid Christie's introduction of the candidate. Christie presented Kennedy as "truly the man of the hour," then addressed the religious issue, saying that "I have told him that his candidacy would be judged on its merits—not on bigotry and intolerance."[181]

That night Kennedy told an audience that "I am delighted to submit my political fate to the people of West Virginia."[182] Certainly submitting his future in McDowell County to Christie served him well.[183] Kennedy would carry the county with 80 percent of the vote. The following year, President Kennedy would ask for the appointment of Christie to federal judge.[184]

Wednesday, May 4

On Wednesday, both candidates spent the day campaigning before traveling to Charleston for the televised debate in the evening. While Humphrey visited the Ohio River towns of Henderson and Point Pleasant, and then went on to Ripley, Kennedy headed south on an itinerary that included six towns in three counties.[185]

After a speech at Concord College, Kennedy traveled to Hinton to make up for the visit he'd missed a week earlier. On a sunny day in the railroad town of 6,000, Kennedy was greeted at the Summers County Courthouse Park by a high school band and a crowd of 600. The makeup visit "blossomed into a three-pronged affair" with the senator, his younger brother Ted, and Franklin D. Roosevelt Jr.[186]

Still nursing an ailing throat, Kennedy spoke briefly from the bed of a truck parked in front of the post office, but it was enough time to promote the possibility of tourism as the new industry for Summers County.

After the candidate spoke, Frank Roosevelt and Ted Kennedy filled in. The format followed a familiar one-two-three presentation, where the candidate would start, the former president's son would follow, and the younger brother would finish. Each person in this campaign troika had a job. The powerful trio allowed the audience to hear about policy from the candidate, a promise from the candidate's brother, and an attack on the candidate's opponent delivered by a president's son.

Brother Ted promised future friendship saying that "if Jack is successful here he will win the nomination . . . and you can rest assured you will have a friend in the White House."[187]

Roosevelt's role was to play the hatchet man, taking down the opponent. In this case, he told the audience that "You either are going to throw your vote down the drain next week by voting for a straw man, or you have a choice of voting for the next president of the United States." [188]

After his Hinton visit, the Kennedy motorcade left for the Greenbrier Valley to visit the string of towns of Alderson, Ronceverte, Lewisburg, and White Sulphur Springs that had been rescheduled from the previous week.[189] At each stop he drew large crowds, including an overflow crowd at the Alderson High School gymnasium and an audience of 1,000 at Ronceverte.[190]

That evening of May 4, more than a half million viewers watched the two Democratic contenders, Kennedy and Humphrey, debate at the studio of WCHS in Charleston. The lackluster affair had no brass-knuckle surprises.[191]

Thursday, May 5

The day after the debate, both candidates returned to the campaign trail with five days remaining. While Kennedy toured Raleigh County on Thursday, his opponent returned to the Northern Panhandle for a grueling eleven-hour tour that included visits to three towns, three college campuses, and one factory. The long day didn't end until Humphrey returned to Washington where he joined Kennedy for a Friday morning vote on the economic development bill.[192]

Humphrey's schedule appears all the more remarkable when one considers that he didn't arrive at the Wheeling Ohio County Airport until 4:00 a.m. Thursday morning. He was supposed to reach Wheeling at midnight, but a missed flight (and a refusal from Bobby Kennedy to provide air transportation to Wheeling on the Kennedy campaign plane) caused a delayed arrival.[193] Yet the senator appeared cheerful and wide awake at an early-morning press conference, even before he had his morning coffee.

That Thursday morning, he spoke at two colleges in the Northern Panhandle, but at neither assembly did he did focus on state issues. At Wheeling College, the state's newest college, Humphrey talked about cancer, promising that if elected president he would call a White House conference early in 1961 "to bring together the best medical and scientific brains in this country to plan an accelerated attack upon this disease."[194] His only reference to the state came when he dedicated his talk to the deceased former US senator M. M. Neely of West Virginia, who had "led the fight for cancer research on the floor of Congress . . . until he himself was cut down by this dreadful disease."[195]

The student audience that Thursday may have been partisan, but they proved enthusiastic. His speech on nuclear arms met with sustained applause. He was called back three times for further comments by the enthusiasm of the crowd.[196]

Although Humphrey got the attention of the students, he didn't get the level of media attention that Kennedy received when he toured the region earlier, accompanied by reporters from the major wire services and national newspapers. Humphrey was covered that day by only one wire service—a journalist for United Press International.[197]

While Humphrey hunted for votes in the Northern Panhandle and Morgantown, Kennedy visited Beckley for the third time.[198] Kennedy then went on to Oak Hill, where he spoke to an overflow crowd at the Collins High School gymnasium.[199] He reminded his audience that he had visited in April, which meant he was the only presidential candidate who had twice visited their high school. He referred to the student body as the best cheering section for Kennedy in the nation.[200]

In his upbeat message, he denied that West Virginia was a dying state, asserting that all it lacked was an opportunity to move ahead. This opportunity, he implied, would be available if he was elected. As a reporter observed, he "left no doubt in the minds of the hundreds who gathered in the Collins High School gymnasium that he considers a great majority in West Virginia's primary next Tuesday a key factor in his campaign to win the nomination at the Democratic national convention."[201]

Kennedy returned to Charleston for a reception at the Civic Center, but he and Humphrey had to bring their campaigns to a sudden halt when they left that night for a Friday morning vote in Washington on the area redevelopment bill, a measure each had promoted across West Virginia. "This is one of the bills I have been talking about which would do something concrete for the depressed state of the West Virginia economy," said Kennedy.[202]

Friday, May 6

After both candidates cast their votes Friday morning in the Senate chamber, they returned to West Virginia for the last four days of the primary campaign. Kennedy went west. For the fifth time he visited Huntington, speaking on the lawn of the Cabell County Courthouse. Afterward he stopped at Ceredo and

Kenova in Wayne County along the Ohio River before returning to Charleston for a televised rally.[203]

Humphrey headed south for his last tour of the southern counties. He and Muriel flew from Washington to the Welch Municipal Airport in McDowell County.[204] He then went by helicopter to a rally at Williamson in Mingo County, addressing fewer people than Kennedy had a week earlier.[205] This time a tight schedule forced Humphrey not to meet with Christie, who had endorsed Kennedy a few days earlier.[206] Afterward Humphrey traveled by car to Pineville in Wyoming County, his final destination that day, for a dinner to honor Judge R. D. Bailey. In attendance that night was a virtual Who's Who of state politics. But the focus was on the judge, not the candidate. While Humphrey's presence was noted by dinner organizers, he made only a few remarks, as did John Kennedy's representative, Bobby Kennedy. The main speaker that evening was FDR Jr.'s brother, California congressman James Roosevelt.[207]

In all, the May 6 trip was less successful than Humphrey's southern counties tour at the start of his West Virginia campaign in April. Four weeks previous, he had been greeted by enthusiastic crowds; he'd dined with Sid Christie, the political boss of McDowell County; and he'd returned from that tour feeling like a "triumphant Caesar."[208] But now there was no sense of momentum, and the southern counties would overwhelmingly support his opponent in the Tuesday primary. Kennedy would win Wyoming by 65 percent, Mingo by 60 percent, and McDowell by 75 percent.[209]

The difference in the candidates' activities that evening of May 6 was striking. While Humphrey was at a dinner with the political establishment, honoring a judge and saying little, Kennedy was on television doing a call-in show with area voters. The half-hour program, which ran from 8:30 to 9:00 p.m., featured a rally held at the Dickinson Street parking lot next to the Kanawha County Library.[210] It was advertised in the *Charleston Gazette* and broadcast on three different stations: WCHS, WHTN (now WOWK), and WSAZ. The format was interactive, as Kennedy took phone calls live on the air.

Friday, May 6, would also mark the most controversial episode of the 1960 West Virginia primary. During the last days of the campaign, arguments between the two candidates grew more numerous and more intense. But the last-minute focus on Humphrey's draft status became the most infamous as Roosevelt implied that Humphrey several times had sought a deferments during World War II. [211]

The accusation remained part of the political landscape in the closing days of the campaign.

An angry Humphrey recalled that after he corrected the record with the Kennedy brothers, they "never shut FDR Jr., up, as they easily could have. It was a dishonest and a politically unnecessary thing to do, but it persisted."[212] A month later Roosevelt apologized to Humphrey.

Saturday, May 7

Bad weather on Saturday forced Kennedy to cancel his flight from Charleston to Elkins for a campaign rally. The campaign sent Franklin D. Roosevelt Jr. in his place. At the event, Kennedy spoke by phone to the audience gathered at Tygart Hotel, his voice broadcast over a loudspeaker.[213] Due to the schedule change, Kennedy went on a one-day swing through five cities in Kanawha County—Spencer, Elkview, Cotton, Walton, and Clendenin—and visited the Libby-Owens-Ford glass plant in Charleston. The stops were mostly handshaking opportunities. Kennedy's only speech that day was at the Roane County Courthouse in Spencer.[214]

Humphrey used Saturday for a visit to Clay in the morning and a rally in Clarksburg in the afternoon. He was given a hero's welcome on his first visit to Clarksburg as the Jane Lew band met him at the edge of the city and escorted him to the county courthouse. After his speech he took a street tour, shaking hands. Later that evening he attended a dance at the Moose Hall.[215]

The big event on Saturday was the Clarksburg Democratic fundraiser featuring Senate Majority Leader Lyndon Baines Johnson. An estimated 5,000 people attended the $10-a-plate Jefferson-Jackson fundraiser event dinner held at the Clarksburg Masonic Temple.

Johnson didn't come alone. He brought a planeload of other US senators. The eight senators at the dinner that night included two of Kennedy's rivals for the 1960 Democratic presidential nomination—one present (Humphrey) and one future (Johnson)—as well as Kennedy's West Virginia adversary, Robert C. Byrd, and the state's other US senator, Jennings Randolph.[216]

It is interesting to note that Kennedy wasn't one of the senators at the Clarksburg dinner. As with any event where he would play second fiddle, Kennedy chose not to attend. While FDR Jr. represented him at the fundraiser, Kennedy did a one-day campaign visit in Nebraska, where he was unopposed on the May 10 ballot.

Lyndon Johnson's visit to West Virginia had been arranged months before anyone knew that the state's presidential primary would attract national attention. The press approached the dinner in the same way they did the debate, as a newsworthy event that could be a defining moment in the campaign, but like the debate, there were no fireworks that night. Johnson remained quiet, both about his future challenge to Kennedy and about Humphrey's present campaign.

Press attention that night settled on Humphrey's hostility to Frank Roosevelt a day after he made his statement about Humphrey's war record. As AP reporter

Arthur Edson said, "Anyone who doubts the sting of these [Roosevelt's words], at least on Hubert H. Humphrey, needed only to spend a weekend in Clarksburg."[217] The reporter noted that Humphrey's body language spoke volumes. He was hesitant to shake hands with Roosevelt, refused to pose with him for a photograph, and later stayed outside the Masonic auditorium until Roosevelt had finished his remarks. When it was his turn to speak, Humphrey summoned up some joviality as he told the crowd he remembered when Roosevelt campaigned for him. "Ah, those were happy days," Humphrey said sarcastically.[218]

Johnson was the star that night, as he always was, and there would be no spotlight on Humphrey, even though the Kennedy camp promoted the idea of a "gang-up" conspiracy against their candidate. As Humphrey accurately observed, "If Lyndon wants to give me his blessing that night, that'll be fine. But I think that the only blessing he'll give will be on Lyndon."[219]

Humphrey did pose for a picture with Senator Johnson, his supposed partner in the "Stop-Kennedy" conspiracy. The cameras clicked as Senator Humphrey threw his arms around the Senate majority leader and said, "I have been a friend of Lyndon Johnson a long time. . . . He is the kind of Democrat I like because we can disagree without being disagreeable."[220]

Sunday, May 8

On Sunday, Mother's Day, Hubert Humphrey wore a red carnation in honor of his mother living in Huron, South Dakota. He took Muriel and two of his children to a Methodist church service in Clarksburg. He had been scheduled to attend a Mother's Day tea in Huntington, sponsored by the Democratic Women's Club at the Junior League Community Center. It would mark his fourth trip to the Ohio River city. When weather conditions grounded their plane at Clarksburg, they drove 80 miles to Parkersburg and chartered a plane to Huntington.[221]

Sunday's bad weather also altered John Kennedy's schedule. Scheduled for an afternoon open house in Clarksburg at the Stonewall Jackson Hotel, he was unable to attend when his plane was grounded in Charleston. Once again family took his place, as Bobby Kennedy and a cousin, Polly Fitzgerald, met the crowd. Between 2,500 and 3,000 people shook hands with Bobby Kennedy in Clarksburg.[222] It was a much larger group than the hundred people who had greeted John Kennedy two weeks earlier at a coffee stop when the senator visited the city for the first time.

That Sunday night, Kennedy again went on television to answer a series of prepared questions offered by a supportive questioner, Franklin Delano Roosevelt Jr.[223] Theodore White and many Kennedy advisors considered the program the turning point in the primary. It was his most dramatic presentation on the religious issue, and it was the most controlled.

Almost all of the 30-minute program centered on religion, but the candidate also gave a "sixty-day promise," pledging that "within sixty days of the start of my administration, I will introduce a program in Congress for aid to West Virginia."[224]

Kennedy's Sunday television program contrasted Humphrey's telethon. Seen locally in the Kanawha region, the eleventh-hour show was poorly planned. The studio had a chair, a desk, a manual telephone with two lines, and the candidate poised to answer questions. But the calls were unscreened and the result was embarrassing.[225]

A backdrop to Humphrey's telethon effort was his campaign's lack of funds. Theodore White relates how he watched Humphrey respond angrily when an aide told him that the television stations required a deposit that morning. It was one of the few times that White saw the senator lose his temper. After his outburst, Humphrey pulled out his own checkbook, and as Mrs. Humphrey watched, he wrote a check for $750 of the $1,500 cost. "One had the feeling that the check was money from the family grocery fund," White said, "or the money earmarked to pay for the wedding of their daughter who was to be married the week after the primary."[226]

Election Eve, May 9

On election eve, most of the pieces of the Kennedy strategy devised at the Kanawha Hotel a month before were in place. The Sunday television program focusing on the religious issue reflected the confrontational strategy. The "sixty-day" promise and the last-minute FDR/FDR Jr. newspaper ad identified the candidate indirectly with food, the first of the three-F issues. The ad featured a drawing of FDR's face and the signature of FDR Jr. which asserted that John F. Kennedy "would do for West Virginia in the '60s what FDR did for West Virginia in the '30s." And the war service smear against Humphrey escalated the flag issue—the second F.

The only piece of the puzzle missing was the third F—family. Jackie Kennedy had left the state nine days earlier and wouldn't return until after the election. But she'd already established her presence in the Mountain State through days of campaigning. While his sisters' role was smaller than in Wisconsin, the two Kennedy brothers practically lived in the state for the duration of the campaign.

The day before the election there was evidence from a number of sources that Kennedy had gained in the last weeks. On Monday, the *Fayette Tribune* reported its final and unscientific county straw poll, which showed Senator Kennedy leading Humphrey for the first time. An earlier poll released on

April 25 had shown Humphrey leading by an 85 to 57 count. The final poll had 68 people for Kennedy, 43 for Humphrey, and 70 undecided. But the paper pointed out that the large number of undecided voters made any prediction uncertain.[227]

Kennedy's pollster, Lou Harris, also discussed a last-minute switch based on his survey of selected precincts in Kanawha County. He gave credit to the senator's Sunday television program for undermining the earlier voiced concerns about the impact of his religion on his actions as president.[228] Harris's poll of selected precincts on Saturday, May 7, showed Humphrey at 45 percent, Kennedy at 42 percent, and 13 percent undecided. A selected precinct poll taken after the Sunday night program showed Kennedy with a slight lead. Straw polls, television time, large crowds—all appeared to favor the Massachusetts senator. But those measurable items were offset by the immeasurable: how many West Virginia Democrats would vote their religious fears and prejudice?

The lack of any statewide scientific polling data ensured that uncertainty would mark the Tuesday election when the five-week campaigning came to an end. This uncertainty was reflected in the effort of Kennedy to lowball expectations by raising the possibility of a 40 per cent showing. *Charleston Gazette* reporter Don Marsh wrote that 40 percent was " like having a previously prepared position to retreat to." Marsh reported that in more private discussions Kennedy estimated that 45% was about the best he could accomplish.[229] Kennedy told W. H. Lawrence that he doubted the he could "get beyond 46 or 47 percent of the vote . . . If I get that close , maybe I can still survive."

Humphrey publicly predicted a close victory, saying, "We ought to be able to squeak through."[230] In private, he told close friend Joseph Rauh that "he was going to lose."[231] In the weeks leading up to the primary election, Humphrey repeatedly told Rauh that "it was going badly in West Virginia."[232]

The last day of campaigning was "raw and cold" in parts of the state. Monday found Humphrey and his wife visiting five towns in the Charleston area: Nitro, Kanawha City, South Charleston, Dunbar, and Campbell's Creek. Their itinerary included stops at four industrial plants and one school—Midway Junior High on Campbell's Creek.[233]

Meanwhile, his opponent toured the Ohio Valley in the western part of the state for the last time. The visit marked Kennedy's sixth visit to Huntington and his third visit to Parkersburg. In the morning he went to three factories in Huntington. He then flew to Parkersburg, where he greeted workers at a American Viscose Corporation plant and, an hour later, students at Parkersburg High School. His final event of the primary campaign was a parade through the town, led by Parkersburg High's Big Red Band. After a 20 to 30 minute concert, Kennedy gave his last speech of the West Virginia primary.[234]

There was a dramatic contrast in location between the two candidates' final campaign speeches. Humphrey spoke at Campbell's Creek, a small school in a small community. Kennedy spoke at Parkersburg, a large city, and was preceded by a parade.

That Monday evening both candidates returned to Charleston. Almost five weeks after the Wisconsin presidential primary, they would await the outcome of the West Virginia presidential primary. The unexpectedly intense campaign in the Mountain State had come to an end.

Chapter 6

LEGACY

Ted [Kennedy] told me, "I don't think you know how important West Virginia was to us," and I told him, "I don't think you know how important Kennedy is to us in West Virginia."

—Governor Joe Manchin III, West Virginia Public Radio, April 10, 2010

John F. Kennedy won the West Virginia presidential primary in a rout. One newspaper described his victory as "Kennedy's sparkling ballot blitz."[1] In American politics, 55 percent is considered a landslide; Kennedy won 61 percent of the primary vote and carried 50 of the state's 55 counties. The final vote total was 236,510 ballots for Kennedy to 152,187 for Hubert Humphrey.[2] A reporter described the winner as "grinning like a schoolboy with a fistful of 'A's' as he accepted the noisy greetings and backslaps from his supporters . . ."[3]

In his victory remarks, Kennedy first expressed his thanks to the people of West Virginia, saying, "Despite all that has been written about the people here, after traveling to every corner of the state and meeting you, I had no doubt that you would cast your vote on the basis of the issues and not on any religious prejudice."[4]

He then reaffirmed his promises, saying, "I pledge again tonight that I will not forget the people of West Virginia, nor will I forget what I have learned here. On my television show last night I said that if elected I would work to help West Virginia. This I will do."[5]

The record shows that this is what he did, taking action to pay back that debt to the state. Part of it was paid in coin of the realm—appropriations or appointments. On the county level, Logan County got a new courthouse, and McDowell County chairman Sid Christie was considered for a federal judgeship. But most of the debt was paid in historic federal intervention in the state and the region. The millionaire senator who had never confronted poverty before, came, saw and, as president, acted. Bob McDonough, Kennedy's campaign manager during the primary, noted that while West Virginia at that time lacked a powerful senator who could intercede for the state, the state had something better: "what we had was that powerful president interested in our problems."[6]

Short-Term Legacy

Influencing Public Policy

In January 1961, John Kennedy's first action as president was related to food commodities, an issue he'd repeatedly made a priority during his campaign in West Virginia. As candidate, he held up a can of powdered milk during a televised debate and complained about inadequate food commodities. As president, he issued an executive order to double federal government food rations and expand coverage to four million needy people. Arthur Schlesinger Jr. believed that such action was "in response to his memories of West Virginia and the pitiful food rations doled out to the unemployed miners and their families."[7]

In February, the president implemented the national food stamp program that Hubert Humphrey had promoted during the primary.[8] The first step was the creation of pilot food stamp programs in eight selected counties across the nation.[9] One of those counties, McDowell, was in southern West Virginia. On May 29, 1961, Kennedy sent his secretary of agriculture to Welch, West Virginia, to deliver the nation's first food stamps to Alderson Muncy, an unemployed coal miner with 13 children. Muncy made the nation's first food stamp transaction when he bought a can of pork and beans at Henderson's Supermarket.[10]

For Kennedy, Muncy's transaction brought the food issue full circle. In May of 1960 during a televised debate, John Kennedy read a letter from an unemployed West Virginia coal miner who received food commodities. Now another unemployed West Virginia miner would be the first food stamp recipient. By May 1970, participation in the program would number six million households.[11]

Ironically, the cabinet member who gave Muncy the stamps was former Minnesota governor Orville Freeman, who campaigned for Humphrey in West Virginia. In that primary contest, Freeman championed Humphrey's call for a food stamp program. Now he returned to the Mountain State to begin a historic program that Humphrey had long promoted.

The food stamp initiative was only a part of a massive intervention. Bob McDonough believed that West Virginia got more federal assistance in the three years John Kennedy was president than any of the 15 years before. Under the Kennedy administration, he recalled there was "a flood of federal favor."[12] He kept track of this funding stream, and calculated that West Virginia was allocated almost $600 million in federal funds, allocated to defense contracts, road money, and varied public works.[13] So much money was coming in that

Governor Wally Barron funded a state liaison office at the Congressional Hotel on Capitol Hill. Under the guidance of Paul Crabtree, the office facilitated the flow of federal funds to West Virginia.[14] The Governor also paid the expenses of Kennedy's campaign manager in the state primary, Robert McDonough, to make hundreds of trips to Washington in the interests of West Virginia.[15]

In the case of funding highways, McDonough recalled that under that Eisenhower administration West Virginia was "low man on the totem pole" in terms of road mileage allotment. But Kennedy "could and would and did keep directing the attention of the Bureau of Public Roads to the fact that West Virginia needed roads."[16]

In all, federal funds for West Virginia went from $70 million in 1959 to $93 million in 1964.[17] Nearly 50 percent of state revenue came from federal money.[18] Such an increase reflected Washington's change in attitude in regard to federal intervention. The symbol of Washington neglect—"Eisenhower curtains" (boarded up windows on vacated homes)—was replaced by a series of programs. Critics argued that such expenditure efforts were not enough. Washington politicians needed to address the root causes of the poverty such as overly powerful private industries that took profits out of the state, or ran local governments.[19] But such attempts to address structural changes were not part of the new president's, and his administration's, vision. Kennedy focused on a historic series of actions to address the paradox of regional poverty in a prosperous nation—a situation brought to attention by a shocked candidate and powerful media focus.

On the state level, Kennedy's actions lived up to the primary election-eve promise that "his first order of business will be to give West Virginia a fair break."[20] His most recognized act was the release of federal funds for the construction of Interstate 79, a proposed four-lane highway up the middle of the state from Charleston to the Pennsylvania border going through the towns of Sutton, Clarksburg, and Morgantown.

The new president's proactive stance on transportation stood in sharp contrast to the inaction of the Eisenhower administration. West Virginia had been largely left out of the 1956 Interstate Highway Act. Of the 41,000 miles designated for construction, the allotment for West Virginia by the end of 1960 was only 306 miles. A year earlier Eisenhower's secretary of commerce, Sinclair Lewis, dashed hopes for I-79 when he told the press that West Virginia was not likely to get more mileage because most of the miles had been allocated for other locations.[21]

This changed when John Kennedy became president. He acted in response to a request from his West Virginia campaign manager, Bob McDonough. It was an unselfish request, as McDonough lived in the far western part of the state. But like many others, he recognized the positive impact an interstate would have through the center of the state. McDonough would call the construction of I-79 the most important benefit the state received as a result of the Kennedy administration. When he died in 1965, McDonough requested that his ashes be scattered along the highway.[22]

The Kennedy administration's efforts reflected the bureaucratic-realism perspective that would be shared by many government agencies in the 1960s. According to this perspective, the essential characteristics of poverty in Appalachia weren't fundamentally different from those of poverty elsewhere: unemployment was the principal cause, economic development the cure. Highways would provide a way for employers to reach those in isolated pockets of poverty.[23]

Federal investments by ARC in transportation, as well as in education and health were designed to overcome isolation and stimulate economic development.

Some studies have shown that such highways did increase development.[24] But critics like Ron Eller have argued that Washington politicians didn't address the counterview that the problems of the West Virginia coalfields lay in economic exploitation rather than economic isolation. They pointed out road improvement did not address the real problems.[25]

The highway initiative focused on cities, so-called federally designated "growth centers," rather than to connecting small towns and making them less isolated. Resources were channeled to cities rather than to the "dying mining camps and fading rural hollows."[26] This emphasis on urbanization—encouraging rural dwellers to move to medium-sized cities—prompted concern in the *Charleston Gazette* that funds for potential growth areas meant that public dollars would not go to the poorest areas of the states. These were the very areas that motivated John Kennedy and other Washington politicians to intervene in the region.[27]

While the debate over merits of construction continues today, West Virginia during the Kennedy administration enjoyed a road construction bonanza that provided the state with a series of viable transportation routes. The interstate was only part of the Mountain State's highway construction in the following years. As the only state to reside entirely in the federally defined borders of the Appalachian region, West Virginia received much of the funds allotted to the development of the Appalachian Highway system, a network of corridor highways that connected distressed areas of Appalachia with the outside world in order to spur economic growth. Of the one billion dollars allocated to build the Appalachian Highway system, 24 percent was set aside for West Virginia.[28] By 2015, 424 miles of corridor roads had been built in the state.[29]

If the construction of I-79 stands as the most visible benefit of the Kennedy administration, the Area Redevelopment Act is arguably the most important. This effort to aid targeted, depressed areas constituted a milestone in federal intervention. The idea of assistance to "poverty pockets" was first introduced in the 1950s by Illinois senator Paul Douglas and sponsored by seven Democrats, including John Kennedy.[30] However, President Eisenhower vetoed the bill three times. The last time occurred during the West Virginia primary, prompting both Kennedy and Humphrey to suspend their campaigns and return to Washington in an unsuccessful effort to override the president's action. At that time, Kennedy declared, "This is one of the bills I have been talking about which would do something concrete for the depressed state of the West Virginia economy."[31]

After his election in November of 1960, Kennedy was ready to act on West Virginia's behalf. Even before his inauguration, he appointed a task force headed by both West Virginia senators, Robert C. Byrd and Jennings Randolph, to construct an economic recovery plan in economically depressed areas. The task force proposed up to $75 million be allocated to more than a hundred such areas across the United States as part of the Area Redevelopment Act. Many of the targeted counties were located in the Appalachian regions of Pennsylvania, Kentucky, and West Virginia.[32] Enacted in May of 1961, the law constituted the first legislative achievement of President Kennedy's "New Frontier" agenda.[33]

John Kennedy's support of the bill isn't surprising given his view on government's role in the economy and his experience in West Virginia. According to Ted Sorensen, being in West Virginia had "made him more attuned to specific solutions for specific problems such as depressed areas, untrained workers, substandard wages."[34] Kennedy recognized and was ready to deal with what economists called the problem of "structural unemployment," a concept that recognized that as jobs increased in new industries, they decreased in old ones—such as coal and textiles." While Keynesians hoped that effective fiscal and monetary policies would allow most of the structurally unemployed to find work, they acknowledged that a hard core would remain jobless.[35]

Many economists viewed the dynamic with pessimism, but the new president apparently saw it as a challenge. On signing the bill, he remarked, "A wise public policy uses economics to create hope—and not to abet despair." The optimistic president then declared, "We are not helpless before the iron laws of economics."[36]

Unfortunately, the number of counties targeted during the act's four-year existence increased from 114 to 500 and then to 1,000. In the end, it covered a third of the nation's counties. Such increases diluted the intended impact on critical areas of unemployment and the original intention to target a limited area of high need.[37]

This dilution prompted a group of governors to lobby the president to create a separate program specifically for the Appalachian region. The result led to the creation of the Appalachian Regional Commission (ARC) during the Johnson administration.[38] By 1980, this dramatic experiment in public policy helped narrow the differential between Appalachia and the rest of country in terms of income, employment opportunity, education, and health.[39] But critics have questioned the program both in its inception and in its operation.

The 1962 Manpower Retraining Act represented another effort to tailor legislation to help the victims of economic forces. The act provided $434 million for those who had lost jobs, such as the miners displaced by mechanization of the coalfields. Of the 138 programs, ten were in West Virginia. Kennedy considered such displacement to be one of the most important issues ever addressed by Congress. "It is a bill," he said, "which will eliminate waste of human resources."[40]

During the primary campaign Kennedy often asked, "What happens when machines take the place of ten miners?" He understood that loss of job meant loss of identity. Since coal mining was a male-only occupation, the loss of a coal-mining job implied a loss of masculinity. In this way, Kennedy mobilized the West Virginia male breadwinner who was unable to perform his traditionally manly role. It is interesting that in his introductory remarks at the televised debate in Charleston with Humphrey, Kennedy equated West Virginia miners with West Virginians who served in the military. Each profession was one of risk and service.[41]

As a candidate in West Virginia, Kennedy saw a "waste of human resources." As president, he was ready to promote federal action. The theme of more direct help to the state had been a constant in his primary campaign speeches, and now he as president he could deliver. As a candidate, he coupled his praise for the state's record of military service to the promise of more defense contracts. As president, Kennedy announced that West Virginia in 1960 "was at the bottom—50th in percentage of attention it received from the national government—it is a fact that in 1963 it has moved up to 30th."[42]

The rest of the 1960s would see increased congressional attention on and funding for a region long neglected by Washington.[43] The most important was the War on Poverty, whose origins have been traced to literature rather than politics. Debora McCauley, however, argues that credit for "starting" the War on Poverty in Appalachia goes not to the publication of Harry M. Caudill's *Night Comes to the Cumberlands* or Jack Weller's *Yesterday's People*, but rather the "education" of John Kennedy: "The seed planted for the War on Poverty is attributed to the shock John F. Kennedy felt at the poverty he saw when he campaigned in West Virginia."[44]

Others also observed Kennedy's reaction to West Virginian poverty. According to Ted Sorensen, Kennedy was appalled by "the pitiful conditions he saw, by the children of poverty, by the families living on surplus lard and cornmeal, by the waste of human resources."[45] Teddy White noted that "Kennedy's shock at the suffering he saw in West Virginia was so fresh that it communicated with the emotion of original discovery."[46] John Kennedy in 1960 was a "man who had never wanted for anything and, in his political life to this point, had rarely bothered to consider anyone who did." Now he came from a visit to a Cabin Creek school muttering, "Imagine, just imagine kids who never drink milk."[47]

During his administration, Kennedy took a number of steps in dealing with poverty through targeted economic redevelopment programs. By the end of 1963 he was ready to consider a more comprehensive attack. Just before he left for Texas in November of that year, the president had discussed possible programs with Walter Heller, chairman of the Council of Economic Advisors. But the plan he outlined to Heller wasn't the one envisioned by Lyndon Johnson and passed by Congress in 1964. While Kennedy pictured a pilot program that could impact a handful of cities, President Lyndon Johnson enlarged the scope, promoting an "unconditional war on poverty" as if it had been Kennedy's final wish. Larry Sabato notes that this extension of Kennedy's legacy was a marriage of conviction and convenience because it was useful to both JFK's historical image and LBJ's presidency."[48]

Also useful to the effort was the face given to the program. Because of Kennedy's weeks of campaigning in West Virginia, the nation connected poverty to white Appalachians. Adam Yarmolinsky, a key architect of the program, noted that "the original picture of the poverty program in the public eye was Appalachia." Ian Harman points out that such identification had political benefits. The poster children for the War on Poverty were those rugged descendants of Daniel Boone and Davy Crockett. The West Virginia mountaineers and Kentucky frontiersmen were the "ideal symbols to rally a nation around a novel set of social and economic policies."[49]

Ian Hartman observes that President Johnson didn't "stroll down a street in Washington to find poverty," but instead went 500 miles to Inez, Kentucky, to visit Tom Fletcher, an unemployed coal miner, for a photo op. Such optics "ensured that economic inequality would receive a thorough public hearing in the early 1960s." But another result was the whitewashing of poverty through its association with so many white faces. The whitewashing effort also led ongoing stereotyping of Appalachia as entirely poor and white, when it is actually a region with much diversity.

Hartman points out that this period "was not the first time that poverty exposed a crisis of white masculinity and raised the possibility of Anglo-Saxon collapse." That bell had been rung several times before, much to the alarm of many in the nation. He argues that one should locate the "rediscovery" of poverty in the 1960s upland South in the cultural legacy of frontier masculinity and racial discourse—an unsettling perspective on the origin of the War on Poverty and the decade's liberalism.[50]

Long-Term Legacy

Perpetuating Regional Stereotypes

The short-term legacy of Kennedy's primary victory in West Virginia can be measured by programs and funding. The long-term impacts are harder to measure, but probably more important. These include the primary's impact on the image of the state and region, the conduct of future presidential campaigns, and the Catholic factor in the selection of presidential nominees.

In terms of image, the 1960 West Virginia primary did have a positive effect on the state and region by defying the low expectations that outsiders had of West Virginians, and reaffirming the enduring belief that America is equipped to overcome longstanding biases and prejudices to adapt to a changing world.[51] For the outcome of the primary contest undermined the stereotype of Appalachians as religious bigots holding a jug of moonshine in one hand and a Bible in the other. As Charleston reporter L. T. Anderson argued, "Sen. Kennedy's victory proves what some of us have been trying to say all along. That West Virginia is not the hotbed of religious prejudice some of our distinguished visitors have supposed it to be. We have our religious feelings, to be sure, and here and there they run deep and bitter, but in a purely political campaign, they are not decisive."[52]

After the election, the *Wall Street Journal* published an editorial apology to the citizens of West Virginia who, the editorial acknowledged, had been allocated a "stereotyped role." An example of media misrepresentation was that the press had overlooked the fact that Catholic Al Smith had won the Democratic presidential primary in 1928. Such information was a fact "that was forgotten in the soap-opera script of this year's primary."[53]

Apologies aside, the negative press coverage that focused on stereotypes had a lasting effect on West Virginia's image as an impoverished state. Appalachia had always been victim of caricature, and the virtual invasion of the national press in April and May of 1960 would only make the stereotyping worse.[54] Although Ben Bradlee pointed out the economic differences between "the boom-town northern half and the ghost-town southern half" of the state,[55] most press attention focused on the southern coal counties and ignored the other areas. This focus prompted an editorial in the *Charleston Daily Mail* with a headline "On The Other West Virginia: The Figures Tell A Far More Encouraging Story." The editorial noted that West Virginia's story had two sides, one of which was often invisible to outside press. The editorial went on to cite overlooked positive statistics, such as the fact that personal income in Kanawha County had been increasing steadily since 1953, with two exceptions, 1954 and 1958.[56]

Writing in 1963, Roy Lee Harmon, journalist and poet laureate of the state, argued that "No state in the nation has been as much maligned as West Virginia." He remembered working public relations for the Humphrey campaign during the 1960 presidential primary. His job included making sure that "big time" journalists and TV men had seats on the bus and were briefed about the towns they were visiting. His exposure was not a happy one. "Practically every writer who came down here came looking for ignorance, poverty and religious prejudice." Not surprisingly, Harmon, after ten days, could barely stay "on speaking terms with most of the big-headed, big-time boys" who wanted to smear West Virginia.[57]

Such information was not highlighted, as the press appeared to only strengthen negative stereotypes. While the national attention paid to West Virginia during the primary campaign meant that many Americans no longer thought that Richmond was West Virginia's capital and cotton the state crop, they now thought of Cabin Creek as the state capital and poverty as the state's only industry. Former West Virginia Congressman Alan B. Mollohan argues that the stereotyping of a highly diverse region as "stark pictures of ramshackle homes, populated by struggling families" was overpowering. They seared a perception in the public mind "of a place of utter poverty, and in desperate need of outside help." Yet while such pictures, he noted, did help trigger support for federal intervention, they also supported a stereotype.[58]

The Appalachian stereotype promoted by the national press became a part of people's everyday lives in the 1960s and 1970s as a number of popular television programs like *The Beverly Hillbillies* and *The Real McCoys* attracted large audiences. [59] Anthony Harkins notes that the success of such shows with Mountaineer characters "reflected the national media fascination with this 'white other,'" those isolated people outside the mainstream. Such a one-dimensional perspective ignored the rich history of the region, which included actions and protests. "We were presented on TV as having no history and no culture," notes Denise Giardina. "The main thing the people knew about us was what they saw on the *Beverly Hillbillies*, Jethro Bodine, Granny, and her raccoon recipes—so it was a very difficult time in the that sense. The nation was looking at us, laughing at us, or pitying us."[60]

Foreshadowing Political Campaigns

The Kennedy campaign in West Virginia previewed what Ralph McGill calls "the latest scientific mechanisms" of political campaigns in its use of polling, television, and computers.[61] The first presidential contender to have his own private pollster, Kennedy used Lou Harris throughout his quest for the presidency. Soon such access to polling was obligatory for any future presidential candidate. Ironically, the only statewide poll in the West Virginia contest was conducted by Harris in December of 1959. But too often his later surveys of selective precincts in the state, showing Kennedy behind 60–40 and then gaining, are cited as if they were statewide polling efforts. [62]

In regard to television, Kennedy was among the first prominent American politicians to understand and use the new medium. It is not surprising that in office the candidate would be known as the first television president.[63] In West Virginia, his campaign exploited television though ads, programs, and a historic debate. These mechanisms, plus the large expenditures and selection of primaries as the path to presidential nomination, would become part of presidential campaigns for the rest of the twentieth century and beyond.

Advancing Religious Tolerance

Regarding the religious issue, Kennedy's victory triggered an outpouring of self-congratulation among the press, politicians, and scholars. Charlie Peters argued that one of the greatest social changes in the twentieth century was the rapid decline between 1960 and 1965 in anti-Catholicism. He credits it to the "two Johns"—John XXIII and John Kennedy.[64] For in the 1960s both the Pope and the President defied "stereotypes of Catholicism's hostility toward the modern, secular world."[65] Father Andrew Greeley even suggested canonization because John Kennedy had "put to rest forever the fear that Catholicism was an alien religion and that Catholic political leaders would use their positions to interfere with American freedoms."[66]

It's hard to reassess the conventional wisdom on religion that followed the 1960 presidential election. Teddy White saw Kennedy's victory as an event that "turned the hinge" in American history by removing the political taboo against a Catholic running for president.[67] But some scholars have wondered how far that door was opened. "If 1960 represented a turning point for American Catholics," Thomas J, Carty argues, "how do we explain the failure of any Catholic—in over 40 years—to repeat Kennedy's accomplishment?"[68] Carty's perspective is supported by Michael Massa's controversial claim that, by downplaying his faith, the way John Kennedy ran and ruled made it harder for future Catholic candidates. [69]

The future intersection between American presidential politics and Roman Catholicism remains an open question, but there remains a consensus that John Kennedy's electoral successes in May and then in November of 1960 exorcised the ghost of Al Smith and undermined the unwritten law that a Catholic could not reach the White House. As Martin Marty noted, "His inauguration symbolized the end of 'Protestant America.'"[70]

The majority of opinion, at the time and at the present, acknowledges the significant role West Virginia played in John Kennedy's political career. As Daniel B. Fleming Jr. says, "An irony in American politics is that in 1960 a poor, Protestant state in the Bible Belt made it possible for the first Roman Catholic to be elected president."[71]

The Return and the End

To celebrate the centennial of West Virginia, President John Kennedy returned in 1963 on his first official visit since his inauguration.

As a candidate in the state's primary, he had often cited a number of statistics detailing the economic distress of West Virginia, but as president he came with favorable numbers to tout. The state's unemployment had been cut in half, its job and income numbers were up, and the state no longer ranked last in getting defense contracts.

But the key to the president's address was acknowledgement of his political debt to the state, saying, "I would not be where I now am, I would not have some of the responsibilities which I now bear, if it had not been for the people of West Virginia."

The man who, as candidate, had always found room in his speeches to praise West Virginians did so again in a memorable line. "The sun does not always shine in West Virginia," Kennedy told the large crowd standing in the pouring rain, "but the people always do, and I am delighted to be here."[72]

He added more compliments as he spoke of West Virginia's history. "In many other places this crowd would long ago have gone home, but this state was born in a period of difficulty and tension. Three extraordinary events marked 1863—the birth of this state, the Emancipation Proclamation, and the battle of Gettysburg." He continued by declaring, "This state was born to turmoil. It has known sunshine and rain in a hundred years, but I know of no state, and I know this state well, whose people feel more strongly, who have a greater sense of pride in themselves, in their state and in their country, than the people of West Virginia. And I am proud to be here today."

The president closed with a nod to the state's motto, "Mountaineers are always free," saying, "I salute West Virginia and I join you, and I will carry on Saturday when I go to Europe the proud realization that not only mountaineers, but also Americans, are always free."[73]

The address was to be John F. Kennedy's last speech in West Virginia. The president would travel four months later to Texas and not come back alive. His assassination in November of 1963 would end the unlikely but very special relationship between the 35th president and the 35th state—a relationship that began with the primary that made a president.

NOTES

Introduction

1. John Kennedy (speech, Kennedy Library, Charleston, WV, June 22, 1963).
2. Ben Bradlee, "Now West Virginia," *Newsweek*, April 18, 1960, 35.
3. Ken Kurtz, "West Virginia History and Culture," W-SAZ, Primary Election Coverage, May 10, 1960. According to Kurtz, "Jack Kennedy's role as the underdog in West Virginia is a new one for the frontrunner for the Democratic nomination. His strength may hinge on a much publicized if little understood factor: how his Roman Catholic religion will sit at the polls with West Virginia's heavily Protestant voters. Kennedy has steadfastly denied that this religion should have or has had much influence on the election."
4. Kennedy won 236,505 votes to Humphrey's 152,187. J. Howard Myers, *West Virginia Blue Book 1960* (Charleston, WV: Jarrett, 1960), 723.
5. Harry Hoffmann, "Kennedy Win Gives His Driver Impetus," *Charleston Gazette*, May 12, 1960.
6. Helen O'Donnell with Kenneth O'Donnell Sr., *The Irish Brotherhood: John F. Kennedy, His Inner Circle, and the Improbable Rise to the Presidency* (Berkeley, CA: Counterpoint, 2015), 328–329.
7. Kenneth P. O'Donnell and David F. Powers, *Johnny We Hardly Knew Ye* (New York: Pocket Books, 1973), 200.
8. Ralph McGill, "Organization Won for Jack," *Charleston Gazette*, May 14, 1960.
9. Richard J. Whalen, *Founding Father: The Story of Joseph P. Kennedy* (New York: New American Library, 1964), 456.
10. McGill, "Organization."
11. Whalen, *Founding Father*, 457.
12. Ted Sorensen, *Kennedy: The Classic Biography,* (New York: Harper, 1965), 397, 404.
13. "When West Virginia Lost Its Voice," *USA Today*, October 27, 2013.
14. Don Marsh, "Jack Happy Fate Is Here," *Charleston Gazette,* May 4, 1960.
15. Richard N. Goodwin, *Remembering America: A Voice from the Sixties,* (Boston: Little, Brown and Co., 1988).
16. Editorial, "West Va. Will Be Winner," *Raleigh Register* (Beckley, WV), May 6, 1960.
17. Editorial, "West Va. Will Be Winner."
18. Don Marsh, "Jack Happy Fate Is Here," *Charleston Gazette*, May 4, 1960; "Collins Students Hear Sen. Kennedy," *Raleigh Register* (Beckley, WV), April 21, 1960; Sorenson, *Kennedy*, 140.

19. Ian C. Hartman, *In the Shadow of Boone and Crockett: Race, Culture, and the Politics of Representation in the Upland South* (Knoxville: University of Tennessee Press, 2015), 88–92, 158.

20. Boyd Creasman, *Writing West Virginia: Place, People, and Poverty in Contemporary Literature from the Mountain State* (Knoxville: University of Tennessee Press, 2016), 3–4.

21. L. T. Anderson, "Religious Issue," *Charleston Gazette*, May 10, 1960.

22. Denise Giardina, letter to author, March 8, 2002.

23. L. T. Anderson, "Religion Issue May Not Be Dead," *Charleston Gazette*, May 12, 1960.

24. Benjamin C. Bradlee, *Conversations With Kennedy* (New York: W.W. Norton & Company, 1975), 16.

25. "Man from Minnesota," *Time*, January 11, 1960; "Man from Massachusetts," *Time*, January 11, 1960; Carl Solberg, *Hubert Humphrey: A Biography* (New York: W.W. Norton, 1984), 34–46; Robert Dallek, *An Unfinished Life: John F. Kennedy, 1917–1963* (Boston: Little, Brown, and Company, 2003), 26–54.

26. William H. Lawrence, *Six Presidents, Too Many Wars* (New York: Saturday Review Press, 1972), 232.

27. Solberg, *Humphrey*, 34–46, 160–176.

28. Sorensen, *Kennedy*, 138, 144.

29. "Mrs. Frances Howard Honored at Ronceverte Dinner," *Beckley (WV) Post-Herald*, May 3, 1960. Humphrey's sister remembered the influence of her father in providing a solid political background, noting that while most children are read fairy tales at bedtime, her father used to read her the life of Thomas Jefferson and various other historical items. "My father was a William Jennings Bryan man and, although he was a druggist, I always said, 'With every pill he sold, he sold a new political idea.'" Albert Eisele, *Almost to the Presidency: A Biography of Two American Politicians* (Blue Earth, MN: Piper, 1972), 14–15.

30. Ralph McGill "One Straight, Other Folksy," *Charleston Gazette*, May 4, 1960.

31. "A Small State Takes the Limelight," *Life*, May 9, 1960.

32. Hugh Sidey, interview by Robert Rupp, May 8, 1992, Buckhannon, WV.

33. "Mrs. Frances Howard Honored."

34. Sidey, interview.

35. "Humphrey Insists He's an Underdog: Renews Attack on Kennedy Wealth as He Pushes His West Virginia Campaign," *New York Times*, April 27, 1960.

36. W. H. Lawrence, "Kennedy Backers in Debt, They Say: Supporters Report Spending 20% Less Than Humphrey Forces in West Virginian," *New York Times*, May 4, 1960.

37. Edson, "Mountain Feudin.'"

38. W. H. Lawrence, "Roosevelt Hits Humphrey," *New York Times*, May 7, 1960.

39. Lawless, "Ward Bond."

40. "A Study of Voter Attitude in West Virginian on Presidential Preferences," Lou Harris and Associates, January, 1960; O'Donnell and Powers, *Johnny*, 195.

41. Harry W. Ernst, *The Primary That Made a President: West Virginia 1960*, vol. 26 of *Eagleton Institute Cases in Practical Politics*, ed. Paul Tillett (Rutgers, NJ: McGraw-Hill, 1962), 5–7.

42. Ernst, *Primary*, 32. Although in 1968 Ernst would coauthor a favorable campaign biography on Hubert Humphrey, he believed that "too often during the campaign, Humphrey acted as if he were not a serious candidate." On the other hand, "the Kennedy camp missed few tricks. No possibility was too small to ignore."

43. Theodore H. White, *The Making of the President* (New York: Athenaeum House, 1961), 97–114.

44. Scott Porch, "The Book That Changed Campaigns Forever: How Teddy White Revolutionized Political Journalism," *Politico*, April 22, 2015, 5–7.

45. White, *Making*, 96–114.

46. Porch, "The Book That Changed Campaigns."

47. Stephen Ambrose, *Nixon: The Triumph of a Politician, 1962–1972* (New York: Simon & Schuster, 1989), 609.

48. Sorensen, *Kennedy*, 138–147.

49. Edmund F. Kallina Jr., *Kennedy v. Nixon: The Presidential Election of 1960* (Gainesville: University Press of Florida, 2010), 62–67; William Rorabaugh writes that his book (*The Real Making of the President*) offers "a corrective to White."

50. W. J. Rorabaugh, *The Real Making of the President: Kennedy, Nixon, and the 1960 Election* (Lawrence: University of Kansas Press, 2009).

51. Edmund F. Kallina, *Kennedy v. Nixon: The Presidential Election of 1960* (Gainesville, University of Florida Press, 2010), 61–67.

52. Thomas Oliphant and Curtis Wilkie, *The Road to Camelot: Inside JFK's Five-Year Campaign* (New York: Simon & Schuster, 2017), 21.

53. David A. Corbin, "John F. Kennedy Plays the 'Religious Card': Another Look at the 1960 West Virginia Primary," *West Virginia History: A Journal of Regional Studies* 9, no. 2 (2015).

54. Gary A. Donaldson, *The First Modern Campaign: Kennedy, Nixon, and the Election of 1960* (New York: Rowman & Littlefield, 2007), 60.

55. "Results of 1960 Presidential Election Primaries," John F. Kennedy Library, Boston, MA.

56. "Meeting West Virginia Primary, April 8, 1960," Robert F. Kennedy Pre-Administration Papers, Box 39, Memos: RFK Incoming, January 1960-August 1960, John F. Kennedy Library, Boston, MA.; Dan. B. Fleming, Jr., *Kennedy vs. Humphrey, West Virginia, 1960: The Pivotal Battle for the Democratic Presidential Nomination* (Jefferson, NC: McFarland, 1992), 32–33; O'Donnell and Powers, *Johnny*, 183–185.

57. John F. Kennedy, "Television as I See It: A Force That Has Changed the Political Scene," *TV Guide*, November 14, 1959. 5–8. The senator noted how the new technology illuminated political personalities, and the more congenial, compassionate, and intelligent candidate would fare better than a bombastic orator. Advice that he would follow in his televised debate

Chapter 1

1. Rorabaugh, *Real Making*, 43.

2. Douglas W. Johnson, Paul R. Picard, and Bernard Quinn, *Churches and church Membership in the United States: An Enumeration by Region, State, and County, 1971* (Washington, DC: Glenmary Research Center, 1974), 218–21, table 3.

3. W. H. Lawrence, "Kennedy Tackles Issue Of Religion: Meets Anti-Catholic Feeling in West Virginia Visit—Statement Applauded," *New York Times*, April 12, 1960; "Humphrey, in Coal Fields Tour, Feels Like 'Triumphant Caesar,'" *New York Times*, April 12, 1960.

4. Henry Clay McDougal, *Recollections, 1844–1909* (Kansas City, MO: Franklin Hudson, 1910), 146.

5. Phil Conley and William Thomas Doherty, *West Virginia History* (Charleston, WV: Education Foundation, 1974), 207–248; Otis K. Rice and Stephen W. Brown, "History of West Virginia" in *The West Virginia Encyclopedia*, ed. Ken Sullivan (Charleston, WV: West Virginia Humanities Council, 2006), 337–339; Louis H. Manarin, "Sectionalism and the Virginias," in Sullivan, *West Virginia Encyclopedia*, 646.

6. Richard A. Brisbin Jr., et al., *West Virginia Politics and Government* (Lincoln: University of Nebraska Press, 2008), 19–22; Charles Henry Ambler, *Sectionalism in Virginia from 1776–1861* (New York: Russell & Russell, 1964), 175–218, 273–299.

7. Robert Rupp, "Politics," in Sullivan, *West Virginia Encyclopedia*, 575–576.

8. Rupp, "Politics," 575–576.

9. John Alexander Williams, *West Virginia: A History* (Charleston: West Virginia Press, 2001), 203. The history of Virginia has been characterized by sectional antagonism—the natural features of her territory and the different elements of her politics and population made such conflicts inevitable. Ambler, *Sectionalism in Virginia*, 3.

10. John C. Campbell, *The Southern Highlander and His Homeland* (Lexington: University of Kentucky Press, 1908). This book promoted the lasting image of Appalachia as a region apart, an "other" in the heart of America.

11. Henry D. Shapiro, *Appalachia on Our Mind: The Southern Mountains and Mountaineers in the American Consciousness, 1870–1920* (Chapel Hill: University of North Carolina Press, 1978). Shapiro's pathbreaking study of Appalachia traced the effort to portray the region as myth.

12. Ronald L. Lewis, *Transforming the Appalachian Countryside: Railroads, Deforestation, and Social Change in West Virginia* (Chapel Hill: University of North Carolina Press, 1998); Ronald D. Eller, *Miners, Millhands, and Mountaineers: The Industrialization of the Appalachian South* (Knoxville: University of Tennessee Press, 1982); Dwight B. Billings, "Introduction: Writing Appalachia: Old Ways, New Ways, and WVU Ways," in *Culture, Class, and Politics in Modern Appalachia*, ed. Jennifer Egolf, Ken Fones-Wolf, and Louis C. Martin (Morgantown: West Virginia University Press, 2009).

13. Ronald L. Lewis, "Beyond Isolation and Homogeneity: Diversity and the History of Appalachia," in *Back Talk from Appalachia: Confronting Stereotypes*, ed. Dwight

B. Billings, Gurney Norman, and Katherine Ledford (Lexington: University of Kentucky Press, 1999), 37.

14. John Gaventa, *Power and Powerlessness: Quiescence and Rebellion in an Appalachian Valley* (Urbana: University of Illinois Press, 1980); James Green, *The Devil Is Here in These Hills: West Virginia's Coal Miners and Their Battle for Freedom* (New York: Atlantic Monthly Press, 2015).

15. Rupp, "Politics," 576–577.

16. Brisbin et al., *West Virginia Politics*, 22.

17. Rupp, "Politics," 576–577.

18. Rupp, "Politics," 575–576. Democratic domination would continue through the twentieth century. With two exceptions (Cecil Underwood and Arch Moore), all the governors during this period (1932–2000) were Democrats.

19. Rupp, "Politics," 575–576. See also Rupp, "Democratic Party," 191, and "Republican Party," 612–13 in Sullivan, *West Virginia Encyclopedia*.

20. Don Chapman, interview by Robert Rupp, March 10, 1990, Welch, McDowell County, West Virginia.

21. Rupp, "Politics," 191. One could argue that the decentralized nature of the state party and lack of all powerful politicians enabled the Democratic Party to weather several internal crises in West Virginia, including the 1950s controversy surrounding Governor Marland's attempt to impose major taxes on the coal industry.

22. Daniel B. Fleming, *Kennedy vs. Humphrey, West Virginia, 1960: The Pivotal Battle for the Democratic Presidential Nomination* (Jefferson, NC: McFarland, 1992), 14–15. The election of 1956 proved to be an electoral aberration. Democrats would rebound in 1960, retaking the governorship and supporting the Democratic presidential ticket while retaining control of the legislature.

23. Lawrence O'Brien, *No Final Victories: A Life in Politics—from John F. Kennedy to Watergate* (New York: Doubleday & Co., 1974), 67. "Sheriffs and county clerks controlled patronage, but presidential candidates meant little or nothing to them."

24. Base map, US Geological Survey, West Virginia.

25. Myers, ed., *West Virginia Blue Book 1960*, 710.

26. Brisbin et al., *West Virginia Politics*, 105–115. The prohibition against reelection was a carryover from the Virginia constitution. It was lifted in the 1970s by a constitutional amendment.

27. Brisbin et al., *West Virginia Politics*, 220–231.

28. White, *Making*, 97. White excludes from this list the "baroque courthouse states of the South."

29. H. John Rogers, "Political Corruption," in Sullivan, *West Virginia Encyclopedia*, 574–575.

30. Jack Canfield, "William Barron," in Sullivan, *West Virginia Encyclopedia*, 44–45; Richard Grimes, "Arch Moore," in Sullivan, *West Virginia Encyclopedia*, 496–497.

31. Don Wilson, "In Logan County, the Half-Pint Vote, Slating and Lever Brothers," *Life*, May 9, 1960, 26–27.

32. Wilson, "Half-Pint Vote," *Life*, 26–27.

33. Fleming, *Kennedy vs. Humphrey*, 12–13.

34. Fleming, *Kennedy vs. Humphrey*, 14.

35. "Voters Urged to Study Sample Ballot in Advance," *Charleston Gazette*, May 5, 1960.

36. "Sample Ballot: The Democratic Party Primary Election May 10, 1960," *Charleston Gazette*, May 8, 1960.

37. White, *Making*, 99–100.

38. Wilson, "Half-Pint Vote,"; "National Magazine Takes Look at 'Bible Belt': Vote Buying, Bigotry Seen in Logan," *Charleston Gazette*, May 6, 1960.

39. Rorabaugh, *Real Making*, 54.

40. Chapman interview.

41. Bob Barrie, telephone interview with Daniel B. Fleming, September 4, 1985, cited in Fleming, *Kennedy*, 122.

42. Ray Chafin and Topper Sherwood, *Just Good Politics: The Life of Raymond Chafin, Appalachian Boss* (Pittsburgh: University of Pittsburgh Press, 1994), 130–50.

43. Ken Kurtz, panel discussion, "Celebrating the Primary that Made a President," Division of Culture and History and West Virginia Wesleyan College, Charleston, West Virginia, May 15, 1990.

44. Hubert Humphrey, *The Education of a Public Man: My Life and Politics* (New York: Doubleday, 1976), 157–58, 216.

45. Fleming, *Kennedy vs. Humphrey*, 121.

46. O'Brien, *No Final Victories: A Life in Politics—from John F. Kennedy to Watergate* (New York: Doubleday & Co., 1974), 68–69.

47. "A Plunge into Eyewash," *Time* 59, no. 7 (February 18, 1952): 20.

48. "Democratic Hopefuls," *Time* 72, no. 21 (November 24, 1958): 15–18. Senate majority leader Lyndon Johnson, Missouri senator Stuart Symington, and former presidential nominee Adlai Stevenson did not enter any primaries.

49. White, *Making*, 54–56.

50. White, *Making*, 32–34; Humphrey, *Education*, 149

51. White, *Making*, 55–56. The Mountain State was attractive because it was "a state of vast unemployment, an attractive battleground, and far enough from home so that regional victory there would make Humphrey's appeal seen nationwide."

52. Sorensen, *Kennedy*, 141.

53. Robert Ajemian, "Hubert's Zeal, Jack's Box Score of Delegates, Enthusiastic Catholics," *Life*, March 28, 1960, 29; Sorensen, *Kennedy*, 138.

54. Harry Hoffman, "Primary Won't Elect a President," *Charleston Gazette*, January 26, 1960.

55. "A Study of Voter Attitudes in West Virginia on Presidential Preferences," Louis Harris and Associates, John F. Kennedy Library, January 1960. The poll began on December 10, 1959, and ended at the end of the first week of January 1960. Harris's organization conducted 1,050 interviews in West Virginia, 690 of which were in depth. Among Democratic voters, Adlai Stevenson had a slight lead over Kennedy, but with Stevenson out Kennedy had an almost two-to-one margin over his

chief opponent, Lyndon Johnson. With Humphrey trailing far behind, Kennedy appeared to gather almost half of the Stevenson vote.

	With Undecided In	With Undecided Out
Kennedy	54%	70%
Humphrey	23	30
Undecided	23	—

56. Louis Harris and Associates, "A Study of Voter Attitudes in West Virginia," January 1960, Box 818, PPP, Senate Files.

57. "Strategic Warpath in Wisconsin," *Life*, March 28, 1960, 22.

58. White, *Making*, 94–95; "Results of Presidential Primaries in 1960" and "Results of the 16 Presidential Primaries in 1960," Box 26, David F. Powers Personal Papers, John F. Kennedy Library, Boston, MA.

59. Joseph Alsop, "Wisconsin Results," *Washington Post*, April 1, 1960, 4.

60. White, *Making*, 95.

61. O'Donnell and Powers, *Johnny*, 183; White, *Making*, 94.

62. Chalmers M. Roberts, *First Rough Draft: A Journalist's Journal of our Times* (New York: Praeger, 1973), 179; Henry Cathcart, "Bitterness Develops in W.V. Primary," *In Inside Washington: March of Events, Clarksburg Exponent*, May 3, 1960; Evelyn Lincoln, *My Twelve years with John F. Kennedy* (New York: McKay Co., 1965), 137.

63. Lincoln, *My Twelve Years*, 137.

64. O'Donnell and Powers, *Johnny*, 183.

65. O'Donnell and Powers, *Johnny*, 184–185.

66. O'Donnell and Powers, *Johnny*, 183–185.

67. O'Donnell and Powers, *Johnny*, 185.

68. "Meeting Re: West Virginia Primary, April 8, 1960," Robert F. Kennedy Pre-Administration Papers, Box 39, Memos: RFK Incoming, January 1960–August 1960, John F. Kennedy Library, Boston, MA.

69. White, *Making*, 101.

70. Sid Christie, oral history interview, July 16, 1964, John F. Kennedy Library. Christie's daughter married a Catholic and was told by her father to convert in order to have unity. So his attitude was different from Logan County judge C. C. Chambers—a Mason and openly anti-Catholic.

71. Robert P. McDonough, oral history interview, December 5–6, 1965, John F. Kennedy Library. Not well known statewide, McDonough had a taciturn personality and a businesslike demeanor that disdained small talk and demanded direct answers. After the general election, he became the "West Virginia's key link to the White House." O'Donnell and Powers, *Johnny*, 50.

72. O'Donnell and Powers, *Johnny*, 183.

73. McDonough, oral history interview.

74. O'Brien, *No Final Victories*, 67.

75. McDonough, oral history interview.

76. O'Brien, *No Final Victories*, 67.

77. Memorandum, Ted Sorensen and Bob Wallace to John F. Kennedy, April 22, 1959, Box 969, fol. West Virginia: Organization, 18 February 1959–27 April 1960, PPP, Presidential Campaign Files, 1960..

78. Memorandum, Ted Sorensen and Bob Wallace to John F. Kennedy, April 22, 1959, Box 969, fol. West Virginia: Organization, 18 February 1959–27 April 1960, PPP, Presidential Campaign Files, 1960.

79. Memorandum, Bob Wallace to Robert F. Kennedy, January 5, 1960, Box 969, PPP, Presidential Campaign Files, 1960. First: Ralph Pryor of Wellsburg; second: Jack Morton of Webster Springs; third: Benjamin Stout of Clarksburg; fourth: Bruce Hoff of Parkersburg; fifth: Laurence Tierney of Bluefield; sixth: Mrs. Charles Peters of Charleston. It is interesting to note that the Sixth District, which included Charleston, was headed by delegate Mrs. Charles G. Peters, mother of key supporter and future delegate Charles Peters.

80. Wallace, memorandum. In this memo, Bob Wallace proposed bold organizational goals for "West Virginians for Kennedy." His plan proposed selecting two people in each of the 55 counties who in turn would pick five to ten assistants. The plan envisioned 110 cochairs, at least 275 assistants, and thousands of contact cards.

81. Fred Forbes to Robert McDonough, memorandum, March 27, 1960, West Virginia Campaign Files, John F. Kennedy Library, Boston, MA.

82. Dan. B. Fleming Jr., *Kennedy vs. Humphrey, West Virginia, 1960: The Pivotal Battle for the Democratic Presidential Nomination* (Jefferson, NC: McFarland, 1992), 119–22.

83. Chafin and Sherwood, *Just Good Politics*, 130–150; Fleming, *Kennedy vs. Humphrey*, 104.

84. Matt Reese Jr., interview by Robert Rupp, May 5, 1990, Boston, MA. Reese, a former head of the Young Democrats, became the first paid employee of the West Virginians for Kennedy organization in late 1959 and was hired full-time in early 1960 with the title of executive director.

85. White, *Making*, 103.

86. William L. Jacobs, oral history interview, July 6, 1964, John F. Kennedy Library; "Claims W. Va. Insult: Says Kennedy Downgrades Intelligence," *Clarksburg (WV) Exponent*, April 18, 1960.

87. "Sen, Wylie to Head Kennedy Campaign," *Charleston Gazette*, April 7, 1960; Fleming, *Kennedy vs. Humphrey*, 21.

88. Fleming, *Kennedy vs. Humphrey*, 21; Homer Bussa (United Steelworkers, Wheeling, WV) letter to Frank Hoffman (United Steelworkers, Washington, DC), January 22, 1960, Box 968, fol. West Virginia: Labors, 23 December 1959–7 April 1960, PPP, Presidential Campaign Files, 1960.

89. Fleming Jr., *Kennedy vs. Humphrey*, 21; Sorensen and Wallace to Kennedy, memorandum.

90. Harry Hoffman, "'Poll Came Out As Byrd Wanted,'" *Charleston Gazette* (Charleston, WV), March 1, 1960; "Sen. Byrd's Poll Favoring Johnson Ruffles Democrats," *Charleston Gazette* (Charleston, WV), March 1, 1960; "Byrd Defends Disputed

Poll of Democrats," *Charleston Gazette* (Charleston, WV), March 4, 1960; Thomas
Stafford, "Byrd Steering Mighty Shaky Craft," *Charleston Gazette* (Charleston, WV),
April 17, 1960.

Chapter 2

1. Stacey Bredhoff, *Winning West Virginia: JFK's Primary Campaign* (Washington,
   DC: Foundation for the National Archive, 2010), 15.
2. Dave Powers, interview by Robert Rupp, May 5, 1990, Boston, MA.
3. "The Campaign of Issues," *Time* 75, no. 1 (February 15, 1960): 22.
4. "Transcript: JFK's Speech on Religion," NPR, last modified December 5, 2007,
   https://www.npr.org/templates/story/story.php?storyId=16920600.
5. Mark S. Massa, *Anti-Catholicism in America: The Last Acceptable Prejudice* (New
   York: Crossroads Publishing Co., 2003), 83–85.
6. "JFK's Speech on Religion," NPR.
7. Sorensen, *Kennedy*, 299. The format in Houston differed dramatically from his
   May 8 telecast to West Virginia voters. For the Charleston broadcast he was in
   a studio with no audience and answering prepared questions from a friendly
   anchor. But in Houston, Kennedy spoke with Protestant ministers and submitted
   himself to any questions a skeptical if not hostile audience might ask.
8. "The Defeat of the Happy Warrior," *Time*, April 18, 1960, 19.
9. Jay Dolan, "The Right of a Catholic to Be President," *Notre Dame Magazine*, Au-
   tumn 2008, https://magazine.nd.edu/news/1155; Christopher M. Finan, *Alfred E.
   Smith: The Happy Warrior* (New York: Hill and Wang, 2002), 215.
10. Robert A. Slayton, *Empire Statesman: The Rise and Redemption of Al Smith* (New
    York: Free Press, 2001), xii; Matthew Josephson, Hannah Josephson, and Frances
    Perkins, *Al Smith: Hero of the Cities* (Boston; Houghton Mifflin, 1969), 383.
11. Alfred E. Smith, *Campaign Addresses of Governor Alfred E. Smith* (Washington,
    DC: Democratic National Committee, 1929), 43–59; Robert A. Slayton, "Smith
    and Kennedy," 210–23. Smith's Oklahoma City speech was a single shot leveled at
    a historic and pervasive prejudice. It was an ineffective effort delivered in a hostile
    territory without evidence of careful planning or a plan for follow-through.
12. Finan, *Happy Warrior*, 217; "Straton Raps Smith in Oklahoma City," *New York
    Times*, September 22, 1928.
13. Marc Schulman "1928 Election Results Hoover vs. Smith." History Central. Ac-
    cessed March 17, 2019 https://www.historycentral.com/elections/1928.html
14. O'Donnell and Powers, *Johnny*, 182.
15. Paul A. Carter, "The Campaign of 1928 Re-Examined: A Study in Political Folk-
    lore," *Wisconsin Magazine of History* 46, no. 4 (Summer 1963): 263–272.
16. Fletcher Knebel, "Democratic Forecast: A Catholic in 1960," *Look* 23 (March 3,
    1959): 13–17.
17. Thomas J. Carty, *A Catholic in White House? Religion, Politics, and John F. Kenne-
    dy's Presidential Campaign* (New York: Palgrave Macmillan, 2004), 27.

18. Knebel, "Democratic Forecast," 13–17.

19. Abigail McCarthy, *Private Faces: Public Places* (Garden City, NY: Doubleday & Co., 1972), 236.

20. Carty, "Catholic," 27.

21. Joe Alsop told John Kennedy of an encounter he had with McCarthy when riding on a plane in 1960. When Alsop objected to McCarthy telling anti-Kennedy stories, the Minnesota senator went off in a pout to read his Missal. Jack responded with a P.J. Kennedy story." Well Joe, he said to Alsop, "my grandfather always used to say, 'Always mistrust a Catholic politician who reads his Missal on a trolley car.'" Peter Collier and David Horowitz, *The Kennedys: An American Drama* (New York: Encounter Books, 1984), 309n. Of McCarthy, Bobby Kennedy quipped that "He felt he should have been the first Catholic president because he knew more the teachings of St. Thomas Aquinas better than my brother..." (309).

22. Michael O'Brien, *John F. Kennedy: A Biography* (New York: St. Martin's Press, 2005), 419. Just as interesting as the criticism from Catholics over his policy positions was the criticism by Protestants over his implied dismissal of the role of religion in his actions. Martin Marty, associate editor of the liberal *Christian Century*, called Kennedy "spiritually rootless and politically almost disturbingly secular."

23. Knebel, "Democratic Forecast," 13–17.

24. Matt Reese, oral interview, October 24, 1964, John F. Kennedy Presidential Library. According to Reese, Ken O'Donnell asked him, "Why the hell did you get a Catholic for the invocation? We're trying to duck this Catholic issue as much as we can."

25. Patricia Barrett, *Religious Liberty and the American Presidency: A Study in Church-State Relations* (New York: Herder and Herder, 1963), 270.

26. Carty, "Catholic," 172.

27. Doris Fleeson, "Religion Useful in '56," *Charleston Gazette*, April 2, 1960.

28. O'Donnell and Powers, *Johnny*, 183–84.

29. White, *Making*, 106. The Kennedy campaign camp had remained divided on the confrontational strategy. West Virginians and pollster Lou Harris had urged the candidate to tackle the issue head-on, while his Washington staff believed that the issue was too explosive to address in public.

30. O'Donnell and Powers, *Johnny*, 191. "When we got into the car to drive to the next town on our schedule, Kennedy said, 'How did it go?' . . . 'I could see that he was pleased with himself. He talked again about his religion and the right of a Catholic to run for the president at every other stop that day, and in almost every speech that he made from then on until the primary.'"

31. Herb Little, "Angry Sen. Kennedy Brings Up Religion," *Charleston Daily Mail*, April 19, 1960.

32. Herb Little, "Kennedy Shifts Tactics Discusses Religion Issue," *Beckley (WV) Post-Herald*, April 19, 1960.

33. Kathleen Hall Jamieson, *Packaging the Presidency: A History and Criticism of Presidential Campaign Advertising* (New York: Oxford University Press, 1992), 128–29.

34. White, *Making*, 323; "Dr. Peale Unconvinced Kennedy Free of Church," *Clarksburg (WV) Exponent*, April 13, 1960.

35. Cleveland Amory quoted in Herbert S. Parmet, *Jack: The Struggles of John F. Kennedy* (New York: Dial Press, 1980), 515.

36. L. T. Anderson, "In Reverse; They're Trying to Shame Us Into a Kennedy Vote," *Charleston Gazette-Mail*, April 17, 1960.

37. White, *Making*, 106–107.

38. "Byrd Says Kennedy Made Religion Issue, "*New York Times*, April 22, 1960. He said he would not support Kennedy even if the candidate was a missionary Baptist. The second part of Byrd's charge also appeared true, for the Kennedy camp was preparing an alibi in case he lost. Such an excuse was provided daily in the national press's focus on bigotry. The alibi was also aided by a *Life* article that portrayed the corruption and bigotry in Logan County.

39. White, *Making*, 108.

40. "Kennedy Side Accused of Viewing West Virginia Foes as Intolerant," *Clarksburg (WV) Exponent*, April 19, 1960; Jacobs, oral history interview.

41. "The Kennedy Speech," *New York Times*, April 22, 1960; "Texts of Speeches by Kennedy, Symington and Humphrey at Editors' Conventions," *New York Times*, April 22, 1960.

42. "Texts of Speeches," *New York Times*, April 22, 1960.

43. White, *Making*, 96

44. National Editors Association speech, April 21, 1960; John F. Kennedy; "The Religious Issue in American Politics," *U.S. News and World Report*, May 2, 1960, 92.

45. James Reston, "How to Clear the Air and Muddy the Waters," *New York Times*, April 22, 1960.

46. Doris Fleeson, "Religion Useful in '56," *Charleston Gazette*, April 2, 1960. "The relevant point today is that the Sorensen memorandum was not a hidden persuader, clandestinely employed. It was openly and cleanly used to strengthen Kennedy's case. Among those was John Bailey, Dem. State chairman active in 1960."

47. John F. Kennedy, "Religion Advertisement #1, Divided Loyalties," Spring 1960, Directed by Jack Denove, Phil Smith Collection, West Virginia State Archives, Charleston, WV.

48. Donahue interview, May 12, 1990.

49. John F. Kennedy, "Religion Advertisement #2, Morris Harvey College," Spring 1960, Directed by Jack Denove, Phil Smith Collection, West Virginia State Archives, Charleston, WV.

50. Kennedy, "Religion Advertisement #2, Morris Harvey College." The ad summarized Shepard's question. Rather than recording him asking it, the ad said, "Here is Walton Sheppard-Charleston, attorney, asking in effect how the senator's religion will affect his duties as president."

51. Kennedy, "Religion Advertisement #2, Morris Harvey College."

52. Kennedy, "Religion Advertisement #2, Morris Harvey College."

53. Franklin Delano Roosevelt Jr., "Religion Advertisement #1," Spring 1960, Directed by

Jack Denove, Phil Smith Collection, West Virginia State Archives, Charleston, WV. "My friends, my family came here in 1621 to escape religious persecution in Europe. I have been brought up to believe that the Constitution means what it says—that every citizen has the right to worship or not to worship as he sees best for himself."

54. Franklin Delano Roosevelt Jr., "Religion Advertisement #2," Spring 1960, Directed by Jack Denove, Phil Smith Collection, West Virginia State Archives, Charleston, WV.
55. Jamieson, *Packaging*, 126–127. Roosevelt Jr. started the program asking other questions, but three to four minutes into the broadcast, he asked the first of many questions on religion, which would take up ten to twelve minutes.
56. Sorensen, *Kennedy*, 145.
57. Jamieson, *Packaging*, 126; Sorensen, *Kennedy*, 139.
58. White, *Making*, 107–8.
59. Garry Wills, *Bare Ruined Choirs* (Garden City, NY: Doubleday, 1972), 91.
60. Arthur Schlesinger Jr, *Robert Kennedy and His Times* (Boston: Mariner, 1978), 17, 600–602; Albert J. Menendez, *John F. Kennedy: Catholic and Humanist* (Buffalo, NY: Prometheus Books), 66–67. Menendez argues that Kennedy "made some sort of intellectual accommodation with his heredity faith before embarking on his political career." And that he "accepted the religion he had inherited without feeling either superior or inferior about it. He never apologized for his religion nor did he boast about it."
61. Sorensen, *Kennedy*, 19. As president, Kennedy would shake hands with Pope Paul rather than kiss his ring. 365.
62. Sorensen, *Kennedy*, 19.
63. Arthur M. Schlesinger Jr., *A Thousand Days: John F. Kennedy in the White House* (Boston: Houghton Mifflin, 1965), 20.

Chapter 3

1. Fleming Jr., *Kennedy vs. Humphrey*, 32–33; O'Donnell and Powers, *Johnny*, 183–185.
2. O'Donnell and Powers, *Johnny*, 183.
3. "Meeting Re: West Virginia Primary, April 8, 1960," Box 39, fol. Memos: RFK Incoming, January 1960–August 1960, Robert F. Kennedy Pre-Administration Papers.
4. "Tough Testing Ground," *Time* 75, no. 1 (March 28, 1960): 23.
5. Bradlee, "Now West Virginia."
6. "Remarks of Senator John F. Kennedy in Welch, West Virginia, May 3, 1960," Box 909, PPP, Senate Files.
7. "Remarks of Senator John F. Kennedy in Welch, West Virginia, May 3, 1960," Box 909, PPP, Senate Files.
8. "Remarks of Senator John F. Kennedy in Welch, West Virginia, May 3, 1960," Box 909, PPP, Senate Files.
9. Mary Chilton Abbot, "Mary Chilton Abbot's Washington Watch: Ike's Memory Short on W. Va," *Charleston Gazette*, May 2, 1960. "Cecil Given Vow by Ike," *Charleston Gazette*, May 5, 1960.

10. "Kennedy Chides Governor in Third Visit to Beckley," *Beckley (WV) Post-Herald*, May 6, 1960.

11. Herb Little, "Kennedy Bewails Lack of Proper Food for Needy," *Charleston Daily Mail*, April 20, 1960; John F. Kennedy, Mt. Hope speech. He tied this issue, as he would do many others, to the Cold War. "Why should there be hungry people in this state," he asked, "while $9 billion worth of surplus is rotting in warehouses? . . . Why should miners be out of work, and mines and mills be idle at a time when this nation needs all of its powers and energies to match the growing menace of the Soviet Union?"

12. John F. Kennedy, "Economic Advertisement #3, Slab Fork Mine," Spring 1960, Directed by Jack Denove, Phil Smith Collection, West Virginia State Archives, Charleston, WV.

13. "Underwood Sees Concern for State Purely Political," *Charleston Gazette*, May 10, 1960. Senator Kennedy did not endorse Humphrey's bill to make the food stamp plan mandatory in industrial areas of chronic unemployment and in rural areas of low farm income. Governor Underwood argued that Humphrey's bill would have little impact since it would not increase the amounts of surplus foods or the quantity and variety. Or increase the number of individuals or families eligible to receive food. On the other hand, the plan would place the costs of distribution on the federal government.

14. James A, Haught, "Humphrey Purchases Monthly Allotment of Commodity at Charleston Grocery," *Charleston Gazette*, April 28, 1960. "Here's what they are," he said. "Ten pounds of flour, five pounds of corn meal, one pound of lard, one pound of rice, 13 ounces of dry eggs and four and a half pounds of dry milk. I'll let the people themselves judge how adequate a diet that is for a month."

15. Thomas F, Stafford, "Kennedy, Humphrey Attack Ike, Nixon on TV Debate," *Charleston Gazette*, May 5, 1960. There would not be a visual aid brought to a presidential televised campaign debate until Ross Perot attempted to bring a chart to the presidential debate during the 1992 general election.

16. Hartman, *In the Shadow*, 88–96.

17. Sorensen, *Kennedy*, 136, 148.

18. Don Marsh, "Jack Happy Fate Is Here," *Charleston Daily Mail*, May 4, 1960.

19. "Huge Crowd Greets Kennedy: Candidate, Wife Meet Local Voters," *Morgantown (WV) Post*, April 19, 1960. Kennedy said the president is responsible for the freedom of the United States, and he should be a representative of the people.

20. "Bob Kennedy Returns," *Clarksburg (WV) Exponent*, April 26, 1960.

21. Herb Little, "Jack Continues Blast of Administration," *Charleston Gazette*, April 26, 1960.

22. "Memo from Lou Harris on the Last Week's Campaigning," n.d., Box 27, David R. Powers Personal Papers, John F. Kennedy Library, Boston, MA; "A Ten Point Program for West Virginia," April 25, 1960, Box 535, Pre-Presidential Papers, Presidential Campaign Files, 1960, John F. Kennedy Library, Boston, MA (hereafter cited as PPP).

23. "Humphrey Proposes Solution to Coal Problems, Mine-Mouth Power Stations 'Could' Provide the Answer," *Morgantown (WV) Dominion News*, May 6, 1960.

24. Thomas F. Stafford, "Humphrey Finds Cheer," *Sunday Gazette-Mail* (Charleston, WV), April 10, 1960. During the last week of the campaign, Humphrey offered a ten-point program. Among his recommendations was a "a federal commission that would provide a plan for new coal uses and markets."

25. Kennedy, "Economic Advertisement #3, Slab Fork Mine."

26. "Economic Advertisement #3, Slab Fork Mine." In addition to the Slab Fork television commercial, the Kennedy campaign made two more ads that featured the coal industry and Kennedy's plan to protect and promote it.

27. L.T. Anderson, "Kennedy Promise," *Charleston Gazette*, May 2, 1960. Bobby Kennedy stressed this theme when he spoke at Clarksburg. "We had the same economic problems in the state of Massachusetts that you have here in West Virginia," he declared, and then stated that "A friendly president can do the same thing for West Virginia. We had greater unemployment at one time since the war than you now have in West Virginia. It was because of the work of my brother, chiefly with the help of other members of Congress from Massachusetts, that Massachusetts was able to revitalize itself." Bobby Kennedy also pointed out that "West Virginia has never had a major role to play in selecting a nominee before," but this time they could do it. "If my brother gets to the White House," Bobby declared, "it is going to be because of West Virginia."

28. "Memo from Lou Harris."

29. Don Marsh, "Aid for State Is Pledged By Kennedy," *Charleston Gazette*, May 10, 1960.

30. "Wiseman to Serve as Co-Chair for Kennedy, Mrs. Humphrey to Meet Many People Here," *Clarksburg (WV) Exponent,* April 16, 1960. "He would sit for hours and talk to me of his personal hero, Franklin Delano Roosevelt. . . . 'That's the man on whose life I want to pattern mine.'"

31. "Humphrey's Address to the State Legislature," West Virginia Film Archives, March 10, 1960.

32. Arthur Edson, "Hubert, Kennedy Return to Stump: Humphrey Strikes 'Poor Man's' Theme," *Charleston Gazette*, April 26, 1960.

33. Thomas F. Stafford, "Humphrey Finds Cheer," *Sunday Gazette-Mail* (Charleston, WV), April 10, 1960; Mary Chilton Abbot, "Sen. Humphrey Speaks His Mind," *Sunday Gazette-Mail* (Charleston, WV), April 17, 1960. Humphrey said that the purpose of the proposal was "to develop and improve our great natural resources, our forests, our lakes, our streams, our parks."

34. "Sen. Kennedy Urges W.Va. 'New Deal,'" *Parkersburg (WV) News*, April 12, 1960; "And Now Is the Time," press release, April 12, 1960, Box 989, PPP.

35. JFK to Fellow Democrats, April 18, 1960, Box 989, PPP.

36. John F. Kennedy, "Economic Advertisement #2," Spring 1960, Directed by Jack Denove, Phil Smith Collection, West Virginia State Archives, Charleston, WV.

37. Peter Lisagor, oral history interview, April 22, 1966, John F. Kennedy Library.

38. Doris Kearns Goodwin, *The Fitzgeralds and the Kennedys: An American Saga* (New York: Simon and Schuster, 1987), 799.

39. Don Marsh, "Aid for State Is Pledged by Kennedy," *Charleston Gazette*, May 10, 1960.

40. Franklin Delano Roosevelt Jr., "Cabin Creek Advertisement #1, Economy," Spring 1960, Directed by Jack Denove, Phil Smith Collection, West Virginia State Archives, Charleston, WV.

41. Roosevelt Jr., "Cabin Creek Advertisement #1, Economy."

42. *Charleston Gazette*, May 10, 1960. The ads featured a picture of FDR and a signed endorsement by FDR Jr. At the bottom it said, "VOTE FOR WEST VIRGINIA VOTE FOR KENNEDY FOR PRESIDENT TOMORROW."

43. "Gridiron Club," *Washington Post*, March 15, 1960; Herbert S. Parmet, *Jack: The Struggles of John F. Kennedy* (New York: Dial Press, 1980), 508.

44. White, *Making*, 92–93.

45. Kate Clifford Larson, *Rosemary: The Hidden Kennedy Daughter* (New York: Houghton Mifflin. 2015), 160–65, 180, 173–192; Peter Collier and David Horowitz, *The Kennedys: An American Drama* (New York: Encounter Press, 2002), 94–95. Rosemary lived to the age of 86, staying at a house on the grounds of an institution in Jefferson, Wisconsin.

46. "The Tragic Story of . . . the Daughter JFK's Mother Had to Give Up," *National Enquirer*, November 5, 1967. Even as late as 1967, the public was not aware of the full story.

47. Rorabaugh, *Real Making*, 253; "On, Wisconsin," *Time*, April 4, 1960, 14.

48. Doris Fleeson, "Money Also Big Issue," *Charleston Gazette*, April 8, 1960.

49. Ralph G. Martin, *Seeds of Destruction: Joe Kennedy and his Sons* (New York: G.P. Putnam's Sons, 1995); Whalen, *Founding Father*, 456. Not only did the father avoid any appearance during his son's run for the nomination, but he was also not present when the family clustered around the candidate at the Los Angeles convention after John won the nomination. As his wife, sons, daughters, and in-laws went to the podium, Joe was watching it on television at the mansion of Marion Davies. Joe would not appear in public with his son until after the general election in November.

50. Rose Kennedy, *Times to Remember* (Garden City, New York: Doubleday & Company, 1974), 363–364. See her obituary from the *Boston Globe*: https://www.jfklibrary.org/learn/about-jfk/the-kennedy-family/rose-fitzgerald-kennedy.

51. "Kennedy Sisters in Lewis," *Charleston Gazette*, May 1, 1960.

52. David Barnett, "Kennedy is Mining Votes With His Change in Tactics," *Charleston Gazette*, April 21, 1960; Laurence Leamer, *The Kennedy Women: The Saga of an American Family* (New York: Fawcett Books, 1996), 498.

53. Kennedy's Sister to Visit Mullens," *Beckley (WV) Post-Herald*, May 5, 1960; "Kennedy's Sister, Mrs. Shribere [sic], is Feted in Pineville," *Beckley (WV) Post-Herald*, May 9, 1960; "Kennedy's Sister, Mrs. Shribere [sic], Honored in Oceana," *Beckley (WV) Post-Herald*, May 10, 1960.

54. On Campaign Trail, https://www.saturdayeveningpost.com/2014/04/on-the-campaign-trail/ Last accessed April 21, 2019.

55. Jean M. Rhodes, "Mrs. Humphrey Is for Candidacy," *Charleston Gazette*, November 23, 1959.

56. Charlie Peters, *Tilting At Windmills: An Autobiography* (Reading, MA: Addison-Wesley, 2002), 55.

57. O'Donnell and Powers, *Johnny*, 188–189.
58. Gary A. Donaldson, *The First Modern Campaign: Kennedy, Nixon, and the Election of 1960* (New York: Rowman & Littlefield, 2009), 55. Her campaign skills captured media attention. A reporter noted that when the candidate's wife learned that a "nice old man said he would love to meet Jackie, but could not leave his invalid wife," she went to their home to visit. "Now I believe in Santa Claus," said the man. "She looks like a real queen." Dallek, *Unfinished Life*, 253; "Jackie in West Virginia," n.d., Box 27, David R. Powers Personal Papers, John F. Kennedy Library, Boston, MA.
59. Dallek, *Unfinished Life*, 254; "West Virginia," May 10, 1960; "Highlights of JFK's Campaign in West Va.," Box 27, David R. Powers Personal Papers, John F. Kennedy Library, Boston, MA. See also Barbara Leming, *Mrs. Kennedy* (New York: Free Press, 2001), 16.
60. "Mrs. Kennedy Now Vital Participant in Campaign; Paid No Attention to Politics Until She Married Jack," *Raleigh Register* (Beckley, WV), April 21, 1960; "Kennedy Comforts Are Wife's Main Aim," *Wheeling (WV) News-Register*, October 11, 1959; "Jack, Wife Tour State This Week," *Charleston Gazette-Mail*, April 17, 1960; "Log of the Roving Reporters," *Wheeling News-Register*, May 6, 1960; Walker Long, "It's Possible for 'Jackie' Kennedy: From Press Photographer to First Lady of the Land," *Huntington (WV) Advertiser*, April 21, 1960.
61. Stacy Bredhoff, *Winning West Virginia—JFK's Primary Campaign* (Washington, DC: Foundation for the National Archives, 2010), 21.
62. Bredhoff, *Winning West Virginia*, 21
63. Don Marsh, "Kennedy's Brother Here—Solon May Try W. Va. Primary," *Charleston Gazette*, January 14, 1960.
64. Joseph Manchin III, interview by Robert Rupp, May 5, 2010; Norman Julien, "A. James Manchin," in Sullivan, *West Virginia Encyclopedia*, 443–44.
65. "Ted Kennedy Sees Hard Fight for Brother in West Virginia," *Clarksburg (WV) Exponent*, April 13, 1960. The much-vaunted Kennedy campaign, however, had problems. Ted Kennedy was originally scheduled to address a Democratic gathering Tuesday night at the Harrison County Courthouse, but plans were changed, and he was to address a rally in Webster Springs instead. In practice, the Kennedy organization did not live up to its reputation.
66. Dallek, *Unfinished Life*, 254; Evelyn Lincoln Diary Notes, April 26, 1960, Box 2, Evelyn Lincoln Papers, John F. Kennedy Library, Boston, MA.
67. Sorensen, *Kennedy*, 139.
68. Stan Bumgardner, "Sam Huff," in Sullivan, *West Virginia Encyclopedia*, 351–52; "Sport: A Man's Game," *Time*, November 30, 1959; "Pro Football: Brawn, Brains & Profits," *Time*, November 30, 1959 .
69. Sam Huff, interview by Robert Rupp, May 10, 2010. According to Huff, when he picked the senator up at the airport, Kennedy asked for advice on how to handle "his people." The response verified the candidate's new strategy of confrontation: raise the issue directly and frame it in terms of fairness.

70. Greg Moore, "Stydahar Not After WVU Job," *Charleston Gazette*, April 19, 1960; "Joe Stydahar" in Sullivan, *West Virginia Encyclopedia*, 689–90.

71. "Stydahar," *Charleston Gazette*, April 19, 1960. A five-time all-National League tackle, Stydahar was named by *Sports Illustrated* as tenth most prominent West Virginia sports figure of the twentieth century. His visit to the capital city allowed him to visit the Civic Center to see the West Virginia Sports Writers Hall of Fame, where he was among 15 charter members. The next day he went to Shinnston.

72. Paul F. Lutz, "William Casey Marland," in Sullivan, *West Virginia Encyclopedia*, 449–50; Paul F. Lutz, *From Governor to Cabby: The Political Career and Tragic Death of West Virginia's William Casey Marland* (Huntington, WV: Marshall University Library Associates, 1996); Jerry Bruce Thomas, *An Appalachian Reawaking: West Virginia and the Perils of the New Machine Age, 1945–1972* (Morgantown: West Virginia Press, 2010), 68–71.

73. Matt Reese, interview by Robert Rupp, Boston, MA, May 5, 1990; Lutz, "Marland," 449–50. Back in Chicago, Marland's drinking problem worsened, and after several hospital stays he joined Alcoholic Anonymous. In 1962, he took a job as a taxicab driver. He gained national attention when *Life* magazine did a feature article in 1965 on the recovered alcoholic who went from the governor's mansion in Charleston to driving a taxicab in Chicago. Less than a year later, Marland died of cancer at the age of 47.

74. Ben Bradlee, "On to West Virginia," *Newsweek*, April 18, 1960.

75. "Sen. Humphrey Banquet Speaker," *Charleston Gazette*, March 21, 1959; "Sen. Humphrey Banquet Speaker Democratic Women's Day Set Saturday," *Charleston Gazette*, March 18, 1959.

76. "Democratic Women's Day." Her dressmaking skills had come in handy when she was given the tour of the Colshire Manufacturing Company and the Morgan Shirt Factory at Sabraton the day before. An article describes her as an accomplished seamstress, and a picture shows her watching closely as Mary Lou Long operates one of the many "button machines. "Of Special Interest," *Morgantown (WV) Dominion News*, April 21, 1960.

77. Grace Joanou, "Mrs. Humphrey Completely Sold on Hubby's Presidential Role: Enthusiastic Over Friendly Welcome in West Virginia; Will Tour Counties in Northern Panhandle Area Today," *Wheeling (WV) Intelligencer*, April 27, 1960; "Muriel Alone—Jackie with Jack," *Morgantown (WV) Dominion News*, April 18, 1960. "His wife Muriel will start a three-day tour Monday on behalf of her husband's candidacy. She will visit Charleston, Clendenin, Gassaway, Sutton, Buckhannon, and Clarksburg. Kennedy's wife, Jacqueline, will campaign with her husband during his three-day stumping of the state this week."

78. "Mrs. Humphrey Visits Grafton, Bridgeport, Morgantown in Day," *Clarksburg (WV) Exponent*, April 20, 1960. The article includes Muriel Humphrey's recipe for beef soup: "Over one and a half pounds stew beef or chuck and one soup bone with cold water in a heavy three quart sauce-pan. Add salt, pepper and two bay leaves. Heat to bubbly stage. Turn heat low and add one half cup chopped onions,

one cup each chopped celery and cabbage, four or five medium sized carrots, sliced, and a pinch of oregano. Simmer at least two and a half hours, or until meat is very tender. Remove bone and bay leaves and cut meat into bit sized pieces. Add contents of a No. 2 can Italian style tomatoes, one tablespoon Worcestershire sauce and one beef bouillon cube. Simmer for one half hour longer and serve."

79. "Mrs. Humphrey Visits Grafton," *Clarksburg (WV) Exponent*, April 20, 1960.
80. "Mrs. Howard Guest in City," *Clarksburg (WV) Exponent*, May 7, 1960; "Mrs. Howard Will Be Here," *Clarksburg (WV) Exponent*, May 6, 1960; "Mrs. Frances Howard Honored at Ronceverte Dinner," *Beckley (WV) Post Herald*, May 3, 1960. She credited her interest in world affairs to her father. While most children were read fairy tales at bedtime, she said that her father would read her the life of Thomas Jefferson and various other historical items. She told a reporter that "my father was a William Jennings Bryan man and, although he was a druggist, I always said, 'With every pill he sold, he sold a new political idea.'"
81. "Mrs. Frances Howard Honored."
82. Ryan Herst, "Political Talk Pushed Aside as Rolvaag Discusses Father," *Fairmont Times-West Virginian*, April 29, 1960.
83. "Minnesota Governor Here to Help Hubert," *Charleston Gazette*, April 29, 1960; Bob Mellace, "Hardship Inexcusable, Minn. Governor Says," *Charleston Daily Mail*, April 29, 1960; "W.Va., Minnesota Unemployment Figures Match Humphry Aide Finds: Presidential Hopeful Has Promised Aid for 'Most Serious Jobless State,'" *Wellsburg (WV) Daily Herald*, April 28, 1960; "Minnesota Governor Speaks Here Saturday," *Calhoun Chronicle* (Grantsville, WV), May 5, 1960; "Minnesota Governor Speaks in Marshall; Freeman Will Kick Off Area Drive for Sen. Humphrey at St. Joseph," *Wheeling (WV) Intelligencer*, April 29, 1960.
84. "Minnesota Governor Likes Jerry," *Charleston Gazette*, April 30, 1960. "Gov. Orville Freeman of Minnesota couldn't have chosen a more popular theme for the people of Chelyan. He talked about Jerry West."
85. "Minnesota Governor."
86. "Rolvaag Adds Literary Turn to Campaign," *Fairmont Times-West Virginian*, April 27, 1960; "Lt. Governor of Minnesota Visits Elkins Today," *Randolph Enterprise* (Elkins, WV), April 28, 1960; "Minn. Lt. Gov is Belington Visitor," *Belington (WV) News*, April 27, 1960; "Rolvaag Joins Democratic Speaker List," *Grafton (WV) Sentinel*, April 25, 1960.
87. "Rolvaag Will Visit Marion: Minn Man to Campaign for Humphrey," *Fairmont Times-West Virginian*, April 28, 1960.
88. Dallek, *Unfinished Life*, 56. "West Virginia Attacks," Box 994, PPP.
89. Paul B. Fay Jr., *The Pleasure of His Company* (New York: Harper & Row, 1966), 19–22.
90. Ernst, *Primary*, 13. The state's declining economy could be seen by the percentage of military payments to veterans of the Korean War that went out of state.
91. "Complete Text of Kennedy-Humphrey Debate," *Charleston Gazette*, May 5, 1960.
92. Ernst, *Primary*, 5.
93. Richard Donahue, interviewed by Robert Rupp, May 15, 1990, Charleston, WV.

94. David Barnett, "Kennedy Is Mining Votes With His Change in Tactics: Switches From Soft Sell," *Charleston Gazette*, April 21, 1960.

95. O'Brien, *No Final Victories*, 72.

96. Robert J. Donovan, *PT 109: John F. Kennedy in World War II* (New York: Mc-Graw-Hill, 1961), 139–48.

97. Donovan, *PT 109*, 149–53; Doris Kearns Goodwin, *The Fitzgeralds and the Kennedys: An American Saga* (New York: Simon & Shuster, 1987), 658–59; Nigel Hamilton, *JFK: Reckless Youth* (New York: Random House, 1992), 577–602; Dallek, *Unfinished Life*, 93–99.

98. Rose Fitzgerald Kennedy, *Times to Remember* (Garden City, NY: Doubleday, 1977), 364–65.

99. Laurence Leamer, *The Kennedy Men, 1901–1963: The Laws of the Father* (New York: Perennial, 2001), 181–84; Ralph G. Martin, *A Hero For our Times* (New York: MacMillan Co., 1982), 43–44.

100. "Kennedy's Son is Hero in Pacific As Destroyer Splits His PT Boat," *New York Times*, August 20, 1943; "Kennedy Erred on Island's Name; Navy Corrects Him on Site of Wartime Experiences," *New York Times*, June 4, 1961.

101. John Hellman, *The Kennedy Obsession: The American Myth of JFK* (New York: Columbia University Press, 1997), 39–41. John Hersey, "Survival," *New Yorker*, June 17, 1944, 31–43. After *Life* magazine turned "Survival" down, it was published in the *New Yorker* on June 17, 1944.

102. Whalen, *Founding Father*, 446.

103. Sorensen, *Kennedy*, 18.

104. Hellmann, *Kennedy Obsession*, 59.

105. Letter. John F. Kennedy Campaign to Veterans of Foreign War Posts, May 3, 1960, Robert F. Kennedy, Pre-Administration Records; Fleming Jr., *Kennedy vs. Humphrey*, 47.

106. Lasky, *J.F.K.*, 343–344.

107. O'Donnell and Powers, *Johnny*, 189. Initially, the former congressman focused on his time with Kennedy in Congress, but in West Virginia he talked about their shared service in the navy during World War II.

108. O'Donnell and Powers, *Johnny*, 189.

109. David Barnett, "Kennedy is Mining Votes With His Change in Tactics; Switches from Soft Sell" *Charleston Gazette*, April 21, 1960. Account noticed that "To the Ivy league accent the candidate has added a sharp bite"; Holmes Alexander, "Catholicism vs. Draft-Dodging: Issue Raised in Primary," *Morgantown (WV) Post*, April 25, 1960. "Members of the Kennedy camp in West Virginia are now sporting PT boat lapel buttons. These depict not only Jack's memorable war service in WWII but call attention to the fact that Humphrey was a wartime stay-at-home."

110. Arthur Edson, "Mountain Feudin' Puts Frost on Hubert," *Charleston Gazette*, May 9, 1960.

111. "Didn't Call Sen. Humphrey Draft Dodger, FDR Jr. Says," *Charleston Gazette*, May 7, 1960.

112. Anderson Edson, "Mountain Feudin."

113. William H. Lawrence, oral history interview, April 22, 1960, John F. Kennedy Library.

114. "Didn't Call Sen. Humphrey," *Charleston Gazette*, May 7, 1960.

115. Victor Lasky, *J.F.K.: The Man and the Myth* (New York: Macmillan Company, 1963), 344–45.

116. "Didn't Call Sen. Humphrey Draft Dodger," *Charleston Gazette*, May 8, 1960; In his autobiography, O'Brien blamed Roosevelt for raising the issue and releasing the Humphrey material without waiting for that low blow. O'Brien, *No Final Victories*, 72–73; Roosevelt blamed Bobby Kennedy, and not John, for instigating the smear and pressuring Roosevelt to raise the issue. Fleming, *Kennedy*, 51.

117. Lasky, *J.F.K*, 344–45.

118. Goodwin, *The Fitzgeralds and the Kennedys*, 799.

119. Albert Eisele, *Almost*, 56. He became first the state director of war production training and reemployment, then state chief of Minnesota's War Service Program, then assistant director of the state's War Manpower Commission.

120. Eisele, *Almost*, 56. In fact, Humphrey had volunteered for service several times, attempting to enter the Naval Reserve Officer program, but he was rejected due to color blindness and a double hernia. The closest Humphrey ever came to serving in the military was in 1943 when he became a political science professor at Macalester College in St. Paul and taught members of the Air Corps training detachment.

121. Eisele, *Almost*, 147.

> Q: Did you forgive him [FDR Jr.] for that?
> Humphrey: Nope.
> Q: That's the only time I've ever heard of someone whom you didn't forgive.
> Humphrey: I did not forgive him for that because I thought it was unconscionable.
> Q: Bobby or FDR Jr.?
> Humphrey: Both, but mostly FDR.

122. O'Donnell, *Irish Brotherhood*, 323.

123. O'Brien, *No Final Victories*, 73.

124. O'Donnell, *Irish Brotherhood*, 323.

125. Don Marsh, "Name-Calling Regretted: Kennedy Takes Friendlier Tone," *Charleston Gazette*, May 9, 1960.

126. Franklin Delano Roosevelt, Jr., "Cabin Creek Advertisement #2, War Records," Spring 1960, Directed by Jack Denove, Phil Smith Collection, West Virginia State Archives, Charleston, WV. "His older brother was in college with me, Joe Kennedy Jr., and I am sorry to say Joe Kennedy lost his life flying a mission over Germany in 1943. Jack Kennedy and I served in the United States Navy for five years. He came out of his navy service a hero, but he also required two years in veteran hospitals for him to recover from the wounds he suffered in the South Pacific. Jack Kennedy was a great hero and a great Navy veteran, and as such he will help and he has the qualifications to lead us to a world of peace."

127. Roosevelt Jr., "Cabin Creek Advertisement #2, War Record."
128. Roosevelt Jr., "Cabin Creek Advertisement #2, War Record."
129. Lawrence, "Roosevelt Hits Humphrey."
130. Edson, "Mountain Feudin'"; Arthur M. Schlesinger, *Robert Kennedy and His Times* (New York: Ballantine, 1978), 201. Humphrey revealed his disgust with both Kennedy brothers at a party fundraiser dinner at Clarksburg on the night of May 7.
131. Joseph A. Loftis, "Kennedy Is Firm on Oath of Office," *New York Times*, May 9, 1960.
132. Loftis, "Kennedy Is Firm"; Dallek, *Unfinished Life*, 256; Schlesinger, *Robert Kennedy*, 201.
133. O'Brien, *No Final Victories*, 73.
134. Schlesinger, *Robert Kennedy*, 217.
135. Humphrey, *Education*, 475.

Chapter 4

1. "It's Respectable to Be Wealthy and Run for President This Year," *Clarksburg (WV) Telegram*, April 11, 1960.
2. "It's Respectable."
3. "It's Respectable." By the late 1950s Joe Kennedy's estimated worth of $200 million made him one of the 20 wealthiest persons in America and certainly the wealthiest Roman Catholic in the nation. Some estimates placed his worth in 1960 at $400 million. Rorabaugh, *Real Making*, 38–39.
4. David E. Koskoff, *Joseph P. Kennedy: A Life and Times* (Englewood Cliffs, NJ: Prentice Hall, 1974), 433. Bill Beckett, cochairman for Humphrey in Cabell County, recalled a meeting where a leader from Wayne County told Bobby, "'We need a lot of money here in Wayne if your brother is to win.' When Bobby replied, 'How much do you need?' the leader asked, 'How much does your daddy have to spend?' Bobby responded, 'All you need!' Beckett believed that the Kennedys could obtain whatever was needed when it was needed." Fleming Jr., *Kennedy vs. Humphrey*, 126.
5. Koskoff, *Joseph P. Kennedy* (Englewood Cliffs, NJ: Prentice Hall, 1974), 433.
6. Tom Carver, "Campaign column: The price of vote," BBC News. Last accessed April 29, 2019 http://news.bbc.co.uk/2/hi/americas/3733180.stm
7. Dallek, *Unfinished Life*, 231; Gridiron speech, March 15, Box 1025, Pre-Presidential Papers, John F. Kennedy Library.
8. "John F. Kennedy and West Virginia: How WV Won JFK the 1960 Democratic Presidential Primary," *The Parts in the Sum of the Whole* (blog), November 15, 2013, https://partsinthesum.wordpress.com/2013/11/15/john-f-kennedy-and -west-virginia-how-wv-won-jfk-the-1960-democratic-presidential-primary/. Last accessed March 17, 2019.
9. W. H. Lawrence, "Kennedy Backers in Debt, They Say; Supporters Report Spending 20% Less Than Humphrey Forces in West Virginia," *New York Times*, April 12, 1960.

10. "Report," *New York Times*, May 4, 1960.

11. Charles Peters, interview by Robert Rupp, December 27, 2002, Washington, DC.

12. "West Virginia Becomes 4-Week Battleground in National Scramble," *Clarksburg (WV) Exponent*, April 7, 1960.

13. Arthur Edson, "Hubert, Kennedy Return to Stump: Humphrey Strikes 'Poor Man's Theme," *Charleston Gazette* (Charleston, WV), April 26, 1960.

14. Denise Giardina, *The Unquiet Earth* (New York: W.W. Norton and Company, 1992), 153–154.

15. Arthur Edson, "Homespun Phraseology Employed By Humphrey; 'I was Poor, too, He Reiterates," *Charleston Daily Mail*, April 28, 1960.

16. Humphrey, *Education*, 151.

17. Smithsonian Air and Space Museum Collection, "Convair 240, 'Caroline.'" Last accessed March 17, 2019 https://airandspace.si.edu/collection-objects /convair-240-caroline.

18. Charlie Collie, "JFK and his Campaign Plane: Caroline," *Holliston (WV) Reporter*, January 30, 2015, available at http://www.hollistonreporter.com/article/10444/jfk -and-his-campaign-plane-caroline.html.

19. "Sen. Kennedy Urges W. Va. 'New Deal,'" *Parkersburg (WV) News*, April 12, 1960.

20. Eisele, *Almost*.

21. "Sen. Kennedy Finds Friends in Wheeling," *Charleston Gazette*, April 19, 1960.

22. Phil Smith, interview by Robert Rupp, May 8, 2010, Charleston, WV.

23. Rorabaugh, *Real Making*, 47.

24. Humphrey, *Education*, 163.

25. C. David Heymann, *RFK: A Candid Biography of Robert F. Kennedy* (New York: Dutton, 1998), 119.

26. Rorabaugh, *Real Making*, 47.

27. Humphrey, *Education of a Public Man*, 159.

28. Humphrey, *Education of a Public Man*, 159.

29. Raymond Chafin and Topper Sherwood, *Just Good Politics: The Life of Raymond Chafin, Appalachian Boss* (Pittsburgh: University of Pittsburgh Press, 1994), 130–35.

30. Victor Gabriel, interview with Dan Fleming Jr., August 22, 1985, in Fleming, *Kennedy vs. Humphrey*, 82.

31. Fleming Jr., *Kennedy vs. Humphrey*, 112–14.

32. Edward T. Folliad, "Reporters Fail to Find Kennedy Bought Victory," *Washington Post*, May 31, 1960.

33. Robert Novak notes that the in-house explanation for not publishing the story was because of the unwillingness of the sources to sign affidavits, but Novak believes the paper withheld the story because of the upcoming Democratic convention and that the editors believed that "it was not the place of the paper 'to decide the presidential nominee.'" Robert D. Novak, *The Prince of Darkness: 50 years of Reporting in Washington* (New York: Crown 2007), 65.

34. Jack Anderson, "The Washington Merry-Go-Round: Here's Top Banana in Tax Bonanza," *Washington Post*, August 9, 1960.

35. Barry Goldwater, *With No Apologies* (New York: William Morrow, 1979), 112–114.
36. John G. Morgan, "Kennedy Didn't Buy Win, He Sold Himself to Voters," *Charleston Gazette*, June 18, 1960; Don Marsh, "Money-Was It the Key: Kennedy Victory 'No Surprise-it was Prue Amazement," *Charleston Gazette*, June 13, 1960. Counties the reporters investigated were McDowell, Raleigh, Mercer, Wyoming, Boone, Fayette, Mercer, Wyoming, Boone, Fayette, Marion, Monongalia, and Ohio.
37. Oliphant and Wilkie, *Camelot*, 210–211. "But there is no direct evidence about Mafia money, or the extent of Joe Kennedy's money or anything else of relevance beyond occasional, wiretapped, and unsupported boasts by gangsters and other hearsay without details or proof" (211); Tom Searls "'The Dark Side of Camelot' Cast West Virginia in Bad Light," *Charleston Gazette*, November 12, 1997. For discussion of the mob money allegations, see Thomas C. Reeves, *A Question of Character: A Life of John F. Kennedy* (New York: Macmillan, 1991), 165–166; Seymour Hersh, *The Dark Side of Camelot*, (New York: Little, Brown, 1997), 100–101. See Fleming, *Kennedy vs. Humphrey*, 69–75.
38. Quoted in Fleming, *Kennedy vs. Humphrey*, 71–72. For a discussion about and dismissal of the allegations of Mafia money see Fleming, Chapter 5.
39. Jimmy Wolford, interview by Robert Rupp, May 10, 2010, Charleston, West Virginia.
40. Humphrey, *Education*, 152.
41. The organizational effort in West Virginia had started in April of 1959, more than a year before the presidential primary, when Bob McDonough of Parkersburg and two Kennedy associates held meetings in four cities. Fleming Jr., *Kennedy vs. Humphrey*, 116.
42. A memo from Ted Sorensen reported and reflected the senator's physical presence in the state, both past and future, noting Kennedy's earlier visits to Morgantown, Parkersburg (1958), and Wheeling (1959) and his planned visits to Wellsburg and Welch. The memo reads:

> *First District* (Northern). This district includes the Northern Panhandle JFK has already visited in Wheeling and will return to Wellsburg on October, 1959. [The memo noted that "rackets are reported to prevail." in this district.]
>
> *Second District* (Eastern). JFK visited Morgantown, summer, 1958. Congressman Staggers is for JFK.
>
> *Third District* (Western). JFK visited Parkersburg, fall, 1958 and Bob McDonough sparkplugs statewide activity from this district.
>
> *Fifth District* (Southern). Includes hard-hit depressed areas including Welch and Bluefield. JFK will visit Welch on May 9, 1960. Sid Christie is very important there.
>
> *Sixth District* (Southwestern). Includes Charleston and Beckley and hard-hit coal mining areas. Memorandum, Ted Sorenson and Bob Wallace to JFK, JFK Library, April 4, 1959.

43. Jacobs, oral history interview.

44. Louis Harris and Associates, "A Study of Voter Attitudes in West Virginia," January 1960, Box 818, PPP, Senate Files. The Harris polling found that the number one issue in the state was the Depressed Areas bill. Harris found that, in addition to disliking foreign aid, the voters disliked reciprocal trade-law tariffs, viewing imports of oil and glass as threats to coal mining and the local glass manufacturing.

45. Memorandum, Chuck Daly to Mike Feldman, "Issues as Seen by Hechler, Bailey and Staggers," Box 989, fol. Campaign Issues, PPP, Presidential Campaign Files, 1960. The most succinct and conservative advice came from Cleve Bailey, who stated, "We don't want any long-haired internationals around here." Bailey's disparagement of "internationals" was a common theme in the primary contest. In fact, one of the first questions asked of Kennedy in the coal mine television ad concerned foreign aid.

46. "Legends profile: Jerry West," NBA.com, last accessed March 17, 2019, https://www.nba.com/history/legends/profiles/jerry-west. West would be a player and a manager in his long career in professional basketball. He earned the nickname Mr. Logo after his silhouette was incorporated into the NBA logo. He also had the nickname Zeke from Cabin Creek, after the creek near his birthplace of Chelyan, West Virginia. The family lived in Chelyan, but collected their mail at the Cabin Creek post office. Norman Julian, "Jerry West," in Sullivan, *West Virginia Encyclopedia*, 748–49.

47. Daly to Feldman, memorandum.

48. "Minnesota Governor Likes Jerry," *Charleston Gazette*, April 30, 1960.

49. Ken Hechler, interview by Robert Rupp, May 2, 2010, Charleston, WV.

50. Hechler, interview.

51. Hechler, interview.

52. Letter, M. Rouch to Dave Hackett, April 13, 1960, Box 968, fol. West Virginia: JFK for President Committee: Headquarters, PPP, Presidential Campaign Files, 1960.

53. Rouch, letter.

54. Hechler, interview.

55. Fleming Jr., *Kennedy vs. Humphrey*, 47.

56. Whalen, *Founding Father*, 446.

57. Henry Fairlie, "Television's Love Affair with John F. Kennedy," *New Republic*, December 26, 1983, 11–16.

58. Jack Denove Collection, UCLA Film and Television Archive, last accessed March 17, 2019, https://www.cinema.ucla.edu/collections/jack-denove.

59. Jamieson, *Packaging*, 167–68. The 1960 Kennedy campaign marked the first extensive use of television in a presidential election. During the primaries and the general election, 200 television ads were produced and a quarter of a million feet of film shot. Jack Denove oversaw this media effort.

60. https://www.jfklibrary.org/learn/about-jfk/the-kennedy-family/joseph-p-kennedy, accessed March 17, 2019.

61. Jamieson, *Packaging*, 164.

62. Phil Smith, interview by Robert Rupp, April 10, 2010, Charleston WV. He told the story of sending Kennedy "down to a chicken farm," but the ad was never shown; instead they filmed Kennedy in a store in Donovan.

63. Smith, interview.

64. Smith, interview.

65. Jamieson, *Packaging*, 164–65.

66. Jamieson, *Packaging*, 164–65.

67. Smith, interview.

68. John F. Kennedy," Introduction-Capitol Steps," Directed by Jack Denove (Spring 1960), 16mm film print, Phil Smith Collection, West Virginia State Archives, Charleston, W.V.; John F. Kennedy, "Religion Ad #1: Divided Loyalties," Directed by Jack Denove (Spring 1960), 16mm film print, Phil Smith Collection, West Virginia State Archives, Charleston, W.V.

69. Roosevelt, Jr., "Religion Advertisement #1," Roosevelt, Jr., "Religion Advertisement #2."

70. John F. Kennedy, "Economic Advertisement #1," Spring 1960, Directed by Jack Denove, Phil Smith Collection, West Virginia State Archives, Charleston, WV.

71. Kennedy, "Economic Advertisement #2."

72. Kennedy, "Economic Advertisement #3, Slab Fork Mine."

73. Kennedy, "Economic Advertisement #3, Slab Fork Mine."

74. John F. Kennedy, "Gallup Poll Advertisement," Spring 1960, Directed by Jack Denove, Phil Smith Collection, West Virginia State Archives, Charleston, WV; "Nixon Is Trailing Kennedy In Poll," New York Times, April 25, 1960.

75. John F. Kennedy, "Gang Up Advertisement," Spring 1960, Directed by Jack Denove, Phil Smith Collection, West Virginia State Archives, Charleston, WV.

76. Kennedy, "Gang Up Advertisement."

77. Kennedy, "Gallup Poll Advertisement."

78. White, *Making*, 111–12.

79. O'Donnell and Powers, *Johnny*, 194.

80. O'Donnell and Powers, *Johnny*, 194.

81. John F. Kennedy's national television appearances prior to 1961, accessed at https://www.jfklibrary.org/learn/about-jfk/life-of-john-f-kennedy/fast-facts-john-f-kennedy/john-f-kennedys-national-television-appearances-pre-1961

82. Victor Lasky, *J.F.K.*, 344.

83. White, *Making*, 107; Donahue, interview, May 12, 1990.

84. Jamieson, *Packaging*, 70.

85. White, *Making*, 106–8; Joseph A. Loftis, "Kennedy is Firm On Oath of Office," *Charleston Gazette*, May 8, 1960.

86. "Two Candidates Debate Tonight," *Charleston Gazette*, May 4, 1960.

87. "Candidates Set TV Debate Rules," *Charleston Gazette*, May 3, 1960.

88. Herb Little, "Kennedy Angrily Accepts Challenge," *Charleston Gazette*, April 20, 1960; Bill Chaddock, "Kennedy Consents to Debate; Humphrey's Challenge Accepted; New Englander Has Full Schedule in Area Today," *Wheeling (WV) News-Register*, April 19, 1920.

89. "Kennedy, Humphrey Set Debate for May 4," *New York Times*, April 24, 1960; Little, "Kennedy Angrily Accepts Challenge."

90. Kathleen Hall Jamieson and David S. Birdsell, *Presidential Debates: The Challenge of Creating an Informed Electorate* (New York: Oxford University Press, 1987), 120. Moderator Quincy Howe asked questions on a range of foreign and domestic issues and warned that the debate must be kept on the issues and not degenerate into personal conflict. As in the West Virginia debate, the candidates found little to disagree about. Jamieson and Birdsell, *Presidential Debates*, 92–93.

91. Jamieson and Birdsell, *Presidential Debates*, 120. Sixty percent of the adult population—around 77 million people—watched the first Kennedy-Nixon debate. Ernst, "Primary," 3.

92. "Kennedy, Humphrey Set Debate"; "Two Candidates Debate Tonight," *Charleston Gazette*, May 4, 1960.

93. "Kennedy-Humphrey: TV Debate Set Here on May 4," *Charleston Gazette*, April 24, 1960. From hundreds of questions submitted, the *Gazette* staff assembled a list. The selected questions came from across the state, and two came from out of state. In the debate, the two-man panel read the question and identified by name and town the person who submitted it. The exception was a hostile question on religion addressed to Kennedy, and the submitter asked not to be identified.

The format did not allow the two-member panel to ask any questions of the candidates, but some of the selected questions were directed to only one candidate while others were directed to both. The only time there was any out-of-line discussion came near the end of the debate when Kennedy asserted that he was the victim of a "gang-up" by his opponents and that Humphrey could not win the nomination—both major talking points of his campaign. "The Complete Text of Kennedy-Humphrey Debate," *Charleston Gazette*, May 5, 1960.

94. "Kennedy-Humphrey Debate."

95. Charles Schussler, phone interview by Robert Rupp, May 6, 2000, Wheeling, WV.

96. Editorial, "Many Observers Missed the Significance of Debate," *Charleston Gazette*, May 11, 1960.

97. Henry W. Battle, interview by Robert Rupp, April 3, 2010, Charleston, WV.

98. Thomas F. Stafford, "Kennedy, Humphrey Attack, Ike, Nixon on TV Debate: Both Senators Avoid Clashing," *Charleston Gazette*, May 5, 1960.

99. Reston, "West Virginia Debate," *New York Times*, May 5, 1960.

100. Film, Kennedy-Humphrey, 1960 WV Primary, May 4, 1960, Victoria Schuck Collection, John F. Kennedy Library, Boston, MA; Stafford, "Kennedy, Humphrey Attack."

101. A. F. Johnston, letter, April 23, 1960, Box 17, West Virginia file, John F. Kennedy Library.

102. Stafford, "Kennedy, Humphrey Attack."

103. George Lawless, "Maybe Ward Bond Will Win-Debate Seemed Boring Gabfest," *Charleston Gazette*, May 5, 1960. Lawless notes that "Reporters were silently cheering for blood; they got strawberry ice cream instead. . . . They were waiting for something to happen. And finally, it did. Someone accidentally kicked over a wastebasket."

104. Film, Kennedy-Humphrey, 1960 WV Primary, May 4, 1960, Victoria Schuck Collection.

105. Eisele, *Almost*, 145.

106. Eisele, *Almost*, 145.

107. Editorial, "Humphreydum and Kennedyee Talk It Over For an Hour without Striking a Spark," *Charleston Daily Mail*, May 5, 1960.

108. "Hardly a Debate," *Morgantown (WV) Post*, May 5, 1960.

109. James Reston, "West Virginia Debate," *New York Times*, May 5, 1960.

110. Jamieson, *Packaging*, 164.

111. Ken Hechler, "Mountaineers Are Always Free," *Congressional Record*, (Washington, December 5, 1963) Vol. 109, No.198.

112. Roul Tunley, "The Strange Case of West Virginia," *Saturday Evening Post*, February 6, 1960, 19–20, 64–66.

113. "50 Years Ago, Magazine Article Proclaimed W.Va. 'a Dying State,'" *Herald-Dispatch* (Huntington, WV), January 31, 2010.

114. "50 Years Ago."

115. Rowland Evans Jr., "Bogus K. of C. 'Oath' Circulated in West Virginia," *Washington Post*, May 1, 1960.

116. Jim Comstock, "Pa Ain't Selling His Vote to No Catholic," *Best of Hillbilly* (New York: Pocket Books, 1969), 80.

117. L. T. Anderson, "Religion Issue May Not Be Dead: Nation Misinformed About State," *Charleston Gazette*, May 12, 1960.

118. Ken Kurtz, panel discussion, "Celebrating the Primary that Made a President," Division of Culture and History and West Virginia Wesleyan College, Charleston, West Virginia, May 15, 1990.

119. L. T. Anderson, "Religion Issue May Not Be Dead: Nation Misinformed about State," *Charleston Gazette*, May 12, 1960.

120. "Eisenhower Taunts Political Forecasters," *New York Times*, May 12, 1960; "Transcript of Eisenhower's News Conference on Foreign and Domestic Matters," *New York Times*, May 12, 1960.

121. Carroll Kilpatrick, "Pressured to Abandon Race, Humphrey Says," *Washington Post*, May 4, 1960; Don Marsh, "One-Sided Victory Looked Impossible: Kenney Genuinely Surprised," *Charleston Gazette*, May 12, 1960.

122. Fleming, *Kennedy vs. Humphrey*, 66.

123. Ralph McGill, "Organization Won for Jack," *Charleston Gazette*, May 14, 1960.

124. McGill, "Organization Won."

125. Ken Kurtz, panel discussion, "Celebrating the Primary that Made a President," Division of Culture and History and West Virginia Wesleyan College, Charleston, West Virginia, May 15, 1990.

126. Fleming Jr., *Kennedy vs. Humphrey*, 64; Arthur Krock, "In the Nation: Pilgrims Progress in the Delectable Mountains," *New York Times* May 12, 1960, 34. Krock suggested that the best source of forecast remained the professional politicians.

127. Christie, oral history interview.

128. Christie, oral history interview.

129. Anne Hearst, oral history interview, July 28, 1964. John F. Kennedy Library.

130. W. E. Chilton III, oral history interview, July 14, 1964, John F. Kennedy Library.

131. Hearst, oral history interview.

132. Chilton, oral history interview.

133. Chilton, oral history interview.

134. W. H. Lawrence, "Survey of West Virginia Shows Conflicting Trends," *New York Times*, May 9, 1960.

135. Lawrence, "Survey of West Virginia"; *West Virginia Blue Book 1960*, ed. J. Howard Myers (Charleston, West Virginia: Jarrett Printing Co., 1960), 723.

136. Lawrence, oral history interview.

137. Myers, ed., *Blue Book 1960*, 723.

138. Lawrence, "Survey of West Virginia," *New York Times*, May 9, 1960. Some contrary evidence collected by the *Times* reporters that Lawrence did use was an unscientific poll of workers at a Wheeling steel-coking plant. Of the 21 questioned, 13 were for Kennedy, none were for Humphrey, and the remaining eight were either undecided or stated no preference. It is interesting to note that the Lawrence article did not highlight the strong support for Kennedy (13 to 0), but rather the large number of undecided (8).

139. Chilton, oral history interview; Lawrence, "Survey of West Virginia."

140. Russell Baker, *The Good Times* (New York: William Morrow and Co., 1989), 317–19.

141. Baker, *Good Times*, 320–21; Lawrence, *Six Presidents*, 230.

142. "Kennedy Charges 'Gang-Up' By Foes: Also Scores Religious Bigotry and Belittles Humphrey in West Virginia Speeches," *New York Times*, April 19, 1960.

143. Fleming Jr., *Kennedy vs. Humphrey*, 124–25; Rowland Evans and Robert Novak, *Lyndon B. Johnson: The Exercise of Power* (New York: New American Library, 1966), 250.

144. Edson, "Mountain Feudin.'"

145. Baker, *Good Times*, 321, 323. Lawrence's closeness to Kennedy would prompt a personal attack by Lyndon Johnson before the *Times* editors. Johnson demanded of the *Times* a public statement criticizing Lawrence by name and explaining that his "sloppy work was the product of reportorial fatigue."

146. Chalmers M. Roberts, *First Rough Draft: A Journalist's Journal of our Times* (New York: Praeger, 1973), 176.

147. Lawrence, oral history interview.

148. Lawrence, oral history interview.

149. Baker, *Good Times*, 319.

150. Anderson, "Religion Issue."

151. Anderson, "Religion Issue"; "Humphrey Insists He's an Underdog," *New York Times*, April 27, 1960.

152. Lawrence, *Six Presidents*, 258–59.

153. Ben Bradlee, *A Good Life: Newspapering and Other Adventures* (New York: Simon and Schuster, 1995), 205.

154. Bradlee, *Conversations*, 26n, 36–37. The families were so close that the president-

elect sent over a Secret Service agent when Bradlee's wife was ready to go the Washington Hospital Center for the birth of their sixth child and Bradlee could not find a babysitter. During the primary campaign, the couples vacationed together at Joseph P. Kennedy's house in Palm Beach, Florida.

155. Bradlee, *Good Life*, 208; Ben and Antoinette Bradlee, interview with Arthur Schlesinger Jr., March 26. 1964, in Jeff Himmelman, *Yours in Truth: A Personal Portrait of Ben Bradlee* (New York: Random House, 2012), 78–79; Ben Bradlee, *Conversations*, 26–28.

156. Bradlee, "Now West Virginia," 34. For example, he cited several prejudiced clergy including William Ferrey, a Presbyterian minister in Parkersburg who said that the nation "could not afford a Roman Catholic as President."

157. Bradlee, "Now West Virginia," 34.

158. Ben Bradlee, "Best Underdog in Show," *Newsweek*, May 9, 1960, 34; "Humphrey Insist He's An Underdog," *New York Times*, April 27, 1960.

159. Lawrence, "Kennedy Claims," *New York Times*, April 12, 1960.

160. Bradlee, "Now West Virginia," 34–35.

161. Jacobs, oral history interview, July 6, 1964, John F. Kennedy Library, 29; Fleming Jr., *Kennedy vs. Humphrey*, 46.

162. Bryon York, "Ben Bradlee: A Cautionary Tale of Kennedy's Courtier," *Washington Examiner*, October 31, 2014.

163. Robert W. Merry, *Taking on the World: Joseph and Stewart Alsop—Guardians of the American Century* (New York: Viking Press 1996), xvii, xx–xxii.

164. Merry, *Taking*, 341.

165. Merry, *Taking*, xxiii.

166. Merry, *Taking*, 342.

167. Joseph P. Alsop, and Adam Platt. *"I've Seen the Best of It": Memoirs* (New York: Norton, 1992), 418, 420.

168. Merry, *Taking*, 342, 375. His brother, columnist Stewart Alsop, worried that Joe was "trimming a bit" in terms of getting too close to John Kennedy.

169. Chilton, oral history interview.

170. Joe Alsop, "Bigotry as Humphrey's Ally," *New Republic*, May 2, 1960, 11–12.

171. Joseph Alsop, "Anti-Catholic Trend in Slab Fork Termed Humphrey Windfall by Joseph Alsop" *Charleston Daily Mail*, April 15, 1960.

172. Alsop, "Poll Gives."; "Slab Fork-Kennedy won 100 to 36," *Charleston Gazette*, May 11, 1960.

173. "Slab Fork—Kennedy," *Charleston Gazette*, May 11, 1960.

174. "The Question of Bigotry," *New Republic*, April 25, 1960, 5–6.

175. "Question of Bigotry."

176. Alsop, "Anti-Catholic."

177. Anderson, "Religion Issue."

178. Alsop, "Bigotry," 11–12.

179. Oliphant and Wilkie, *Camelot*, 205; Matt Reese, oral history interview, May 5, 1990.

180. Chilton, oral history interview.
181. Chalmers M. Roberts, *First Rough Draft: A Journalist's Journal of Our Times* (New York: Praeger Publishers, 1973), 176.
182. "Un-American Slab Fork Floods Jack," *Charleston Gazette,* May 12, 1960.
183. Anderson, "Religion Issue."
184. Hugh Sidey, *John F. Kennedy, President* (New York: Athenaeum, 1964), 40–41.
185. Joseph W. Alsop and Adam Platt, *I've Seen the Best of It: Memoirs"* (New York: Norton & Company, 1992), 43; Barbara Leming, *Mrs. Kennedy: The Missing History of the Kennedy Years* (New York: Free Press, 2011), 36–39.

Chapter 5

1. Tom Cummings, "Sen. Humphrey Campaign Gets Big Start," *Charleston Daily Mail,* April 8, 1960; "Humphrey in Coal Fields Tour, Feels Like 'Triumphant Caesar,'" *New York Times,* April 12, 1960.
2. Cummings, "Sen. Humphrey Campaign."
3. Cummings, "Sen. Humphrey Campaign."
4. Cummings, "Sen. Humphrey Campaign."
5. "Humphrey, in Coal Fields, Feels Like 'Triumphant Caesar," *New York Times,* April 1, 1960.
6. "Kennedy V. Humphrey: The 50th Anniversary of the West Virginia Democratic Primary," Kennedy Library Forums, May 12, 2010, 10.
7. "FDR Jr. Talk Opens Drive for Kennedy: Dinner at Monongah Will Kick Off Presidential Campaign in State," *Fairmont (WV) Times,* April 8, 1960.
8. "Sen. Kennedy Urges W. Va. 'New Deal," *Parkersburg (WV) News,* April 12, 1960; "600 On Hand To Greet Sen. John F. Kennedy: Pledges New Deal For W.Va.," *Parkersburg (WV) Sentinel,* April 11, 1960.
9. Bob Mellace, "Kennedy Meets Religious Issue," *Charleston Daily Mail,* April 11, 1960.
10. O'Donnell and Powers, *Johnny,* 187.
11. Betty Crickard, "The Mountain State," in *Mountain Heritage,* ed. B. B. Maurer (Parsons, WV: McClain, 2006), 199–213.
12. Fleming Jr., *Kennedy vs. Humphrey,* 34; W. H. Lawrence, "Kennedy Tackles Issue of Religion," *New York Times,* April 12, 1960.
13. "Peale Scores Move Made by Sen. Kennedy," *Clarksburg (WV) Exponent,* April 13, 1960; "Dr. Peale Unconvinced Kennedy Free of Church," *Clarksburg (WV) Telegram,* April 13, 1960; "Dr. Peale Raises Catholic 'Ghost,'" *Raleigh Register* (Beckley, WV), April 13, 1960.
14. "Dr. Peale Unconvinced," *Clarksburg (WV) Exponent,* April 13, 1960; "The Religious Issues: Should the Pope Speak Out," *U.S. News and World Report,* April 25, 1960, 56.
15. Louis Cassels, "Methodists Reject Slap at Sen. Kennedy," *New York Times,* May 3, 1960.

16. "Stop Signs," *Time*, April 25, 1960.
17. "Humphrey, in Coal Fields," *New York Times*, April 11, 1960.
18. W. H. Lawrence, "Humphrey 'Broke,' Cuts His Staff 50%," *New York Times*, April 15, 1960; "West Virginia Becomes 4-Week Battleground," *Clarksburg (WV) Exponent*, April 7, 1960.
19. "Humphrey Cash Short, Adequate," *Clarksburg (WV) Telegram*, April 15, 1960.
20. Jacobs, oral history interview.
21. "Sen. Kennedy Finds Friends in Wheeling," *Charleston Gazette*, April 19, 1960.
22. Bob Mellace, "W. Va. Poll Rocks Kennedy's Hopes: Catholic Faith Swaying Many, Group Learns," *Charleston Daily Mail*, April 14, 1960.
23. Bob Mellace, "Humphrey Has Big Lead in State Poll," *Charleston Daily Mail*, April 15, 1960.
24. Mellace, "W. Va. Poll." "The findings confirmed that four weeks before the vote, most the Democrats knew Kennedy's religion was Catholic and very few knew Humphrey's was Congregational."
25. Thursday's poll results (Kennedy 66 / Humphrey 62 / Undecided 17) were based on interviews of Democrats in two targeted communities—the Fifth Ward in Huntington, Cabell County, and the community of Slab Fork in Fayette County. Friday's numbers included the addition of two more communities of Layland in Fayette County and Chesapeake in Kanawha County.
26. Mellace, "W. Va. Poll."
27. Mellace, "Humphrey Has Big Lead." In Chesapeake, pollsters worked two selected blocks of houses after the supper hour and contacted 19 voters (14 declared for Humphrey and four for Kennedy; one was undecided). Their efforts at gender balance were questionable. The paper explained that "housewives [in the Huntington Fifth Ward] constituted the majority of those areas polled in the morning hours, and these were balanced by supper-hour polling of men home from work."
28. Mellace, "Humphrey Has Big Lead." Kennedy's itinerary would place him in Clarksburg on Monday, the Northern Panhandle on Tuesday, and in southern West Virginia on Wednesday, where he would tour the Beckley area, Mt. Hope, Oak Hill, and Fayetteville.
29. Mellace, "W. Va. Poll."
30. "Change of Tactics: Sen. Kennedy Finds Friends in Wheeling," *Charleston Gazette*, April 19, 1960.
31. Herb Little, "Angry Sen. Kennedy Brings Up Religion," *Charleston Daily Mail*, April 19, 1960.
32. Herb Little, "Kennedy Shifts Tactics, Discusses Religious Issue," *Beckley (WV) Post-Herald*, April 19, 1960.
33. L. T. Anderson, "In Reverse: They're Trying to Shame Us In to a Kennedy Vote," *Charleston Gazette-Mail*, (Charleston, WV), April 17, 1960,
34. White, *Making*, 106–7.
35. O'Donnell and Powers, *Johnny*, 187; David Barnett, "Kennedy Is Mining Votes

With His Change In Tactics; Switches from Soft Sell," *Charleston Gazette* (Charleston, WV) April 21, 1960.

36. "Sen. Kennedy Tells Clarksbu[r]g That GOP Neglects Welfare of WV," *Clarksburg (WV) Exponent*, April 19, 1960.

37. Barnett, "Kennedy Is Mining"; "Jack Gets His Irish Up: Kennedy will visit in City Tonight," *Huntington (WV) Advertiser*, April 20, 1960.

38. Little, "Change of Tactics."

39. "Kennedy to Fight Religious Issue: Won't Turn Cheek," *Morgantown (WV) Dominion News*, April 19, 1960.

40. "Jack Gets His Irish Up."

41. W. H. Lawrence, "Kennedy Agrees to Face Humphrey," *New York Times*, April 20, 1960.

42. "Kennedy Visits Coal Fields: Value Of Trip Questionable," *Huntington (WV) Herald-Dispatch*, April 21, 1960; Little, "Kennedy Bewails."

43. "Religion Gets Stressed During Kennedy Stops: Southern County Swing Features that Issue," *Clarksburg (WV) Exponent*, April 21, 1960.

44. "Religion Gets Stressed."

45. "Collins Students Hear Sen. Kennedy," *Raleigh Register* (Beckley, WV), April 21, 1960; "John Kennedy Believes He's Only Presidential Candidate Who Ever Has Visited Collins High School Two Times: Jack Kennedy Says He Knows State's Needs," *Fairmont (WV) Times*, April 18, 1960.

46. Mellace, "Humphrey Has Big Lead."

47. Hugh Maxwell, "Parting Swing at Critics: Church No Issue, Kennedy Repeats," *Huntington (WV) Advertiser*, April 21, 1960.

48. Maxwell, "Parting Swing at Critics."

49. "The Kennedy Speech," *New York Times*, April 23, 1960; "The Religious Issue in American Politics," *U.S. News and World Report*, May 2, 1960, 91–92.

50. Arthur Edson, "Kennedy Kin Saying Humphrey Isn't Winner," *Clarksburg (WV) Exponent,* May 2, 1960.

51. Stacey Bredhoff, *Winning West Virginia: JFK's Primary Campaign Foundation* (Washington, DC: Text Foundation for the National Archives, 2010), 14–15.

52. Bredhoff, *Winning West Virginia*, 15.

53. Ted Sorensen, interview by Robert Rupp, May 9, 2010, Charleston, WV. Sorensen noted that at an event in Kanawha County, he delivered remarks from a blank sheet of paper. Since he had written the speech, it was not a problem.

54. After receiving bad news about an unscientific state poll the previous week, Kennedy got good news on Sunday, April 24, from the reputable Gallup poll showing far ahead of Humphrey in a national sample of Democrats. The poll results were Kennedy, 39 percent; Stevenson, 21 percent; Johnson, 11 percent; Humphrey, seven percent; and Symington, six percent. Even better, Gallup showed Kennedy leading Nixon by a 52-to-48 percent margin. This result was quickly turned into a television ad, highlighting Kennedy's electability and saying, "Only Kennedy can beat Nixon;" W. H. Lawrence, "Candidates: Democratic Race Grows

Bitter," *New York Times*, April 24, 1960; "Nixon Is Trailing Kennedy In Poll," *New York Times*, April 24, 1960; Kennedy, "Gallup Poll Advertisement."

55. Wicklein, "West Virginians."

56. W. H. Lawrence, "Humphrey Given Edge by Editors," *New York Times*, April 23, 1960.

57. John Wicklein, "West Virginians Discuss Religion," *New York Times*, April 25, 1960. Wicklein found widespread disagreement among the ministers over voter motives. For instance, Methodist minister George McCune of Ripley said that old fears of the Pope would motivate voters. Methodist minister Ross Culpepper of Charleston, on the other hand, stated that it wasn't at all like the Al Smith campaign. Wicklein did visit several small fundamentalist churches near Charleston that had strong feelings against Catholic candidates. He speculated not just about denominational differences, but also about regional differences, predicting that religion would play a bigger role "in the mid-state regions between Parkersburg and Charleston and south to the Kentucky and Virginia boundaries."

58. Maxwell, "Kennedy Breakfast,"

59. Maxwell, "Kennedy Breakfast."

60. "Dem Candidates Again Tour State," *Charleston Daily Mail*, April 25, 1960. "Among guests at the Huntington breakfast meeting, besides Senator Kennedy and his brother Robert, were Sergeant [*sic*] Shriver, the senator's brother-in-law; Chet Huntley, an NBC news analyst who was in the area to do a report on West Virginia politics; William Battle, son of the former governor of Virginia; and Joe Stydahar of Chicago, a former West Virginia University and Chicago Bears football star."

61. "Warm Welcome Given Kennedy—Senator Met by Crowd of 600 at Courthouse," *Logan (WV) Banner*, April 26, 1960. As was common practice, Sen. Kennedy traveled in a private automobile rather than the chartered bus that carried members of his staff and reporters.

62. Herb Little, "Jack Continues Blast of Administration," *Charleston Gazette*, April 26, 1960; "Kennedy Visits Today," *Bluefield (WV) Daily Telegraph*, April 26, 1960.

63. Richard J. H. Johnston, "Kennedy Pledges WV Aid," *New York Times*, April 26, 1960.

64. Johnston, "Kennedy Pledges WV Aid."

65. Johnston, "Kennedy Pledges WV Aid."

66. "Sen. Kennedy Says Nixon Involved In W.Va. Effort: 'Stop-Kennedy' Move Blasted in Talk Here," *Williamson (WV) Daily News*, April 26, 1960.

67. "Sen. Kennedy Says Nixon Involved."

68. "Sen. Kennedy Says Nixon Involved."

69. "Presidential Hopeful Sen. John F. Kennedy to Visit Logan Today," *Logan (WV) Banner*, April 25, 1960; "Warm Welcome," *Logan (WV) Banner*, April 26, 1960.

70. "Dem Candidates Again Tour State," *Charleston Daily Mail*, April 25, 1960.

71. "Sen. Hubert H. Humphrey," *Charleston Gazette*, April 21, 1960. In this vein, he praised the state, saying, "Too much unfair and untrue has been said about West Virginia and that I come here to praise and honor the state and its people."

72. "Sen. Hubert H. Humphrey."

73. "Sen. Hubert H. Humphrey."

74. "Humphrey Advocates Food Stamp: GOP Ignoring Hungry in W. Va. Campaigner Claims," *Wheeling (WV) News-Register*, April 25, 1960. Humphrey called for a "food stamp" program to enable families of the unemployed or with low income to supplement their diets. The plan would allow recipients to use food stamps to directly buy food at the grocery store.

75. Arthur Edson, "Hubert, Kennedy Return to Stump; Humphrey Strikes 'Poor Man's Theme,'" *Charleston Gazette* (Charleston, WV), April; 26, 1960.

76. "Humphrey Insists He's An Underdog: Renews Attack on Kennedy Wealth as He Pushes His West Virginia Campaign," *New York Times*, April 27, 1960: "I can't afford to run through this state with a little black bag and a checkbook . . . I'm being ganged up on by wealth."

77. "Humphrey Insists."

78. "Humphrey Insists."

79. Bradlee, "Best Underdog," 34.

80. Arthur Edson, "Homespun Phraseology Employed By Humphrey; 'I was Poor, too, He Reiterates,'" *Charleston Daily Mail*, April 28, 1960.

81. Edson, "Homespun Phraseology."

82. "Late Arrival, Small Turnout Fail to Faze Humphrey Here," *Martinsburg (WV) Journal*, April 27, 1960.

83. "Kaleidoscope on a Candidate—Humphrey Visits Charles Town," (Special to the *Journal*), *Martinsburg (WV) Journal*, April 28, 1960.

84. "Sen. Humphrey Visits Springs, Drug Store on Stop in Morgan," (Special to the *Journal*), *Martinsburg (WV) Journal*, April 27, 1960. Many children followed his route to the springs and his bus, seeking autographs and asking questions.

85. "Not 'Rich, Bossed,'" *Martinsburg (WV) Journal*, April 27, 1960.

86. "Kaleidoscope."

87. "Local Poll Indicates Kennedy Will Emerge Winner in County," *Martinsburg (WV) Journal*, May 7, 1960. This poll was in direct contrast with forecasts coming from other parts of the state, which showed Senator Hubert H. Humphrey having a lead in the preferential voting for the Democratic presidential nomination.

88. "Kaleidoscope."

89. Herb Little, "Kennedy, FDR Jr. Combine Forces on Tour," *Raleigh Register* (Beckley, WV), April 26, 1960.

90. "Humphrey in Coal Fields."

91. Richard J. H. Johnston, "Kennedy Hailed in Mining Regions: Crowds in West Virginia Are Large and Enthusiastic—He Stresses Job Losses," *New York Times*, April 27, 1960.

92. Little, "Kennedy, FDR Jr. Combine Forces on Tour."

93. "Kennedy Cuts Tour Short, Doesn't Appear In Hinton," *Hinton (WV) Daily News*, April 27, 1960; Little, "Kennedy, FDR Jr. Combine Forces," *Raleigh Register* (Beckley, WV), April 26, 1960.

94. "Kennedy Cuts Tour Short, Doesn't Appear in Hinton," *Hinton (WV) Daily News*, April 27, 1960.

95. "Kennedy Has Close Call In W.Va.; High Voltage Wire Falls," *Mineral Daily News Tribune* (Keyser, WV), April 27, 1960.

96. "Kennedy Has Close Call." Kennedy hit it off quickly with the 200 miners. He got into the mine car and announced who he was, saying, "I'm a Democratic presidential candidate." One of the miners interrupted to shout, "As long as you're not a damn Republican, fine." Kennedy and the others roared with laughter. Kennedy told them he was intrigued by the modern mine where they worked. "I wish Ike would come down and see it," one man yelled. "You build a damn golf course and he'll be here," yelled another.

97. "Kennedy Has Close Call."

98. "Kennedy Cuts Tour Short."

99. *1960 Population of Census Supplementary Report, Race of the Population of the United States, By States: 1960,* (Washington, DC, September 7, 1961), PC(S1)-10.

100. William Lonesome, oral interview, JFK Library, July 14, 1964; Marjorie McKenzie Lawson, oral interview, October 25, 1965, JFK Library.

101. "Arrangements Completed for Kennedy's Visit Here," *Hinton (WV) Daily News*, April 26, 1960.

102. Richard J. H. Johnson, "Kennedy Breaks Campaign To Vote: Leaves West Virginia to Act on Mine Bill- Returns for Charles Town Rally," *New York Times,* April 28, 1960.

103. "Sen. Kennedy Visitor in City," *Martinsburg (WV) Journal*, April 28, 1960. Kennedy's supporters in the panhandle received renewed assurance that he would fly out of Washington and arrive on time. There had been concern when UPI reported Wednesday morning that he had cancelled the remainder of his state tour to fly back to Washington to vote on a coal mine safety bill.

104. "Episcopal Cleric Backing Kennedy," *New York Times*, April 29, 1960.

105. "Former Bishop Backs Kennedy on Church Issue," *Clarksburg (WV) Exponent*, April 28, 1960.

106. "Kennedys in Charles Town," (Special to *The Journal*), *Martinsburg (WV) Journal*, April 26, 1960. His address was carried by WEPM, a Martinsburg radio station that had broadcast his earlier Q and A session.

107. "Kennedys in Charles Town."

108. "Kennedy Here on Wednesday, Day After Humphrey's Visit," *Martinsburg (WV) Journal*, April 25, 1960.

109. "Kennedy Here on Wednesday."

110. "Kennedy Here on Wednesday."

111. "Sen. Kennedy Visitor in City," *Martinsburg (WV) Journal*, April 28, 1960.

112. "Kennedy Went to Indiana to File in the State's Primary," *New York Times*, April 30, 1960.

113. Haught, "Humphrey Hits Aid."

114. Haught, "Humphrey Hits Aid."

115. Haught, "Humphrey Hits Aid."
116. Haught, "Humphrey Hits Aid." On April 19, students at Korea University began protesting against police violence and called for new elections. The protests were again violently suppressed, leading to a demonstration before the presidential Blue House by thousands of students, who dispersed only when police fired point-blank into their ranks. By April 25, the protests had grown even larger as professors and other citizens joined the students, nearly throwing the country into complete anarchy.
117. Haught, "Humphrey Hits Aid."
118. Haught, "Humphrey Hits Aid." "If we can't win the ancient struggle against disease, poverty, illiteracy and hunger, we can't expect to survive merely by armed strength." The Minnesota senator then made reference to the Bible: "Since Cain and Abel, the Bible has been asking, 'Am I my brother's keeper?' If we don't answer in the affirmative, then our brother will slay us. . . . For the hungry and poverty-ridden world is a world made for the demagogue. Khrushchev knows his communism will win in such a world."
119. Hugh Maxwell, "Humphrey Tours in Area," *Huntington (WV) Advertiser*, April 28, 1960.
120. Maxwell, "Humphrey Tours."
121. Maxwell, "Humphrey Tours." Humphrey will visit seven towns and cities in this area on his campaign tour of WV:

> St. Albans / Hurricane at 9:30 a.m. where he will greet citizens.
>
> Milton—At 10 a.m. he will arrive in to be met by Fire Chief and former Mayor Richard Bias; Democratic Committeeman Sly Sanders, Committeewoman Mrs. Nina Summers and a citizens group.
>
> Barboursville Arrive in Barboursville at 11 a.m. where he will be met by James Brady Jr., and a citizens group.
>
> Tours of streets in both Milton and Barboursville are scheduled. Leave at noon.
>
> Huntington—At 12:20 p.m. for a reception at Humphrey for president head-quarters, 1025 Third avenue. Arrangements are in charge of Norman Rood, county chairman of the Humphrey committee and George Henderson Jr.
>
> Hamlin—After an informal private luncheon in Huntington with staff members, he will leave at 2 p.m. for Hamlin, to be greeted by Circuit Court Clerk George Chandler, and Prosecutor R. A. Woodall for a street tour. Leaves Hamlin at 3:30 p.m. Chapmanville for a 15-minute visit lasting until 4:45 p.m. when he leaves.
>
> Logan—He will be greeted in Logan by County Chairman Raymond Chafin. A private dinner is scheduled for 6 p.m. at the Aracoma Hotel. Mrs. Humphrey will join the senator in Logan.
>
> At 8 p.m. he will speak at the Logan county courthouse. Arrangements are in charge of Judge C. C. Chambers, Thomas Childers and William Turley. /—Leaves at 9:30 p.m. for Beckley where he will stay overnight.

122. "Humphrey Setting Fast Pace, Makes Calls in St. Albans," *Charleston Daily Mail*, April 29, 1960.

123. "Humphrey Setting Fast Pace."

124. "Humphrey Setting Fast Pace."

125. "Humphrey Setting Fast Pace."

126. Hugh Maxwell, "Senator Visits City Again—Humphrey's Third Finds Hospitality," *Huntington (WV) Advertiser*, April 30, 1960.

127. Maxwell, "Senator Visits City Again."

128. "Humphrey Tours."

129. "Sen. Humphrey Takes Off Gloves, Hits Back at Kennedy Accusation," *Logan (WV) Banner*, April 30, 1960.

130. John Kady, "Humphrey and Kennedy Trade Insults in W.Va. Stretch," *Washington Post*, May 1, 1960.

131. "Sen. Humphrey Takes Off Gloves."

132. "Sen. Humphrey Takes Off Gloves."

133. "Sen. Humphrey Takes Off Gloves."

134. "Sen. Humphrey Takes Off Gloves."

135. "'Voiceless' Kennedy in Weirton Today: Supporter Reading Speeches," *Wheeling (WV) News-Register*, May 1, 1960.

136. Carroll Kilpatrick, "Bitterness of West Virginia Battle Begins to Worry Democratic Chiefs," *Washington Post*, May 3, 1960.

137. Kilpatrick, "Bitterness."

138. Kilpatrick, "Bitterness."

139. Kilpatrick, "Bitterness."

140. Hubert Eats Ramps." *Huntington (WV) Herald-Dispatch*, May 1, 1960. Some had left by noon, but there were still 500 cars, trucks, trailers, and other vehicles in the parking lot when Humphrey's bus arrived.

141. "Hubert Eats Ramps,"

142. "Hubert Eats Ramps"; Jim Comstock, "Ramps II," *West Virginia Hillbilly*, April 20, 1989, 24.

143. "Humphrey Meets FDR Jr.," *Huntington (WV) Herald-Dispatch*, May 1, 1960.

144. "FDR Jr., to Be in This Region for Kennedy," *Clarksburg (WV) Exponent*, April 29, 1960. His visit was part of a Saturday tour that would take him to Camden-on-Gauley (noon), Cowen (1:00 p.m.), and Parsons in Tucker County (4:00 p.m.). He would then fly to Greenbrier County for a final rally at Rainelle (again shadow) starting at 8:00 p.m. Roosevelt would ironically end the day where Humphrey started out—Rainelle in Greenbrier County.

145. "Elaborate Reception Planned For Kennedy's Visit Sunday," *Ravenswood (WV) News*, April 28, 1960.

146. "Hubert Eats Ramps."

147. "Hubert, Jack Scout Votes Across State," *Huntington (WV) Herald-Dispatch*, May 1, 1960.

148. Matt Reese, interview by Robert Rupp, May 5, 1990, Boston, MA.

149. James Green, *The Devil Is Here in These Hills: West Virginia's Coal Miners and Their Battle for Freedom*, (New York: Atlantic Monthly Press, 2015), 5. The strike resulted in at least 50 deaths and was prelude to the conflict at Blair Mountain less then a decade later.

150. "Kennedy at Cabin Creek," *Charleston Gazette*, May 2, 1960.

151. "Sen. Kennedy Will Address Unitarians," *Charleston Gazette*, April 28, 1960. The tour included his first campaign visit to a church, the Unitarian Church in North Charleston. "2 Presidential Hopefuls Push Campaign," *Charleston Daily Mail*, April 28, 1960.

152. "Enjoys Largest Rally Here: Kennedy Confident," *Parkersburg (WV) News*, May 2, 1960.

153. "Kennedy Visit Here Draws 1,200 [*sic*] People," *Ravenswood (WV) News*, May 5, 1960. Caroline, who was running a temperature, prompted Jackie to fly back to Washington on Saturday night after a television appearance in Charleston.

154. "Kennedy Visit."

155. "Largest Rally."

156. "Kennedy Speaks at Ox Roast: Record-Breaking Crowd Attends Rally at City Park," *Wheeling (WV) News-Register*, May 1, 1960; "Largest Rally."

157. "Largest Rally."

158. "Largest Rally."

159. "Largest Rally."

160. "Largest Rally." Harley E. Bailey of the Jefferson Baptist Temple gave the invocation.

161. Arthur M. Schlesinger Jr., *Robert Kennedy and His Times* (Boston: Houghton Mifflin, 1978), 167–69, 195–96.

162. "Kennedy Speaks at Ox Roast.

163. "Kennedy Speaks at Ox Roast."

164. "Kennedy Speaks at Ox Roast."

165. Schlesinger Jr., *Robert Kennedy*, 104–8, 117–20.

166. *New York Times*, "Mrs. Roosevelt Lauds Humphrey; Says He Comes Closest to 'Spark of Greatness' Next President Will Need," December 8, 1958.

167. "Courage," handout, West Virginia Files, John F. Kennedy Library.

168. John Weyland, "Labor's Aid Requested by Hubert," *Charleston Gazette*, May 10, 1960.

169. "Humphrey Campaigns in Parkersburg: Will Deliver Major Address at VFW Hall Tonight," *Parkersburg (WV) Sentinel*, May 2, 1960.

170. "Sen. Humphrey Will Campaign Here," *Parkersburg (WV) News*, May 2, 1960.

171. "VFW Hall: Humphrey Addresses Rally," *Parkersburg (WV) News*, May 3, 1960.

172. "Largest Rally"; Weyland, "Labor's Aid."

173. Richard K. Boyd, "Humphrey Draws 10,000 in Cabell: Free Rides for All," *Huntington (WV) Dispatch*, May 2, 1960. Park manager Robert Burley estimated the gathering at nearly 10,000.

174. Boyd, "Humphrey Draws 10,000."

175. Fleming Jr., *Kennedy vs. Humphrey*, 124–25; Rowland Evans and Robert Novak,

Lyndon B. Johnson: The Exercise of Power (New York: New American Library, 1966), 259.

176. Evans, *Lyndon B. Johnson*, 259.
177. Evans, *Lyndon B. Johnson*, 259.
178. "Annotated Timeline of Campaign Stops: June 1958–May 10, 1960, Battleground West Virginia: Electing the President. West Virginia Achives and History On-line Exhibit. http://www.wvculture.org/history/1960presidentialcampaign/1960 presidentialcampaign.html. Last accessed April 20, 2019; Christie, oral history interview.
179. Don Marsh, "Jack Happy Fate is Here," *Charleston Gazette*, May 4, 1960.
180. Marsh, "Jack Happy."
181. Marsh, "Jack Happy."
182. Marsh, "Jack Happy."
183. Marsh, "Jack Happy."
184. Myers, ed., *West Virginia Blue Book 1960*, 723.
185. "Battleground, West Virginia: Electing the President in 1960," West Virginia Archives and History, accessed at http://www.wvculture.org/history/1960presidential campaign/1960presidentialcampaign.html
186. "Senator John Kennedy Visits In Hinton Today," *Hinton (WV) Daily News*, May 4, 1960.
187. "Senator John Kennedy Visits In Hinton Today," *Hinton (WV) Daily News*, May 4, 1960.
188. "Senator John Kennedy Visits In Hinton Today," *Hinton (WV) Daily News*, May 4, 1960.
189. "Sen. Kennedy Speaks Briefly At Local High School Wed." *Alderson (WV) Times*, May 5, 1960.
190. "Greenbrier Boy Asks For Autograph," *Beckley (WV) Post Herald*, May 5, 1960.
191. Lawless, "Ward Bond."
192. "Humphrey," *Wheeling (WV) Intelligencer*, May 4, 1960; Thomas A. Stafford, "Hubert Stops Tour to Push Area Aid Bill," *Charleston Gazette*, May 6, 1960. At the panel he again proposed that West Virginia become the nation's center for mine-mouth power plant development. "It is obvious that 'mine-mouth' electric power stations," he said, "represent an exciting new possibility for the growth of the coal industry and the revitalization of West Virginia's economy."
193. Heymann, *RFK*, 119.
194. Stafford, "Hubert Stops Tour."
195. Stafford, "Hubert Stops Tour." When Humphrey spoke at Bethany College, he showed a sense of humor and an understanding of his audience. Introduced to the overflowing crowd of students at the college auditorium, he smiled at the applause and said, "I could make a fiery and probably a razzle-dazzle political speech here today and probably convince all eight or nine Democrats out there to save the political souls of your Republican brethren." He was referring apparently to the poll of Bethany students that showed 375 Republicans and only 87 Democrats.

196. Stafford, "Hubert Stops Tour."

197. Stafford, "Hubert Stops Tour." The UPI reporter was John Kady, a former resident of nearby Glen Dale, West Virginia. None of the national newspapers had correspondents covering the Humphrey tour that day.

198. "Kennedy Lashes Ike, Underwood From Courthouse Steps," *Raleigh (WV) Register*, May 6, 1960. A rally in Raleigh County was the first recorded instance of the candidate being kissed. He had just completed his brief speech to a crowd of upwards of 1,000 at the courthouse steps when a middle-aged lady kissed him on his left cheek. The press reported that the "boyish Kennedy was a marked man with the lipstick" as he walked down from the steps and shook hands for 40 minutes.

199. "Kennedy Lashes Ike."

200. "Kennedy Lashes Ike."

201. "Kennedy Lashes Ike."

202. "Candidates Go to Washington to Cast Votes; Bill to Assist Areas with High Idleness Up," *Clarksburg (WV) Exponent*, May 6, 1960.

203. "Kennedy Lands for 5th Visit," *Huntington (WV) Advertiser*, May 6, 1960.

204. "Humphrey Says No Need For Poverty Here," *Charleston Daily Mail*, May 7, 1960.

205. "Humphrey Says No Need."

206. Wayne Phillips, "Humphrey Hits 'Political Payola' In Kennedy's Primary Spending," *New York Times*, May 7, 1960.

207. "Tribute Posed to Judge Bailey at Pineville Dinner," *Welch (WV) Daily News*, May 7, 1960.

208. "Humphrey in Coal Fields Tour: Feels Like 'Triumphant Caesar,'" *New York Times*, April 12, 1960.

209. Myers, ed., *West Virginia Blue Book 1960*, 723.

210. Humphrey, *Education*, 363n4.

211. Lawrence, "Roosevelt Hits Humphrey." One document he cited was a letter from the dean of Macalester College, where Humphrey once taught political science, requesting a deferment for Humphrey.

212. Humphrey, *Education*, 363.

213. "Kennedy Speaks," *Inter-Mountain* (Elkins, WV), May 8, 1960.

214. "Kennedy Visits," *Charleston Gazette*, May 8, 1960.

215. "Annotated Timeline of Campaign Stops: June 1958–May 10, 1960, Battleground West Virginia: Electing the President. West Virginia Achives and History Online Exhibit. http://www.wvculture.org/history/1960presidentialcampaign/1960presidential campaign.html. Last accessed April 20, 2019; "It's No Waltz: Harrison County Labor Federation Dance," *Charleston Gazette*, May 9, 1960.

216. "10 U.S. Senators Will Visit Clarksburg: Johnson Will Give Address For Dems Here," *Clarksburg (WV) Exponent*, April 14, 1960. Also attending were B. L. Bartlett of Alaska, Allen Bible of Nevada, Dennis Chavez of New Mexico, J. Allen Frear of Delaware, Theodore Francis Green of Rhode Island, Vance Hartke of Indiana, and Oren B. Long of Hawaii. According to a statement by Harrison County Democratic Chairman Ben B. Stout, "These senators and congressmen represent a good

cross-section of the United States, including all the great religious faiths and political thought of the whole country."

217. Edson, "Mountain Feudin.'"

218. Edson, "Mountain Feudin.'"

219. Edson, "Mountain Feudin.'"

220. "More Than 500 at Dinner for Sen. Johnson," *Clarksburg (WV) Exponent*, May 10, 1960.

221. Richard K. Boyd, "Integrity Lost, Says Humphrey," *Huntington (WV) Herald-Dispatch*, May 9, 1960.

222. "More Than 2,500 Present at Kennedy Open House Here," *Clarksburg (WV) Exponent*, May 10, 1960.

223. Ad for television, *Charleston Gazette*, May 9, 1960; White, *Making*, 107; Kenneth O'Donnell, Rowland P. Evans, and Tom Wicker, "TV in the Political Campaign," *Television Quarterly* (Winter 1966): 21. The format worked so well in West Virginia that it was duplicated in the Oregon primary using Congresswoman Edith Green in place of Franklin Roosevelt Jr.

224. O'Donnell, "TV in the Political Campaign," 21.

225. White, *Making*, 110–12.

226. White, *Making*, 110.

227. "Poll Shows Kennedy Winning—but Voters Make Choice Tomorrow," *Fayette Tribune* (Oak Hill, WV), May 9, 1960. "If we add the two polls up together, Humphrey would win. But the results would be so close, 128–125. So maybe we ought to call the race 50–50, and neither Senator Humphrey nor Senator Kennedy would feel bad."

228. O'Donnell and Powers, *Johnny*, 165.

229. Don Marsh, "One-sided Victory Looked Impossible: Kennedy Genuinely Surprised," *Charleston Gazette*, May 12, 1960.

230. Lawrence, *Six Presidents*, 233.

231. Joseph L. Rauh Jr., oral history interview, December 23, 1965, John F. Kennedy Library. Humphrey later admitted that "I never said it publicly or to my staff, but I felt were licked in the last week. I just felt it was over. There was nothing to be done at that point but to see the damn thing through." Helen O'Donnell, *Irish Brotherhood*, 328.

232. Rauh Jr., oral history interview.

233. "Humphrey Visits," *Charleston Gazette*, May 9, 1960.

234. "Kennedy Pays Final Visit to Parkersburg: Presidential Candidate Winding Up Campaign," *Parkersburg (WV) Sentinel* May 9, 1960.

Chapter 6

1. George Lawless, "Some Happy and Some Sad; Pros Being picking at Political Carcass," *Charleston Gazette*, (Charleston, WV), May 12, 1960.

2. Myers, ed., *West Virginia Blue Book 1960*, 723.

3. Jack David, "Kennedy Accepts Hurrahs, Backslaps," *Charleston Daily Mail*, May 11, 1960.

4. "Winner, Loser Say:" *Charleston Daily Mail,* May 11, 1960; "Kennedy Winner, Humphrey Quits," *Charleston Daily Mail,* May 11, 1960.

5. "Winner, Loser Say:" *Charleston Daily Mail,* May 11, 1960.

6. "Federal Judicial History," FJC, accessed at https://www.fjc.gov/history/judges /christie-sidney-lee. On April 15, 1964, Christie was nominated by President Lyndon B. Johnson to a seat on the United States District Court for the Southern District and the Northern District of West Virginia, both vacated by Harry E. Watkins. Christie was confirmed by the United States Senate on April 30, 1964, and received his commission on May 1, 1964. He served as chief judge from 1971–1973 and continued on the bench until his death.

7. Schlesinger, *A Thousand Days,* 166.

8. Jim Haught, "Humphrey Hits Aid."

9. Sorensen, *Kennedy,* 397.

10. "A Short History of SNAP," USDA, https://www.fns.usda.gov/snap/short-history -snap; "Farming in the 1950s & 60s: Food Stamps," Wessels Living History Farm, https://livinghistoryfarm.org/farminginthe50s/money_09.html.

11. "A Short History of SNAP"

12. Robert McDonough, oral history interview, February 13, 1965, JFK Library.

13. McDonough, oral history interview, Feb. 13, 1965, JFK Library.

14. William Wallace Barron, oral history interview, August 10, 1965, JFK Library; Thomas F. Stafford, *Afflicting the Comfortable: Journalism and Politics in West Virginia* (Morgantown: West Virginia University Press, 2005), 80.

15. McDonough, oral history interview, Feb. 13, 1965, Parkersburg, WV. McDonough would later recall that "very little differed in a politician's mind if he gives you a thousand-dollar favor or a hundred-million-dollar favor." He was "determined to get the million-dollar favors more than the five-dollar favors."

16. One of the objections to the north-south road was that the original plan did not connect military or industrial centers, so Charleston was selected instead of Beckley as an end point. McDonough, oral history, Feb. 13, 1965.

17. J. Howard Myers, ed, *West Virginia Blue Book 1959.* (Charleston, WV: Jarrett Printing, 1959), 860; J. Howard Myers, ed, *West Virginia Blue Book 1964.* (Charleston, WV: Jarrett Printing, 1964), 918.

18. Richard A. Brisbin, Jr et al., *West Virginia Politics and Government* (Lincoln: University of Nebraska Press, 2008), 180. By 1974 the share of federal funds increased from 37% to 47% per cent.

19. Ron Eller argued in 2013 that "Many public policies are still based on the naïve assumptions that poverty can be seriously addressed without structural change . . ." Ron D. Eller, *Uneven Ground: Appalachia Since 1945* (Lexington, KY: University Press of Kentucky, 2013), 5–8.

20. Don Marsh, "Aid for State Is Pledged by Kennedy," *Charleston Gazette,* May 10, 1960.

21. Thomas, *An Appalachian Reawakening,* 73–74.

22. Matt Reese, interview by Robert Rupp, Boston, MA, May 5, 1990.

23. Roger A. Lohmann, "Four Perspectives on Appalachian Culture and Poverty,"

Journal of Appalachian Studies Association 2 (1990): 76–91. For a critique of assumptions of the early ARC programs and the economic thinking during the 1960s, see David Whisnant, *Modernizing the Mountaineer: People, Power, and Planning in Appalachia* (Knoxville: University of Tennessee Press, 1994), 129–46.

24. Fred D. Baldwin, "Appalachian Highways: Almost Home but a Long Way to Go," Appalachian Regional Commission. Last accessed April 29, 2019, https://www.arc .gov/magazine/articles.asp?ARTICLE_ID=168. A 1995 study in the *Journal of the American Planning Association* found that the 110 ARC counties with development highways grew 49 percentage points faster in earnings and 69 percentage points faster in income than counties without such highways.

25. Eller, *Uneven Ground*. "Few questioned the benefit of growth or associated poverty with systemic inequalities in political or economic structures." 63; Dwight B. Billings and Kathleen M. Blee, *The Road to Poverty: The Making of Wealth and Hardship in Appalachia* (Cambridge: Cambridge University Press, 2000), 11–13.

26. Thomas, *Appalachian Reawakening*, 166.

27. "Appalachia Bill Needs Changes," *Charleston Gazette*, February 2, 1965.

28. West Virginia Department of Transportation Planning and Research Division: Intermodal Special Projects Division, *West Virginia National Highway System Report* (Charleston, WV: 2000).

29. Carol Melling, "Appalachian Corridor Highways," in *The West Virginia Encyclopedia*, ed. Ken Sullivan, 646. (Charleston: West Virginia Humanities Council), 2006. 17. Billy Joe Peyton, "Highway Development," in *The West Virginia Encyclopedia*, ed. Ken Sullivan (Charleston: West Virginia Humanities Council), 2006. 331–332; *Status of the Appalachian Development Highway System as of September 30, 2015*, www.arc.gov.

30. Michael Bradshaw, *The Appalachian Commission: Twenty-Five Years of Government Policy* (Lexington: University Press of Kentucky, 1992), 26–31.

31. "Candidates Go to Washington to Cast Votes: Bill to Assist Areas with High Idleness up for Action," *Clarksburg (WV) Exponent*, May 6, 1960.

32. Thomas, *Appalachian*, 130–32. A Task Force met December 9, 1960, Kennedy had a bill sent to Congress soon after his inauguration, and by May of 1960 the Area Redevelopment Administration was organized.

33. John F. Kennedy, Area Redevelopment Act, Pub. Law No. 87–27 (1961), in *United States Statues at Large*, Eighty-Seventh Congress, first session, Vol. 75 (Washington, DC: United States Printing Office, 1962), 61. In his message to Congress on February 2, 1961, Kennedy said that he wanted to "establish an effective program to alleviate conditions of substantial and persistent unemployment and underdevelopment in economically depressed areas."

34. Sorensen, *Kennedy*, 403–4.

35. Irving Bernstein, *Promises Kept: John F. Kennedy's New Frontier* (New York: Oxford University Press), 1991., 160–161. Sorensen relates that when Kennedy was campaigning in West Virginia he remarked "that the thing for many of the men in those deserted mining towns would be to help than out of there." The senator then observed that members of Congress, while willing to support retraining,

were reluctant to support relocation and most of the unemployed were equally reluctant to move. Sorensen, *Kennedy*, 404.

36. Area Redevelopment Act, Pub. Law No. 87–27.

37. "114 Areas Listed For Jobless Help: U.S. Names First Distressed Regions Eligible for Aid," *New York Times*, June 10, 1961. Ronald D. Eller, *Uneven Ground: Appalachia Since 1945* (Lexington: University Press of Kentucky, 2008) provides a critical analysis of the Area Redevelopment Act in southern Appalachia. See also Whisnant, *Modernizing the Mountaineer*, 70–91.

38. *Appalachia: A Report by the President's Appalachia Regional Commission*, 1964 (Washington, DC, 1964).

39. Michael J. Bradshaw, *The Appalachian Regional Commission: Twenty-Five Years of Government Policy*, 14, 96. Michael J. Bradshaw maintains that by 1980, "Appalachian people gained considerable improvement in income, employment opportunity, education and health provision relative to the rest of the country." He notes that the gains were diluted during the 1980s and that the differential between Appalachia and the rest of the country was "almost returning to the 1960 differential."

40. John F. Kennedy Presidential Library and Museum, "Legislative Summary: Labor 1961," accessed with credentials, www.jfklibrary.org.

41. "Debate Transcript," *Charleston Gazette*, May 5, 1960.

42. "President Kennedy's Speech," *Charleston Gazette*, June 2, 1963.

43. Thomas, *An Appalachian Reawakening*, 129–32.

44. Debora McCauley, *Appalachian Mountain Religion: A History* (Urbana: University of Illinois Press, 1995), 482–83n4.

45. Dallek, *Unfinished Life*, 255; "A Ten Point Program for West Virginia," April 25, 1960, Box 535, PPP.

46. Dallek, *Unfinished Life*, 254; "Memo from Lou Harris on the Last Week of the Campaigning," n.d., Box 27, David R. Powers Personal Papers, John F. Kennedy Library, Boston, MA.

47. Heymann, *RFK*, 152.

48. Larry J. Sabato, *The Kennedy Half Century: The Presidency, Assassination, and Lasting Legacy of John F. Kennedy* (New York: Bloomsbury, 2013), 266–67.

49. Hartman, *In the Shadow*, 103.

50. Hartman, *In the Shadow*, 102–3.

51. Denise Giardina, Letter to author, March 20, 2002.

52. L. T. Anderson, "Religious Issue May Not Be Dead," *Charleston Gazette*, May 12, 1960.

53. "The Cleared Air," *Wall Street Journal*, May 12, 1960.

54. Anderson, "Religious Issue."

55. Bradlee, "Now West Virginia," 34.

56. Editorial, "On The Other West Virginia The Figures Tell A Far More Encouraging Story," *Charleston Daily Mail*, April 26, 1960. The editorial also noted that personal income in Cabell and Ohio counties income had more than doubled within the past decade.

57. "Roy Lee Harmon, 80, Dies," *Beckley (WV) Post-Herald,* April 8, 1981; Roy Lee Harmon, "Kennedy Assessed State Better Than Many 'Big Time' Newsmen," *Post Herald and Register,* June 22, 1963. Harmon went on to write that fortunately the reporters' words before and after that campaign "was certainly discounted well by President Kennedy in his brief speech Thursday (his address celebrating the state's centennial)."

58. Alan B. Mollohan, "My West Virginia," in *The Appalachians,* 151.

59. Anthony Harkins, *Hillbilly: A Cultural History of an American Icon* (New York: Oxford University Press, 2004), 186, 184–192; Ian Hartman, *In The Shadow of Boone and Crockett: Race, Culture, and the Politics of Representation in the Upland South* (Knoxville: University of Tennessee Press, 2015), 104–32; Gordon McKinney, 153 in *The Appalachians,* ed. Mari-Lynn Evans, Holly George-Warren, and Robert Santelli (New York: Random House, 2004), 153.

60. Denise Giardina, "West Virginia Resident," in *The Appalachians: America's First and Last Frontier,* ed. Mari-Lynn Evans, Holly George-Warren, and Robert Santelli (New York: Random House, 2004), 153; Giardina, Denise, "Appalachian Images: A Personal History," in *Back Talk from Appalachia: Confronting Stereotypes,* ed. D. Billings, G. Norman, and K. Ledford, (Lexington: University Press of Kentucky [1999] 2001). Originally published as *Confronting Appalachian Stereotypes.*

61. Ralph McGill, "Organization Won for Jack," *Charleston Gazette,* May 14, 1960.

62. Sorenson, *Kennedy,* 139. After citing the state poll which showed Kennedy ahead 70–30, Sorenson goes on to mention that after Wisconsin "a new Harris Poll" showed 60–40 landslide for Humphrey" without explaining the poll was not statewide. The omission has continued to be part of most narratives of the primary.

63. Henry Fairlie,"Television's Love Affair with John F. Kennedy," *New Republic,* December 26, 1983, 11–16.

64. Charlie Peters, interview by Robert Rupp, May 10, 1990, Charleston, WV.

65. Carty, *A Catholic in the White House,* 159.

66. Andrew M. Greeley, *The American Catholic Experience: An Interpretation of the History of American Catholicism* (Garden City, NY: Doubleday and Co., 1967), 274–92; Harry G. Hoffmann, oral history interview August 7, 1964, John F. Kennedy Library.

67. Theodore H. White, *In Search of History* (New York: Warner Books, 1979), 457.

68. Thomas J. Carty, *A Catholic in the White House? Religion, Politics, and John F. Kennedy's Presidential Campaign* (New York: Macmillan, 2004).

69. Mark Steven Massa, *Anti-Catholicism in America: The Last Acceptable Prejudice* (New York: Crossroads, 2003), 83–85.

70. Martin E. Marty, *Modern American Religion,* Vol. 3, *Under God, Indivisible 1941–1960* (Chicago: University of Chicago Press, 1996), 4.

71. Fleming Jr., *Kennedy vs. Humphrey,* x.

72. "President Kennedy Speech," *Charleston Gazette,* June 2, 1963.

73. "President Kennedy Speech," *Charleston Gazette,* June 2, 1963.

SELECTED BIBLIOGRAPHY

Books, Articles, and Dissertations

Ajemian, Robert. "Hubert's Zeal, Jack's Box Score of Delegates, Enthusiastic Catholics." *Life*, March 28, 1960, 29.

Alexander, Herbert E. *Financing the 1960 Election*. Princeton, NJ: Citizen's Research Foundation, 1961.

Alsop, Joseph W., and Adam Platt. *I've Seen the Best of It: Memoirs*. New York: Norton, 1992.

Ambler, Charles Henry. *Sectionalism in Virginia from 1776 to 1861*. New York: Russell & Russell, 1964.

Ambrose, Stephen. *Nixon: The Triumph of a Politician, 1962–1972*. New York: Simon and Schuster, 1989.

Baker, Russell. *The Good Times*. New York: William Morrow and Co., 1989.

Baldwin, Fred D. "Appalachian Highways: Almost Home but a Long Way to Go." Appalachian Regional Commission.

Ballard, Sandra L. "Where Did Hillbillies Come From: Tracing Sources of the Comic Hillbilly Fool in Literature." In *Confronting Appalachian Stereotypes: Back Talk from An American Region*, edited by Dwight B. Billings, Gurney Norman, and Katherine Ledford, 138–149. Lexington: The University Press of Kentucky, 1999.

Balmer, Randall. *Blessed Assurance: A History of Evangelicalism in America*. Boston: Beacon Press, 1999.

———. *God in the White House: How Faith Shaped the Presidency from John F. Kennedy to George W. Bush*. San Francisco: HarperOne, 2008.

———. *Mine Eyes Have Seen the Glory: A Journey into the Evangelical Subculture in America*. New York: Oxford University Press, 1989.

Barrett, Patricia. *Religious Liberty and the American Presidency: A Study in Church-State Relations*. New York: Herder and Herder, 1963.

Baughman, James. *Republic of Mass Culture: Journalism, Broadcasting, and Filmmaking in America since 1941*. Baltimore: Johns Hopkins University Press, 2005.

———. *Same Time, Same Station: Creating American Television, 1948–1961*. Baltimore: Johns Hopkins University Press, 2007.

Bernstein, Irving. *Promises Kept: John F. Kennedy's New Frontier*. New York: Oxford University Press, 1991.

Beschloss, Michael R. *Kennedy and Roosevelt: The Uneasy Alliance*. New York: Norton, 1980.

Billings, Dwight B. "Introduction: Writing Appalachia: Old Ways, New Ways, and WVU Ways." In *Culture, Class, and Politics in Modern Appalachia: Essays in Honor of Ronald L. Lewis*, edited by Jennifer Egolf, Ken Fones-Wolf, and Louis Martin, 1–31. Morgantown: West Virginia University Press, 2009.

Billings, Dwight B., and Kathleen M. Blee. *The Road To Poverty: The Making of Wealth and Hardship in Appalachia*. New York: Cambridge University Press, 2000.

Billings, Dwight B., Gurney Norman, and Katherine Ledford. *Back Talk from Appalachia: Confronting Stereotypes*. Lexington: University Press of Kentucky, 1999.

Billings, Dwight B., and Mary Beth Pudup. "Taking Exception with Exceptionalism: The Emergence and Transformation of Historical Studies of Appalachia." In *Appalachia in the Making: The Mountain South in the Nineteenth Century*, edited by Mary Beth Pudup, Dwight B. Billings, and Altina L. Waller, 1–24. Chapel Hill: University of North Carolina Press, 1995.

Blackwell, Deborah L. "Female Stereotypes and the Creation of the Appalachia, 1870—1940." In *Women of the Mountain South: Identity, Work, and Activism*. Edited by Connie Park Rice and Marie Tedesco, 74–94. Athens: Ohio University Press, 2015.

Blair, Joan, and Clay Blair. *The Search for JFK*. New York: Berkley, 1976.

Bradlee, Ben. "Best Underdog in Show." *Newsweek,* May 9, 1960, 34.

———. *Conversations with Kennedy*. New York: Norton, 1975.

———. *A Good Life: Newspapering and Other Adventures*. New York: Simon and Schuster, 1995.

———. "Now West Virginia." *Newsweek,* April 18, 1960, 34.

Bradshaw, Michael. *The Appalachian Regional Commission: Twenty-Five Years of Government Policy*. Lexington: University Press of Kentucky, 1992.

Brauer, Carl. "Kennedy, Johnson and the War on Poverty." *Journal of American History* 69, no. 1 (1982): 98–119.

Bredhoff, Stacey. *Winning West Virginia: JFK's Primary Campaign*. Washington, DC: Foundation for the National Archive, 2010.

Brisbin, Richard A., Jr., Robert Jay Dilger, Allan S. Hammock, and I. Christopher Plein. *West Virginia Politics and Government*. Lincoln: University of Nebraska Press, 2008.

Burner, David. *John F. Kennedy and a New Generation*. New York: Pearson/Longman, 2005.

Burner, David, and Thomas R. West. *The Torch Is Passed: The Kennedy Brothers and American Liberalism*. New York: Athenaeum, 1984.

Campbell, John C. *The Southern Highlander and His Homeland*. Lexington: University of Kentucky Press, 1908.

Carter, Paul A. "The Campaign of 1928 Re-Examined: A Study in Political Folklore." *Wisconsin Magazine of History* 46, no. 4 (Summer 1963).

"Catholic Hero or Secular Icon? Religion in the Presidency of John F. Kennedy." *Religion and Presidency: Modern Presidents*. C-SPAN, November 18, 2004.

Catte, Elisabeth. *What You Are Getting Wrong about Appalachia*. Cleveland: Belt Publishing, 2018.

Carty, Thomas J. *A Catholic in the White House? Religion, Politics, and John F. Kennedy's Presidential Campaign*. New York: Palgrave Macmillan, 2004.

———. *Catholics and American Politics*. Washington, DC: Georgetown University Press, 2008.

———. *Religion and the American Presidency*. New York: Palgrave Macmillan, 2004.

Casey, Shaun A. *The Making of a Catholic President: Kennedy vs. Nixon, 1960*. New York: Oxford University Press, 2009.

Caudill, Harry M. *Night Comes to the Cumberlands: A Biography of a Depressed Area*. Boston: Little, Brown, 1963.

Chafin, Raymond and Topper Sherwood. *Just Good Politics: The Life of Raymond Chafin, Appalachian Boss*. Pittsburgh: University of Pittsburgh Press, 1994.

Chase, Harold W., and Allen H. Lerman, eds. *Kennedy and the Press: The News Conferences*. New York: Crowell, 1965.

Clinch, Nancy G. *The Kennedy Neurosis: A Psychological Portrait of an American Dynasty*. New York: Grosset and Dunlap, 1973.

Cohen, Dan. *Undefeated: The Life of Hubert H. Humphrey*. Minneapolis: Lerner Publications Company, 1978.

Coles, Robert. *Migrants, Sharecroppers, Mountaineers*. Boston: Little, Brown, 1971.

Collier, Peter, and David Horowitz. *The Kennedys: An American Drama*. New York: Summit, 1984.

Comstock, Jim. "Pa Ain't Selling His Vote to No Catholic." In *Best of Hillbilly: A Prize Collection of 100-Proof Writing from Jim Comstock's West Virginia Hillbilly*, edited by Otto Whittaker, 78–81. New York: Pocket Books, 1969.

———. "Ramps II." *The West Virginia Hillbilly*, April 20, 1989.

Conley, Phil, and William Thomas Doherty. *West Virginia History*. Charleston, WV: Education Foundation, 1974.

Corbin, David. A. *The Last Great Senator: Robert C. Byrd's Encounters with Eleven U.S. Presidents*. Washington, DC: Potomac Books, 2012.

———. "John F. Kennedy Plays the 'Religious Card': Another Look at the 1960 West Virginia Primary." *West Virginia History: A Journal of Regional Studies* 9, no. 2 (2015): 1–35.

Creasman, Boyd. *Writing West Virginia: Place, People, and Poverty in Contemporary Literature from the Mountain State*. Knoxville: University of Tennessee Press, 2016.

Crews. Jr., James McRae, "J.F.K. and the Mountaineers: John F. Kennedy's Rhetoric in the 1960 West Virginia Presidential Primary." PhD. Diss., The Florida State University: College of Communications, 1980.

Crickard, Betty P. "The Mountain State." In *Mountain Heritage*, edited by B. B. Maurer, 199–21. Parsons, WV: McClain Printing Company, 2006.

Dallek, Robert. *An Unfinished Life: John F. Kennedy, 1917–1963*. Boston: Little, Brown and Company, 2003.

Davis, F. Keith. *West Virginia Tough Boys: Vote Buying, Fist Fighting, and a President Named JFK*. Chapmanville, WV: Woodland Press, 2003.

Davis, John H. *The Kennedys: Dynasty and Disaster, 1848–1984*. New York: Mc-Graw-Hill, 1984.

Diamond, Edwin, and Stephen Bates. *The Spot: The Rise of Political Advertising on Television*. Cambridge, MA: MIT Press, 1984.

Dochuk, Darren. *From Bible Belt to Sunbelt: Plain Folk Religion, Grassroots Politics, and the Rise of Evangelical Conservatism*. New York: Norton, 2011.

Dolan, Jay P. *The American Catholic Experience: A History from Colonial Times to the Present*. Garden City, NY: Doubleday, 1985.

———. *In Search of an American Catholicism: A History of Religion and Culture in Tension*. Oxford: Oxford University Press, 2002.

———. *The Irish Americans: A History*. New York: Bloomsbury Press, 2008.

Donaldson, Gary A. *The First Modern Campaign: Kennedy, Nixon, and the Election of 1960*. Lanham, MD: Rowman and Littlefield, 2007.

Donovan, Robert J. *PT 109: John F. Kennedy in World War I*. New York: McGraw-Hill, 1961.

Drake, Richard. B. *A History of Appalachia*. Lexington: The University Press of Kentucky, 2001.

Dunaway, Wilma A. *Slavery in the American Mountain South*. Cambridge: Cambridge University Press, 2003.

Egolf, Jennifer, Ken Fones-Wolf, and Louis C. Martin. *Culture, Class, and Politics in Modern Appalachia: Essays in Honor of Ronald L. Lewis*. Morgantown: West Virginia University Press, 2009.

Eisele, Albert. *Almost to the Presidency: A Biography of Two American Politicians*. Blue Earth, MN: Piper, 1972.

Eller, Ronald. Foreword to *Back Talk from Appalachia: Confronting Stereotypes*, edited by Dwight B. Billings, Gurney Norman, and Katherine Ledford, ix–xi. Lexington: University Press of Kentucky, 1999.

———. *Miners, Millhands, and Mountaineers: The Industrialization of the Appalachian South*. Knoxville: University of Tennessee Press, 1982.

———. *Uneven Ground: Appalachia since 1945*. Lexington: University of Kentucky Press, 2009.

Ernst, Harry W. *The Primary That Made a President: West Virginia 1960*. Vol. 26, Eagleton Institute Cases in Practical Politics, edited by Paul Tillett. Rutgers, NJ: McGraw-Hill, 1962.

Ernst, Harry W., and Charles H. Drake. "The Lost Appalachians: Poor, Proud and Primitive." *The Nation*, May 30, 1959.

Evans, Mari-Lyn, Holley George-Warren, and Robert Santelli. *The Appalachians: America's First and Last Frontier*. With Tom Robertson. New York: Random House, 2004.

Evans, Rowland, and Robert Novak. *Lyndon Johnson: The Exercise of Power*. New York: New American Library, 1966.

Fairlie, Henry. "JFK's Television Presidency." *New Republic*, December 26, 1983.

———. *The Kennedy Promise: The Politics of Expectation*. Garden City, NY: Doubleday, 1973.

Fay, Paul B., Jr. *The Pleasure of His Company*. New York: Harper and Row, 1966.

Finan, Christopher M. *Alfred E. Smith: The Happy Warrior*. New York: Hill and Wang, 2002.

Fleming, Daniel B., Jr., *Kennedy vs. Humphrey, West Virginia, 1960: The Pivotal Battle for the Democratic Presidential Nomination*. Jefferson, NC: McFarland, 1992.

Fones-Wolf, Kenneth, and Ronald L. Lewis, eds. *Transnational West Virginia: Ethnic Communities and Economic Change*. Morgantown: West Virginia University Press, 2003.

Frady, Marshall. *Billy Graham: A Parable of American Righteousness*. Boston, Little, Brown & Co., 1979.

Fried, Richard M. Introduction to *A Guide to the Microform Edition of Presidential Campaigns: The John F. Kennedy 1960 Campaign*, v–ix. Frederick, MD: University Publications of America, 1987.

———. *The Man Everybody Knew: Bruce Barton and the Making of Modern America*. Chicago: Ivan R. Dee, 2005.

Fuchs, Lawrence H. *John F. Kennedy and American Catholicism*. New York: Meredith Press, 1967.

Gallup, George H. *The Gallup Poll: Public Opinion 1935–1971*. New York: Random House, 1972.

Gaventa, John. *Power and Powerlessness: Quiescence and Rebellion in an Appalachian Valley*. Urbana: University of Illinois Press, 1980.

Giardina, Denise. "Appalachian Images: A Personal History". In *Back Talk from Appalachia: Confronting Stereotypes*, edited by Dwight Billings, Gurney Norman, and Katherine Ledford, 161–173.

———. "West Virginia Resident," in *The Appalachians: America's First and Last Frontier*, ed. Mari-Lynn Evans, Holly George-Warren, and Robert Santelli (New York: Random House, 2004), 153.

———. *Storming Heaven*. New York: Norton, 1987.

———. *The Unquiet Earth*. New York: Norton, 1992.

Giglio, James. *John F. Kennedy: A Bibliography*. Westport, CT: Greenwood Press, 1995.

———. *The Presidency of John F. Kennedy*. Lawrence: University Press of Kansas, 1991.

Goldwater, Barry M. *With No Apologies: The Personal and Political Memoirs of United States Senator Barry M. Goldwater*. New York: William Morrow, 1979.

Goodwin, Doris Kearns. *The Fitzgeralds and the Kennedys: An American Saga*. New York: Simon and Schuster, 1987.

Goodwin, Richard N. *Remembering America: A Voice from the Sixties*. Boston; Little, Brown, 1988.

Greely, Andrew M. *The American Catholic Experience: An Interpretation of the History of American Catholicism*. Garden City, NY: Doubleday and Co., 1967.

Green, James. *The Devil Is Here in These Hills: West Virginia's Coal Miners and Their Battle for Freedom*. New York: Atlantic Monthly Press, 2015.

Griffith, Winthrop. *Humphrey: A Candid Biography*. New York: Morrow, 1965.

Guthman, Edwin. *We Band of Brothers: A Memoir of Robert F. Kennedy*. New York: Harper and Row, 1971.

Hamilton, Nigel. *JFK: Reckless Youth*. New York: Random House, 1992.

Harkins, Anthony. *Hillbilly: A Cultural History of an American Icon*. New York: Oxford University Press, 2004.

Harrington, Michael. *The Other America: Poverty in the United States*. New York: Scribner, 1962.

Harris, Lou, "A Study of Voter Attitude in West Virginia on Presidential Preferences." John F. Kennedy Library, January 1960.

Hartman, Ian C. "Appalachian Anxiety: Race, Gender, and the Paradox of 'Purity' in the Age of Empire, 1873–1901." *American Nineteenth Century History* 13, no. 2 (2012): 229–55.

———. *In the Shadow of Boone and Crockett: Race, Culture, and the Politics of Representation in the Upland South*. Knoxville: University of Tennessee Press, 2015.

———. "West Virginia Mountaineers and Kentucky Frontiersmen: Race, Manliness, and the Rhetoric of Liberalism in Early 1960s." *Journal of Southern History* 80, no. 3 (2014): 651–79.

Hechler, Ken. *West Virginia Memories of President Kennedy*. Baltimore: Hechler for Congress Committee, 1965.

Hellmann, John. *The Kennedy Obsession: The American Myth of JFK*. New York: Columbia University Press, 1997.

Henderson, Deirdre, ed. *Prelude to Leadership: The European Diary of John F. Kennedy, Summer 1945*. Chicago: Regency, 1995.

Hersey, John. "Survival." *New Yorker,* June 17, 1944: 31–43.

Hersh, Seymour M. *The Dark Side of Camelot*. New York: Little, Brown & Co., 1997.

Heymann, C. David. *RFK: A Candid Biography of Robert F. Kennedy*. New York: Dutton, 1998.

Himmelman, Jeff. *Yours in Truth: A Personal Portrait of Ben Bradlee*. New York: Random House, 2012.

Hoffman, Joyce Hoffman. *Theodore H. White and the Journalism of Illusion*. New York: Columbia University Press, 1997.

Humphrey, Hubert H. *The Education of a Public Man*. Garden City, NY: Doubleday, 1976.

Jamieson, Kathleen H. *Packaging the Presidency: A History and Criticism of Presidential Campaign Advertising*. New York: Oxford University Press, 1984.

Jamieson, Kathleen H., and David S. Birdsell. *Presidential Debates: The Challenge of Creating an Informed Electorate*. New York: Oxford University Press, 1987.

Johnson, Douglas W., Paul R. Picard, and Bernard Quinn. *Churches and Church Membership in the United States: An Enumeration by Region, State, and County, 1971*. Washington, DC: Glenmary Research Center, 1974.

Jones, Loyal. *Appalachian Values*. Ashland, KY: Jesse Stuart Foundation, 1994.

———. "Mountain Religion: An Overview." In *Christianity in Appalachia: Profiles in Regional Pluralism*, edited by Bill J. Leonard, 91–102. Knoxville: The University of Tennessee Press, 1999.

Josephson, Matthew et. al. *Al Smith: Hero of the Cities.* Boston: Houghton Mifflin, 1969.

Kallina, Edmund F., Jr. *Kennedy v. Nixon: The Presidential Election of 1960.* Gainesville: University of Florida Press, 2010.

Kennedy, John F. Area Redevelopment Act, Pub. Law No. 87–27 (1961), in *United States Statues at Large, Eighty-Seventh Congress, first session, Vol. 75.* Washington, DC: United States Printing Office, 1962, 61.

———. *As We Remember Joe.* Cambridge, MA: Privately printed, 1945.

———. *John Fitzgerald Kennedy: A Compilation of Statements and Speeches Made during His Service in the United States Senate and House of Representatives (88th Cong., 2d sess. Senate document no. 79).* Washington, DC: United States Government Printing Office, 1964.

———. *Profiles in Courage.* New York: Harper, 1956.

———. *Public Papers of the Presidents of the United States: John F. Kennedy; Containing the Public Messages, Speeches, and Statements of the President, 1961–1963.* 3 vols. Washington, DC: Office of the Federal Register, National Archives and Records Service, General Services Administration, 1962–1964.

———. *The Strategy of Peace.* New York: Harper & Brothers, 1960.

———. "Television as I See It: A Force That Has Changed the Political Scene," *TV Guide,* November 14, 1959: 5–8.

———. *Why England Slept.* New York: Wilfred Funk, 1940.

Kennedy, Robert F. *Robert Kennedy, in His Own Words: Recollections of the Kennedy Years.* New York: Bantam, 1988.

Kennedy, Rose Fitzgerald. *Times to Remember.* Garden City, NY: Doubleday, 1974.

"Kennedy v. Humphrey: The 50th Anniversary of the West Virginia Democratic Primary." May 12, 2010, Kennedy Library Forums, Kennedy Library and Museum.

Knebel, Fletcher. "Democratic Forecast: A Catholic in 1960." *Look,* March 3, 1959.

Koskoff, David E. *Joseph P. Kennedy: A Life and Times.* Englewood Cliffs, NJ: Prentice-Hall, 1974.

Krock, Arthur. *Memoirs: Sixty Years on the Firing Line.* New York: Funk and Wagnalls, 1968.

Kurtz, Ken, panel discussion, "Celebrating the Primary that Made a President." Division of Culture and History and West Virginia College, Charleston, West Virginia, May 12, 1990.

———, panel discussion, "1960 West Virginia: The Primary Made a President and Changed a Nation." Charleston, WV, May 7, 2010.

Larson, Kate Clifford. *Rosemary: The Hidden Kennedy Daughter.* New York: Houghton Mifflin, 2015.

Lasky, Victor. *J.F.K.: The Man and the Myth.* New Rochelle, NY: Arlington House, 1963.

Lavine, Harold. "Boiling Up." *Newsweek,* April 25, 1960: 30–31.

Lawrence, William H. *Six Presidents, Too Many Wars.* New York: Saturday Review Press, 1972.

Leamer, Laurence. *The Kennedy Men, 1901–1963: The Laws of the Father.* New York: Perennial, 2001.

———. *The Kennedy Women: The Saga of an American Family*. New York: Fawcett Books, 1996.

Lee, K. W. "Fair Elections in West Virginia." *Appalachian Lookout*, April 1969.

Leming, Barbara. *Mrs. Kennedy: The Missing History of the Kennedy Years*. New York: Free Press, 2011.

Leonard, Bill J., ed. *Christianity in Appalachia: Profiles in Regional Pluralism*. Knoxville: University of Tennessee Press, 1999.

Lewis, Ronald L. "Beyond Isolation and Homogeneity: Diversity and the History of Appalachia." In *Back Talk from Appalachia: Confronting Stereotypes*, edited by Dwight B. Billings, Gurney Norman, and Katherine Ledford, 21–46. Lexington: University of Kentucky Press, 1999.

———. *Transforming the Appalachian Countryside: Railroads, Deforestation, and Social Change in West Virginia*. Chapel Hill: University of North Carolina Press, 1998.

Lincoln, Evelyn. *My Twelve Years with John F. Kennedy*. New York: David McKay, 1965.

Lohman, Roger A. "Four Perspective on Appalachian Culture and Poverty." *Journal of Appalachian Studies Association* 2 (1990): 76–91.

Lutz, Paul F. *From Governor to Cabby: The Political Career and Tragic Death of West Virginia's William Casey Marland*. Huntington, WV: Marshall University Library Associates, 1996.

Manarin, Louis H. "Sectionalism and the Virginias." In *The West Virginia Encyclopedia*, edited by Ken Sullivan, 646. Charleston: West Virginia Humanities Council, 2006.

Martin, Ralph G. *A Hero For Our Time: An Intimate Story of the Kennedy Years*. New York: Macmillan Publishing Co., 1983.

———. *Seeds of Destruction: Joe Kennedy and His Sons*. New York: G.P. Putnam's Sons, 1995.

Marty, Martin E. *Modern American Religion*. Vol. 3, *Under God, Indivisible 1941–1960*. Chicago: University of Chicago Press, 1996.

Massa, Mark S. *Anti-Catholicism in America: The Last Acceptable Prejudice*. New York: Crossroads, 2003.

———. *Catholics and American Culture: Fulton Sheen, Dorothy Day, and the Notre Dame Football Team*. New York: Crossroads, 1999.

McAndrew, Lawrence J. "Beyond Appearances: Kennedy, Congress, Religion, and Federal Aid to Education." *Presidential Studies Quarterly* 21 (Summer 1991): 545–57.

McCarthy, Abigail. *Private Faces: Public Places*. Garden City, NY: Doubleday & Co., 1972.

McCarthy, Joe. *The Remarkable Kennedys*. New York: Dial Press, 1960.

McCauley, Deborah Vansau. *Appalachian Mountain Religion: A History*. Urbana: University of Illinois Press, 1995.

McDougal, Henry Clay. *Recollections, 1844–1909*. Kansas City, MO: Franklin Hudson, 1910.

McKinney, Gordon. "Major Negative Impact." In *The Appalachians: America's First and Last Frontier*, edited by Mari-Lynn Evans, Holly George-Warren, and Robert Santelli, 153. New York: Random House, 2004.

Melling, Carol. "Appalachian Corridor Highways." In *The West Virginia Encyclopedia*, edited by Ken Sullivan, 17. Charleston: West Virginia Humanities Council, 2006.

Menendez, Albert J. *John F. Kennedy: Catholic and Humanist*. Buffalo, NY: Prometheus Books, 1978.

Merry, Robert W. *Taking on the World: Joseph and Stewart Alsop—Guardians of the American Century*. New York: Viking Press, 1996.

Mollohan, Alan B. "My West Virginia." In *The Appalachians: America's First and Last Frontier*, edited by Mari-Lynn Evans, Holly George-Warren, and Robert Santelli, 151–154. New York: Random House, 2004.

Myers, J. Howard, ed. *West Virginia Blue Book*. Charleston: State of West Virginia, 1959, 1960, 1964.

Novak, Robert D. *The Prince of Darkness: 50 Years Reporting In Washington*. New York: Crown Forum, 2007.

O'Brien, Lawrence F. *Citizens for Kennedy and Johnson Campaign Manual*. Washington, DC: National Citizens for Kennedy, 1960.

———. *No Final Victories: A Life in Politics from John F. Kennedy to Watergate*. Garden City, NY: Doubleday, 1974.

O'Brien, Michael. *John F. Kennedy: A Biography*. New York: St. Martin's Press, 2005.

O'Donnell, Helen. *A Common Good: The Friendship of Robert F. Kennedy and Kenneth P. O'Donnell*. New York: Morrow, 1998.

O'Donnell, Helen. *The Irish Brotherhood: John F. Kennedy, His Inner Circle, and the Improbable Rise to the Presidency*. With Kenneth O'Donnell Sr. Berkeley: Counterpoint, 2015.

O'Donnell, Kenneth, Rowland P. Evans, and Tom Wicker, "TV in the Political Campaign." *Television Quarterly* (Winter 1966).

O'Donnell, Kenneth, and David F. Powers. *"Johnny, We Hardly Knew Ye": Memories of John Fitzgerald Kennedy*. New York: Pocket Books, 1973.

Oliphant, Thomas and Curtis Wilkie. *The Road to Camelot: Inside JFK's Five-Year Campaign*. New York: Simon & Schuster, 2017.

O'Neill, Tip. *Man of the House: The Life and Political Memoirs of Speaker Tip O'Neill*. With William Novak. New York: Random House, 1987.

Painter, Nell Irvin. *The History of White People*. New York: W.W. Norton Press, 2010.

Parmet, Herbert S. *Jack: The Struggles of John F. Kennedy*. New York: Dial Press, 1980.

———. *JFK: The Presidency of John F. Kennedy*. New York: Dial Press, 1983.

Patterson, Thomas, and Robert D. McClure. *The Unseeing Eye: The Myth of Television Power in National Politics*. New York: Paragon Books, 1979.

Peirce, Neal R. *The Border South States: People, politics, power in the five Border South States*. New York: Norton, 1974.

Perry, Lester. *Forty Years of Mountain Politics*. Parsons, WV: McClain Printing Co., 1971.

Peters, Charles. *Tilting at Windmills: An Autobiography*. Reading, MA: Addison-Wesley, 1988.

Peyton, Billy Joe. "Highway Development." In *The West Virginia Encyclopedia*, edited by Ken Sullivan, 331-32. Charleston: West Virginia Humanities Council, 2006.

Pietrusza, David. *1960: LBJ vs. JFK vs. Nixon—The Epic Campaign That Forged Three Presidencies*. New York: Union Square Press, 2008.

Ponton, Anthony W., "John F. Kennedy and West Virginia, 1960–1963." PhD. diss., Marshall University, 2004.

Pool, Ithiel del Sola, Robert P. Abelson, and Samuel L. Popkin. *Candidates, Issues, and Strategies: A Computer Simulation of the 1960 Presidential Election*. Cambridge, MA: MIT Press, 1964.

Porch, Scott. "The Book That Changed Campaigns Forever: How Teddy White Revolutionized Political Journalism." *Politico*, April 22, 2015.

Pudup, Mary Beth, Dwight B. Billings, and Altina L. Waller, eds. *Appalachia in the Making: The Mountain South in the Nineteenth Century*. Chapel Hill: University of North Carolina Press, 1995.

Reeves, Richard. *President Kennedy: Profile of Power*. New York: Simon and Schuster, 1993.

Reeves, Thomas C. *A Question of Character: A Life of John F. Kennedy*. New York: Macmillan, 1991.

Reston, James. *Deadline: A Memoir*. New York: Random House, 1992.

Rice, Otis K. *West Virginia: The State and Its People*. Hugheston, WV: McClain Printing Co., 1972.

Rice, Otis K., and Stephen W. Brown. "History of West Virginia." In *The West Virginia Encyclopedia*, edited by Ken Sullivan, 335–342. Charleston: West Virginia Humanities Council, 2006.

Roberts, Chalmers M. *First Rough Draft: A Journalist's Journal of Our Times*. New York: Praeger Publishers, 1973.

Roosevelt, Eleanor. *On My Own: The Years since The White House*. New York: Harper & Brothers, 1958.

Rorabaugh, William J. *Kennedy and the Promise of the Sixties*. Cambridge: Cambridge University Press, 2002.

———. *The Real Making of the President: Kennedy, Nixon, and the 1960 Election*. Lawrence: University of Kansas Press, 2009.

Rupp, Robert. "Democratic Party." In *The West Virginia Encyclopedia*, edited by Ken Sullivan, 191. Charleston: West Virginia Humanities Council, 2006.

———. "Politics." In *The West Virginia Encyclopedia*, edited by Ken Sullivan, 576–77. Charleston: West Virginia Humanities Council, 2006.

———. "Republican Party." In *The West Virginia Encyclopedia*, edited by Ken Sullivan, 612–13. Charleston: West Virginia Humanities Council, 2006.

Sabato, Larry A. *The Kennedy Half-Century: The Presidency, Assassination, and Lasting Legacy of John F. Kennedy*. New York: Bloomsbury, 2013.

Salinger, Pierre. *With Kennedy*. New York: Doubleday, 1966.

Schlesinger, Arthur M., Jr. *Kennedy or Nixon: Does It Make Any Difference?* New York: Macmillan, 1960.

———. *Robert Kennedy and His Times*. New York: Ballantine Books, 1978.

———. *A Thousand Days: John F. Kennedy in the White House*. Boston: Houghton Mifflin, 1965.

Shapiro, Henry D. *Appalachia on Our Mind: The Southern Mountains and Mountaineers in the American Consciousness, 1870–1920.* Chapel Hill: University of North Carolina Press, 1978.

Sherwood, Topper. "Kennedy in West Virginia," *Goldenseal 26, no. 3* (Fall 2000): 15–19, 21–23.

Sidey, Hugh. *John F. Kennedy, President.* New York: Athenaeum, 1964.

Slayton, Robert A. *Empire Statesman: The Rise and Redemption of Al Smith.* New York: Free Press, 2001

Smith, Alfred E. *Campaign Addresses of Governor Alfred E. Smith.* Washington, DC: Democratic National Committee, 1929.

Smith, Luther A. "The Grand Commander's Message: Catholicism, Religion, the Presidency, Commonsense." *The New Age* 68, no. 2 (February 1960): 3–5.

Smith, William D. "Alfred E. Smith and John F. Kennedy: The Religious Issue during the Campaigns of 1928 and 1960." PhD diss., Southern Illinois University, 1964.

Solberg, Carl. *Hubert Humphrey: A Biography.* New York: Norton, 1984.

Sorensen, Theodore C. *Counselor: A Life at the Edge of History.* New York: Harper-Collins, 2008.

———. *Kennedy.* New York: Harper and Row, 1965.

———. *The Kennedy Legacy.* New York: Macmillan, 1973.

Stafford, Thomas F. *Afflicting the Comfortable: Journalism and Politics in West Virginia,* Morgantown: West Virginia University Press, 2005.

Stein, Jean. *American Journey: The Times of Robert Kennedy.* Edited by George Plimpton. New York: Harcourt Brace Jovanovich, 1970.

Storber, Gerald S., and Deborah H. Storber, eds. *Let Us Begin Anew: An Oral History of the Kennedy Presidency.* New York: HarperCollins, 1993.

Stossel, Scott. *Sarge: The Life and Times of Sargent Shriver.* Washington, DC: Smithsonian Books, 2004.

TerHorst, Jerald. "No More Pork Barrel: The Appalachian Approach." In *Appalachia in the Sixties: Decade of Reawakening,* edited by David S. Walls and John B. Stephenson, 31–37. Lexington: University Press of Kentucky, 1972.

Thomas, Jerry Bruce. *An Appalachia Reawakening: West Virginia and the Perils of the New Machine Age, 1945–1972.* Morgantown: West Virginia University Press, 2010.

Tunley, Roul. "The Strange Case of West Virginia." *Saturday Evening Post* 232, no. 32, February 6, 1960.

Wallace, Elton Harvey. "Alfred E. Smith, the Religious Issue: Oklahoma City, September 20, 1928." PhD diss., Michigan State University, 1965.

Walls, David, and John B. Stephenson, eds. *Appalachia in the Sixties: Decade of Reawakening.* Lexington: University Press of Kentucky, 1972.

Watson, Mary A. *The Expanding Vista: American Television in the Kennedy Years.* New York: Oxford University Press, 1990.

Weller, Jack E. *Yesterday's People: Life in Contemporary Appalachia.* Lexington: University Press of Kentucky, 1965.

West Virginia Department of Transportation Planning and Research Division: Inter-modal Special Projects Division, *West Virginia National Highway System Report.* Charleston, WV: 2000.

Westin, Avram (producer). "Cover Stories Spring 1960." *Our World.* ABC, April 16, 1987.

Whalen, Richard J. *The Founding Father: The Story of Joseph P. Kennedy.* New York: New American Library, 1964.

Whisnant, David E. *All That Is Native and Fine: The Politics of Culture in an American Region.* Chapel Hill: University of North Carolina Press, 1983.

———. *Modernizing the Mountaineer: People, Power, and Planning in Appalachia.* Revised ed. Knoxville: University of Tennessee Press, 1994.

White, Kenneth. *Barack Obama's America: How New Conceptions of Race, Family, and Religion Ended the Reagan Era.* Ann Arbor: University of Michigan Press, 2009.

———. *The New Politics of Old Values.* Hanover, NH: University Press of New England, 1988.

———. *The Values Divide: American Politics and Culture in Transition.* New York: Chatham House, 2003.

White, Theodore H. *In Search of History: A Personal Adventure.* New York: Warner Books, 1979.

———. *The Making of the President 1960.* New York: Atheneum, 1961.

Wicker, Tom. *JFK and LBJ: The Influence of Personality upon Politics.* New York: William Morrow, 1968.

Wicker, Tom, Kenneth P. O'Donnell, and Rowland P. Evans. "TV in the Political Campaign." *Television Quarterly* 5 (Winter 1966): 20–23.

Williams, John Alexander. *West Virginia: A History.* Morgantown: West Virginia University Press, 2001

Wills, Garry. *Bare Ruined Choirs: Doubt, Prophecy, and Radical Religion.* Garden City, NY: Doubleday, 1972.

———. *The Kennedy Imprisonment: A Meditation on Power.* Boston: Little, Brown, 1981.

Wilson, Donald. "In Logan County, the Half-Pint Vote, Slating and 'Lever Brothers.'" *Life,* May 9, 1960.

Wofford, Harris. *Of Kennedys and Kings: Making Sense of the Sixties.* New York: Farrar, Straus, and Giroux, 1980.

Wyckoff, Gene. *The Image Candidates: American Candidates in the Age of Television.* New York: Macmillan, 1968.

Young, William Lewis. "The John F. Kennedy Library Oral History Project: The West Virginia Democratic Presidential Primary, 1960." PhD. diss., The Ohio State University, 1982.

Collections Consulted

Barron, William W. Papers. West Virginia State Archives, Charleston, WV.

Freeman, Orville L. Papers. Minnesota Historical Society, St. Paul, MN.

Humphrey, Hubert H. Papers. Minnesota Historical Society, St. Paul, MN.

Kennedy, John F. Oral History Collection. John F. Kennedy Library, Boston, MA.
———. Pre-Presidential Papers, Presidential Campaign Files, 1960. John F. Kennedy Library, Boston, MA.
———. Pre-Presidential Papers, Senate Files, Polls of Political Opinion. John F. Kennedy Library, Boston, MA
Kennedy, Robert F., Pre-Administration Papers. John F. Kennedy Library, Boston, MA.
Look Magazine. Photographs. John F. Kennedy Library, Boston, MA.
McCarthy, Eugene J. Papers. Minnesota Historical Society, St. Paul, MN.
Moore, Arch. A., Jr. Papers. West Virginia Regional and History Collection, West Virginia University, Morgantown, WV.
Political Campaigns. Audio-visual Collection. West Virginia State Archives, Charleston, WV.
Powers, David F. Personal Papers. John F. Kennedy Library, Boston, MA.
Schlesinger, Arthur M., Jr. Personal Papers. John F. Kennedy Library, Boston, MA.
Smith, Hulett C. Papers. West Virginia State Archives, Charleston, WV.
Sorensen, Theodore C. Personal Papers. John F. Kennedy Library, Boston, MA.
Walnum, Sven. Photograph Collection. John F. Kennedy Library, Boston, MA.
West Virginia Photograph Collection. West Virginia State Archives, Charleston, WV.

National Newspapers

Baltimore Sun
New York Herald
New York Times
Wall Street Journal
Washington Examiner
Washington Post

West Virginia Newspapers

Alderson Times (Alderson, WV)
Beckley Post-Herald (Beckley, WV)
Bluefield Daily Telegraph (Bluefield, WV)
Charleston Daily Mail (Charleston, WV)
Charleston Gazette (Charleston, WV)
Charleston Gazette-Mail (Charleston, WV)
Clarksburg Exponent (Clarksburg, WV)
Clarksburg Telegram (Clarksburg, WV)
Elkins Inter-Mountain (Elkins, WV)
Fairmont Times (Fairmont, WV)
Fayette Tribune (Oak Hill, WV)
Grafton Sentinel (Grafton, WV)

Hinton Daily News (Hinton, WV)
Huntington Advertiser (Huntington, WV)
Huntington Herald-Dispatch (Huntington, WV)
Logan Banner (Logan, WV)
Martinsburg Journal (Martinsburg, WV)
Mineral Daily News Tribune (Keyser, WV)
Morgan Messenger (Berkeley Springs, WV)
Morgantown Dominion News (Morgantown, WV)
Morgantown Post (Morgantown, WV)
Parkersburg News (Parkersburg, WV)
Parkersburg Sentinel (Parkersburg, WV)
Raleigh Register (Beckley, WV)
Randolph Enterprise (Elkins, WV)
Ravenswood News (Ravenswood, WV)
Richwood News Leader (Richwood, WV)
Spirit of Jefferson (Charles Town, WV)
Weirton Daily Times (Weirton, WV)
Welch Daily News (Welch, WV)
Weston Democrat (Weston, WV)
Wheeling Intelligencer (Wheeling, WV)
Wheeling News-Register (Wheeling, WV)
Williamson Daily News (Williamson, WV)

Interviews at JFK Library

Barron, William Wallace. August 10, 1965, Charleston ,WV.
Chilton W. E., III. July 14, 1964, Charleston, WV.
Christie, Sidney L. July 16, 1964, Bluefield, WV.
Ellis, Claude. September 9, 1964. Logan, WV.
Hearst, Anne. July 28, 1964, Morgantown, WV.
Hoffmann, Harry G. August 7, 1964, Charleston, WV.
Jacobs, William L. July 6, 1964, Parkersburg, WV.
Lawrence, William H. April 22, 1966, Boston, MA.
Lawson, Marjorie McKenzie. October 25, 1965, Morgantown, WV.
Lisagor, Peter. April 22, 1966, Boston, MA.
Lonesome, William. July 14, 1964, Charleston, WV.
McDonough, Robert P. Dec. 5–6, 1964, Feb. 13, July 3, 1965, Parkersburg, WV.
Rauh, Joseph L. Jr., December 23, 1965, Boston, MA.
Reese, Matthew A., Jr. October 24, 1964, Washington, D.C.
West, Marshall G. July 13, 1964, Charleston, WV.

Interviews by the Author

Battle, Henry W. April 3, 2010, Charleston, WV.

Bradlee, Ben. March 18, 2002, Washington, DC.

Donahue, Richard. May 12, 1990, Charleston, WV.

Haught, James F. May 9, 1990, Charleston, WV.

Hechler, Ken. May 2, 2010, Charleston, WV.

Huff, Sam. May 10, 2010, Charleston, WV.

Humphrey, Hubert H. "Skip," III. January 14, 2016, Minneapolis, MN.

Manchin III, Joseph. May 5, 2010, Charleston, WV.

Mondale, Walter. January 14, 2016, Minneapolis, MN.

Peters, Charles G. Jr. December 27, 2002, Washington, DC; May 10, 2010, Charleston, WV.

Powers, David F. May 5, 1990, Boston, MA.

Reese, Matthew A., Jr. May 5, 1990, Boston, MA.

Schussler, Charles. Phone interview, May 6, 2000, Wheeling, WV.

Shriver, Sargent. May 12, 1960, Charleston, WV.

Smith, Oce. May 6, 2001, Charleston, WV.

Smith, Phil. April 10, 2010, Charleston WV.

Sorensen, Ted. May 7, 2010, Charleston, WV.

Wolford, Jimmy. May 10, 2010, Charleston, WV.

Kennedy Television Ads

Kennedy, John F. 16mm film print, "Economic Advertisement #1." Directed by Jack Denove, Spring 1960. Phil Smith Collection. West Virginia State Archives, Charleston, WV.

Kennedy, John F. 16mm film print, "Economic Advertisement #2." Directed by Jack Denove, Spring 1960. Phil Smith Collection. West Virginia State Archives, Charleston, WV.

Kennedy, John F. 16mm film print, "Economic Advertisement #3, Slab Fork Mine." Directed by Jack Denove, Spring 1960. Phil Smith Collection. West Virginia State Archives, Charleston, WV.

Kennedy, John F. 16mm film print, "Gallup Poll Advertisement." Directed by Jack Denove, Spring 1960. Phil Smith Collection. West Virginia State Archives, Charleston, WV.

Kennedy, John F. 16mm film print, "Gang Up Advertisement." Directed by Jack Denove, Spring 1960. Phil Smith Collection. West Virginia State Archives, Charleston, WV.

Kennedy, John F. 16mm film print, "Introduction-Capitol Steps Advertisement." Directed by Jack Denove, Spring 1960. Phil Smith Collection. West Virginia State Archives, Charleston, WV.

Kennedy, John F. 16mm film print, "Religion Advertisement #1, Divided Loyalties." Directed by Jack Denove, Spring 1960. Phil Smith Collection. West Virginia State Archives, Charleston, WV.

Kennedy, John F. 16mm film print, "Religion Advertisement #2, Morris Harvey College." Directed by Jack Denove, Spring 1960. Phil Smith Collection. West Virginia State Archives, Charleston, WV.

Roosevelt, Franklin Delano Jr. 16 mm film print, "Cabin Creek Advertisement #1, Economy." Directed by Jack Denove, Spring 1960. Phil Smith Collection. West Virginia State Archives, Charleston, WV.

Roosevelt, Franklin Delano Jr. 16 mm film print, "Cabin Creek Advertisement #2, War Records." Directed by Jack Denove, Spring 1960. Phil Smith Collection. West Virginia State Archives, Charleston, WV.

Roosevelt, Franklin Delano Jr. 16 mm film print, "Religion Advertisement #1." Directed by Jack Denove, Spring 1960. Phil Smith Collection. West Virginia State Archives, Charleston, WV.

Roosevelt, Franklin Delano Jr. 16 mm film print, "Religion Advertisement #2." Directed by Jack Denove, Spring 1960. Phil Smith Collection. West Virginia State Archives, Charleston, WV.

INDEX

Page numbers in **boldface** refer to illustrations.

Howard, Frances Humphrey, 61, 162n29, 177n80

Howe, Quincy, 186n90

Huff, Sam, 59, 176n69

Humphrey, Bob, 60

Humphrey, Douglas, 60

Humphrey, Hubert: at Barboursville, WV, 131, 196–97n121; and Wallace "Wally" Barron, 30; at Beckley, WV, 6, 112, 131; at Berkeley Springs, WV, 125; "black bags of cash," 7, 83, 124, 194n76; at Bluefield, WV, 112; at Cabin Creek, WV, **70**, 112; campaign finance, 7, 23, 31, 81, 82–83, 104, 115, 146; at Campbell's Creek, WV, 147; at Chapmanville, WV, 131, 196–97n121; at Charles Town, WV, 123, 125; at Charleston, WV, 49, **78**, 93–98, 112, 121, 129, 131, 141, 148; at Clarksburg, WV, **75**, 85, 104, 144–45, 180n130; at Clay, WV, 144; at Dunbar, WV, 147; endorsement by Raymond Chafin, 30–31, 132; at Fairmont, WV 123; food stamp program proposal, 49, 53, 124, 150, 173n13, 194n74; at Hamlin, WV, 131, 196–97n121; at Henderson, WV, 140; at Huntington, WV, 121, 131–32, 139, 196–97n121; at Hurricane, WV, 131, 196–97n121; at Kanwaha City, WV, 112, 147; at Keyser, WV, 7, 124; at Kingwood, WV, 7, 124; at Logan, WV, 112, 121, 131, 132, 196–97n121; at Madison, WV, 88; at Marmet, WV, 112; at Martinsburg, WV 125; at Milton, WV, 131, 196–97n121; at Morgantown, WV 142; at Nitro, WV, 147; at Parkersburg, WV 138–39; at Pineville, WV, 143; at Point Pleasant, WV, 140; at Rainelle, WV, 134, 197n144; at Richwood, WV, 121, 134; at Ripley, WV 140; service in World War II, 7, 62–67, 104, 143–45, 146, 179n109, 179–80n116, 180nn119–121, 200n211; and slating, 23–24; at South Charleston, WV, 147; at St. Albans, 131, 196–97n121; at Summersville, WV, 123; telethon (May 7, 1960), 89, 92, 146; televised debate with Kennedy (May 4, 1960), 11, 13, **78**, **79**, 89, 93–98, 154; at Webster Springs, WV, 124; at Welch, WV, 112, 143; at Wheeling, WV, 141; at Williamson, 112, 143; Wisconsin presidential primary, 1–2, 8, 15, 25–28, 34, 41, 83, 115, 130

Humphrey, Hubert "Skipper," III, 60

Humphrey, Muriel, 53, 57, 60, 143, 145, 177nn77–78; at Buckhannon, WV 61, 177n77; at Campbell's Creek, WV, 147; at Charleston, WV, 60; at Clarksburg, WV, 60–61, 145, 177n77; at Clendenin, WV, 61, 177n77; at Dunbar, WV, 147; at Gassaway, WV, 177n77; at Grafton, WV, 61; at Kanawha City, WV, 147; at Morgantown, WV, 61; at Nitro, WV, 147; and slating, 23; at South Charleston, WV, 147; at Sutton, WV, 61, 177n77; at Welch, WV, 143

Humphrey, Nancy, 60

Huntington, WV, 82, 87, 116, 119–20, 121, 122, 131, 132, 139, 142, 145, 147, 191n25, 191n27, 193n60, 196–97n121; and demographics, 19–20

Huntington Herald-Dispatch, 119

Huntington Kiwanis Club, 139

Huntley, Chet, 193n60

Hurricane, WV, 131, 196–97n121

Hutchinson, Elizabeth, 131

Hyannis Port, MA, 103, 105

Hylton, Charlie, 133

Indiana Catholic and Record, 37

Inez, KY, 155

Interstate Highway Act, 151

Interstate 79, 151–52

Island Creek Coal Company, 85